THE SCANDAL OF THE SCANDALS

The Secret History of Christianity

MANFRED LÜTZ

THE SCANDAL OF THE SCANDALS

The Secret History of Christianity

In collaboration with
Arnold Angenendt

and

Translated by
Beata Vale

IGNATIUS PRESS   SAN FRANCISCO

Title of the German original:
Der Skandal der Skandale. Die geheime Geschichte des Christentums
© 2018 by Verlag Herder GmbH
Freiburg im Breisgau, Germany

Except in chapter XI, part 3, all sources and all uncited material have been drawn from Arnold Angenendt, *Toleranz und Gewalt. Das Christentum zwischen Bibel und Schwert* (Münster: Aschendorff Verlag, 2007). Specific authors can be found through the index.

Cover art:
Saint John Chrysostom and Empress Eudoxia
Jean-Paul Laurens (1838–1921)
Musée des Augustins, Toulouse, France
© Photo Josse / Bridgeman Images

Cover design by John Herreid

CONTENTS

PREFACE

Christianity is the least known religion of the Western world. This is not due to a shortage of information. On the contrary, it is due to an overabundance of information. However, this information usually has a peculiar characteristic: it is ridiculously wrong.

This is not so troubling in itself. One can live well enough with false convictions. For a long time, people believed that air flows through human arteries, and for an even longer time it was commonly accepted that dragons exist. Not even the conviction that the earth was a disk stopped people from leading meaningful lives.

Fake news can even be entertaining. After all, who wants to see the world the way it is all day long? On a personal level, too, suppression is an important skill for coping with life. Walking around with the burden of one's own history, with all its dark sides, makes for a hard life.

Yet the misinformation about Christianity does not simply amount to some small mistakes, amateurish hoaxes, or harmless cheating. This misinformation has deeply shaken Christianity at its core and has made it, for many, absolutely unbelievable.

Sure, people admire Pope Francis and publicly revere Mother Teresa; this is no contradiction. They are esteemed and venerated not *because of*, but *in spite of* the fact that they are Christians. It isn't held against them, so to speak. The charitable work of Christian institutions is respected, too, as are what many call "Christian values"— whatever those might be. But as for the Christian faith, the history of the Christian churches, Christianity itself, people consider these embarrassing at best. In intellectual debates, a confession of Christian faith is often tacitly regarded as unworthy of discussion. In common parlance, the term "fundamentalism" not only applies to fanatical believers, but has been extended to every religious and Christian confession that does not merely describe religion from the perspective of religious studies, but actually holds it to be true. This is the end of real Christianity as a culturally defining force.

9

One could object: at least the Christian churches can still boast respectable institutions that—in Germany for example—have enormous financial means at their disposal. Yet let us not overlook how much energy goes into dismantling formerly large national churches, or the fact that new movements tend to sprout up on the margins of institutional Christianity. The Christian mission is most likely to be successful where people are spoken to directly on a spiritual level and experience a community of convinced believers, and can thereby rejuvenate their personal life. Indeed, as paradoxical as it might sound, Christianity, its history, its institutions, and its representatives rather serve as an obstacle to the Christian mission in our parts of the world—or at least do not serve as an attraction.

This is because Christianity has been dealt a deadly blow. The now-uncontested conviction that the history of Christianity is a history of scandals truly rattles the core of the Christian faith. For a religion that believes in a God-become-Man, and thus in a God-become-History, surrenders itself without reserve to the critical evaluation of this history. And this evaluation is devastating. In 2000, the philosopher Herbert Schnädelbach published a sensational essay entitled "The Curse of Christianity", which culminates with the proposal that the best thing Christianity could do for mankind would be ... to dissolve! And the reasons he brought forth for this death sentence were not primarily philosophical or theological. Schnädelbach did not voice any doubt about the Trinity or about the Incarnation of God, for example. Rather, his arguments were almost exclusively historical. He did not refer to any scholarly studies; instead, he based his claim on a broad consensus in society about the scandalous history of Christianity. Citing the outrageous Crusades, the brutal Inquisition, and the devastating history of anti-Semitism, this highly educated philosopher presented all these facts as being just as unquestionable as anything else we take for granted today: that the moon orbits the earth, for instance, or that Mount Everest is the highest mountain on our planet. No proofs are needed for these claims, either. In this respect, his essay did no more than neatly capture what everyone else was already thinking anyway.

Coming ten years after the collapse of Communism, this text was a socially charged [*engagierter*] obituary for Christianity.

That could have been it, then. As with Communism, there are always some who do not heed the signs and, wearing blinders, press

on nostalgically as if nothing had happened. In truth, though, Schnädelbach's piece struck the heart of the Christian religion. If Schnädelbach was right, Christianity was indeed finished, two thousand years
after it had begun.

But was he right? After the publication of this essay, something
spectacular and completely unexpected took place. An internationally renowned historian accepted the challenge, and armed with
contemporary scholarship, he painstakingly worked his way to the
bottom of Schnädelbach's accusations: What was true and what was
not? This historian was Arnold Angenendt, who in 2007 released a
powerful book, *Toleranz und Gewalt: Christentum zwischen Bibel und
Schwert* (*Tolerance and Violence: Christianity between the Bible and the
Sword*). Since its publication, this book has become a standard reference for any who wish to grapple critically with Christianity and
the Church. Indeed, Angenendt's scholarly depth led to a very rare
kind of success. Persuading through sober, dispassionate explanation,
Toleranz und Gewalt prompted Schnädelbach to correct himself. The
philosopher thanked Angenendt for "proving that my retrospective
was skewed in several instances". As it turned out, popular assumptions about the history of Christianity simply did not stand up to
serious scholarly examination.

These astonishing results, however, have in no way penetrated
into the general consciousness. After all, only a person who is particularly invested in Christianity for some reason—even simply out
of hatred—would pick up a book of 800 pages and more than 3,000
footnotes.

From this observation arose the question of whether it might be
worth the effort to make the significant results of Angenendt's study
available to a broader public in a more readable format. After all, what
had been the case for a highly educated person like Schnädelbach—
who held certain common false assumptions about Christianity to be
unquestionably true—is the case for most other people as well. So
there is simply a need for clarification, in the best sense of the word.

This kind of clarification is urgently necessary because the loss of
Christianity as a unifying power has thrown the whole society into
a serious crisis. People across the spectrum, from the far left to the
far right, openly admit that this is true. At the Evangelische Akademie in Tutzing, the leader of the left, Gregor Gysi, declared that

even though he was an atheist, he was still afraid of a godless society, because it could lose its sense of solidarity. After all, he said, socialism is nothing but secularized Christianity. At the presentation of my book *Gott—Eine kleine Geschichte des Größten* [*God: A Brief History of the Most High*], Gysi candidly declared that when it comes to the question of values in our society, the political left has lost credibility, even for decades to come. The only institutions still relevant in this regard, he said, are the Christian ones, and if atheism means being against the Church, he is not an atheist, but rather a pagan whom the faith has not yet reached. Meanwhile, oddly enough, the right-wing followers of PEGIDA [Patriotic Europeans against the Islamization of the Occident, a German nationalist movement] explicitly celebrate the Christian West, even though they know so little about Christianity that they unabashedly sing Christmas carols during Advent.

However, in this latter instance, it is really an empty shell that is being invoked. Christianity has seemingly discredited itself to such an extent over the course of two thousand years—not just seventy like Communism—that even those who praise it can hardly say what they find in it worth keeping, aside from some humanistic attitudes that even righteous atheists readily display. Anyone who cares about society, even reasonable atheists, should support a clarification of the real truth behind Christianity.

For this reason, Jürgen Habermas, Germany's best-known philosopher, who has declared himself "tone-deaf in the religious sphere",[1] has asked that at the very least a "salvaging translation" be made of the Judeo-Christian concept of man's being in the image of God. Only in this way, Habermas believes, can the general acceptance of the concept of man's dignity, the central concept in our social order, remain safeguarded. And he desires for there to be Christians, whom he perceives as religious citizens, in the public discourse. But this agnostic's pious wish is met with Christians who tend to keep silent about their faith, treating it as a private matter—mostly because they are ashamed of the history of Christianity.

This shame also has to do with the fact that Christians themselves have faced their scandal-ridden history in two basically unconvincing ways. Some have made every effort to wash clean the history of Christianity apologetically and to deny, at all costs, any failures on the side of the Church. But a two-thousand-year uninterrupted "life of the saints" would not at all correspond to what Jesus himself foretold for his Church. The pillars of the Church, the apostles, whom Jesus personally called, were of rather spotty character. Why should this get better with time? Meanwhile, other Christians have focused on the exact opposite. They do not deny Christianity's historical weaknesses; in fact, these even come in handy for them. Against the backdrop of a bygone Christian history full of scandals, they can make their modern, contemporary Christianity look even more brilliant. But this grand gesture is rather naïve: "For two thousand years"—the thinking goes—"Christianity was going astray until I came along, or professor X or Y came along, or the Second Vatican Council." Naturally, any shrewd atheist could only respond: "Let us see, then, if it works better over the next two thousand years, and then we will take it from there."

These two extremely different ways of dealing with one's own past have only reinforced the distorted image of the history of Christianity. In both approaches, history is simply fodder for one's own prejudices—an edifice that could begin to totter with authentic scholarly research.

Arnold Angenendt's approach was quite different. He never whitewashed the Church, but neither did he simply accept scandalous stories because they sounded extra juicy or had been continually rehashed. Instead, this internationally renowned scholar applied his reason and his scholarly expertise, researching the topic in a dispassionate way. The results are impressive. His years of work form the basis of the present book.

Therefore, the goal of this book, too, can only be to tackle Christianity's scandal-ridden history in a way that is free of prejudice and armed with the razor of scholarship. In the end, scandals may turn out truly to be scandals; but of course, even if we find out on the contrary that the historical facts paint a very different picture, a scandal-free history of Christianity would still not be a reason to become a Christian. Even completely nonsensical convictions can have patently beneficial effects on history. So this book is not about creed, but about history, about the incredibly exciting, true history of the greatest religion of all time. And to those so inclined, it is no less about the development of the West and the enlightenment of Europe, in the best sense.

I wrote the text, but the historical scholarship in this book owes a great deal to Dr. Arnold Angenendt and his colleagues, who made sure that it reflects the most current historical research, even beyond *Toleranz und Gewalt*. The book has been completely restructured and filled out with a number of topics, in order to cover as many crucial events in Church history as possible. To make sure everything is accurate, I had the text read by historian of Modernity Dr. Heinz Schilling, Lutheran Church historian Dr. Christoph Markiesch, Catholic Church historian Dr. Hubertus Drobner, contemporary historian Dr. Karl-Josef Hummel, and systematic theologian Dr. Bertram Stubenrauch, all of whom I thank heartily for their work. As usual, my barber has checked it to make sure it remains generally understandable, casual, and readable. Most of all, however, I have told the story of Christianity because history comes alive when it is told, especially a history that has played itself out so dramatically and continues even today to affect all of us, whether we like it or not.

In this way one can experience how a small Jewish sect in the Roman Empire became a world religion, how the Roman Empire turned into a Christian empire, and how in the end it came to pass that the victorious Germanic tribes became Christian Germanic tribes. In this book, one learns what the Crusades were really all about, learns what astonishing insights the latest research has to offer about the Inquisition, the witch hunts, and the Native American missions, and learns what the Enlightenment did for us—as well as what it didn't do. In implementing human rights, did Christianity slam on the brakes or hit the gas—or did it do both? What about the emancipation of women, the sexual revolution? Most pressing of all, what is Christianity's stance on the Holocaust?

In the end, this has become a book for Christians who are not afraid of the truth, as well as for anyone else who wants to understand better where he comes from.

Bornheim, January 1, 2018
Dr. Manfred Lütz

INTRODUCTION

"I Don't Believe You!"

Everything was better before! Since the dawn of history, proponents of the Golden Age theory have uttered this battle cry. For the Greek historian Hesiod, all of history was nothing but a lamentable decline, and in every age, there have been poets and thinkers who saw things exactly the same way—to this very day.

But even in Antiquity, there existed others who saw mankind as on a fixed path of perpetual progress. This happy state at the end of history, this *u-topos* ["no-place"] or utopia, especially fascinated many thinkers in the modern period, not least Communists and Socialists including such simple minds as Erich Honecker [longtime leader of Soviet East Germany], who, shortly before his unexpected resignation, made the following famous toast, holding a glass of champagne: "Neither ox nor mule can stay Socialism's rule." Everything turned out differently in the end, and it wasn't because of an ox or a mule.

For both perspectives, history can act up as much as it wants; as history in itself, it is worthless. It derives its value either exclusively from those precious things it has been able to retain from ancient times, or else from events that bring it closer to its grand finale. History itself is forgettable.

But one cannot live like this. Men without history are seriously impaired, because they do not know who they are. A society that holds nothing but disdain for its history is endangered by an unhealthy mix of nostalgists and utopians, who constantly and aggressively dream themselves out of the present.

This is equally true for a two-thousand-year-old institution like the Church. She, too, is a romping ground for all sorts of radical backward-lookers and radical believers in progress. For both, the real history of the Church is never good enough.

However, if we approach things less radically, it is clear that both of these differing perspectives are necessary for a fair assessment of history. Of course, historical events must first be understood in the context of their own time, but then they also have to be judged from the standpoint of today. If we hold that our concept of human rights today is not just the random result of a random history, but timeless and ever valid, then we must be allowed to evaluate historical events on the basis of how close they come—or not—to today's notion of human rights.

At the same time, the history of the Church in particular has to be viewed from the opposite direction, too: from the point of view of her origins. In this approach, what gets examined is whether or not certain ecclesial developments have strayed from the original idea and mission of the Church as they were intended by Jesus and his first followers. We will have to make use of both these vantage points once the facts have been cleared up.

Of course, one might ask the totally fundamental question of whether Christianity is allowed to develop at all historically. After all, according to the Christian understanding, the definitive revelation of God took place two thousand years ago in the Incarnation of his Son, Jesus Christ, and the Word of God can still be read in the Bible. So would not all the writings and acts of the bishops, popes, and councils during the two thousand years that followed be completely irrelevant—or worse, heresy and apostasy? With this question in mind, some sects have uncompromisingly demanded a return to early Christianity—sometimes even with deadly consequences. Noted Church historian Joseph Lortz has addressed this question. Revelation, according to Lortz, is not merely an isolated event that occurred two thousand years ago. Instead, Christians believe in God's entry into history, which gradually unfolds in the Church over the course of the centuries. Thus, for example, when the Christians' Jewish faith in the Messiah entered into the Greco-Roman intellectual world three hundred years after the founding of Christianity, this was not just some random coincidence. Rather, viewed through the eyes of Christians, this historical process becomes a living event of revelation. In the same way, the early councils with their definitions of the divine Trinity are a manifestation of divine revelation. Other historical developments can take on a revelatory character for Christians, from the rediscovery of Aristotelian philosophy in the Middle Ages, to the development of the concept of the individual at the beginning of the modern period, to the insights of the modern natural sciences—all this can make clearer to Christians the meaning of the original revelation. Revelation, according to Joseph Lortz, is therefore no dead letter, but a living revelation in a living history. That is why history is essential for Christians.

From an outside perspective, Christianity and the Church have another, very different problem: fake news! Anyone who keeps up with what nonsense political parties spread about one another in a six-month federal election campaign, what deliberate distortions of others' positions make up part of the basic toolkit, so to speak, of any competent election campaign—anyone who has witnessed this must keep in mind that Catholics themselves have been in election mode, as it were, for about two thousand years.

Just consider how much nonsense Catholics have unleashed on the world about Protestants, and Protestants about Catholics, over the last five hundred years! Add to that the incredible ideological trash spouted by the right- and left-wing dictatorships of the twentieth century regarding Christianity, which set against their omnipotence an Almighty who absolutely did not fit into their misanthropic systems. To the Nazis, Christianity was a "Judaized" religion, and to the Communists, it was just a wretched drug, opium for the masses. With extremely simplistic arguments and demagogic defamation campaigns, nothing was left undone in order to present Christianity as ridiculous, unmodern, and unscientific—and what counted as "science" was, for instance, what Erich and Margot Honecker thought was science. Both these systems of violence led to a battle of annihilation against Christianity—and were astonishingly successful! Even though professing Christians influenced the resistance against Hitler, and even though the nonviolent revolution of 1989 originated in Christian churches, the atheism preached by the state has survived in the minds of the people, almost the only relic left of these brittle ideologies. And thus it is no wonder that there is probably no institution in the world whose public image is so ludicrously false as that of the Catholic Church, whose history spans not just five hundred years like Protestant churches', but the whole two thousand years of Christianity. The result: rigid stereotypes about

Christian history, which people start to learn as early as in the cradle, as it were.

"I don't believe you", said one student when Arnold Angenendt questioned some of these stereotypes. And it might be the same for some of you at first, dear readers. That is why you will only get something out of this book if you do not merely *believe*, but genuinely want to *know*—that is, if you subject whatever prejudices you might harbor to the cold shower of facts. You will only avoid catching a cold in the process if you can accept the history of Christianity with neither blind love nor blind hatred. The goal of this undertaking is to use contemporary historical scholarship critically to get to the bottom of all the supposed scandals of the Church and thereby bring to light the secret history of Christianity. Brace yourself for some amazing twists and turns. What scholarship today has to say regarding popular ideas about Christianity is really unbelievable, but true.

I

To Hell with Religion

Judaism, Christianity, and Islam—
Monotheism as a Threat to Mankind?

"God is great!" These days, whenever this call suddenly rings out, people spontaneously take cover. For many, Islamist terror has definitively spoiled the reputation of religion. Religion is associated with violence, intolerance, and unreason. Some Christians, wanting to defend the many peace-loving Muslims, are eager to affirm that Christianity, too, has a history of violence. But of course, this does not really make anything better. At the end of the day, when you hear on the news that Hindus are burning mosques in India and the Buddhists in Myanmar are in the process of annihilating an entire Muslim population, the thought might cross your mind that perhaps for the sake of peace we should just try to do without religion altogether. Yet we *did* try this, in the twentieth century—with devastating results. The three dictators Joseph Stalin, Adolf Hitler, and Mao Tse-Tung, with their atheist ideologies, killed some 165 million people altogether. Two thousand years ago, that figure would have made up the entirety of mankind. Still, skepticism about religion persists.

1. Truth and Violence: Killing a Beautiful Theory with an Ugly Fact

Egyptologist Jan Assmann caused an international stir with the thesis that the root of the problem lies in the monotheistic religions' claim to truth. In his opinion, claiming to be in possession of the truth, as believers in one God do, is a scandal with terrible consequences. Philosopher Odo Marquard had already sung the praises of poly-theism, explaining that if people can freely choose their own gods from among many, they certainly will not knock the brains out of those who worship different ones. To each his own. This account seems plausible at first glance. But unfortunately, it does not hold up to reality. Albert Einstein once quipped that scholarship is the act of killing beautiful theories with ugly facts, and indeed, on the ques-tion of polytheism, historical scholarship has something to say. Tribal myths, with their unique heavens and divinities, had a deadly side effect: only the members of one's own people—no one else—possessed rights, especially the right to life. Thus cruel, relentless wars against other nations were the norm. After all, nothing prohibited butchering other people if they did not belong to one's own tribe. In this context, murder was not murder at all.

In tribal societies, the customary term for one's own people was normally "men", which evinces the idea that others are not really men, at least not in the full sense of the word. The American ancient historian Moses Finley sees in the world of the Greeks "no social conscience ..., no trace of the Decalogue, no responsibility other than familial, no obligation to anyone or anything but one's own prowess and one's own drive to victory and power".[1] There was no universal equality, let alone peace or even tolerance. Tribal religion consisted of tales and external rites in which one could take comfort; they explained what the world was like, is like, and would be like in the future. They described the world one lived in and gave instructions on how to get around in it if one did not want to fail. Part of coping with life was being able to "operate" these tribal reli-gions skillfully, the same way one would operate a washing machine today. If you do something wrong, there can be unpleasant conse-quences. That is why we do the right thing even when it's tough. Deep down, one did not believe in these tribal religions any more than one believes in a washing machine; they were simply a part of life, taken for granted.

But suddenly, something enormous happened. Around 1300 B.C.—hazily and uncertainly at first, and then more and more clearly—certain people in certain nations started to believe in *one* God, who had created the whole world, all nations, and all mankind. That was revolutionary! The tribal gods had been responsible only for their own tribes, and often, in the bloody battles between nations, these gods had fought fiercely against the (in their eyes) weakling gods of other nations. And now, suddenly, there was a God for everyone! This probably started in Egypt, under the pharaoh Amenophis IV. The name Amenophis means "Amun is satisfied". One of the countless Egyptian gods, Amun was the god of the kingdom. But Amenophis IV no longer professed a belief in Amun; he now believed in a single sun god, Aton. And because a pharaoh never does anything halfway, he had his name changed to Echnaton, which means "servant of Aton". He built a new imperial capital, Achet-Aton, and developed a new art style that suddenly depicted people realistically, with personal emotions. His wife was Nefertiti, whose charm still delights admiring crowds at the Neues Museum in Berlin. However, Echnaton remained a mere episode in history. After his death, all traces of him and his faith were completely destroyed, and the old pantheon was reinstated.

But the rays of this sun god reached all the way to Mount Sinai, as it were, where a little later Moses received the Tablets of the Law from Yahweh, whose first commandment said loud and clear: "I am the LORD your God.... You shall have no other gods before me" (Ex 20:2–3). Over time, the people of Israel came to understand more and more clearly what this meant, namely, that their God Yahweh was the God of all people.

This marked the breakthrough of monotheism. But it was also much more than that. Now one had to believe, or not believe, in this sole God with one's heart and mind, to obey or disobey him readily, and this was something interior and spiritual, and therefore psychological. And it was something individual. As Jan Assmann writes, man is "emancipated from his symbiotic relationship with the world and develops, in partnership with the One God, who dwells outside the world yet turned toward it, into an autonomous—or rather theonomous—individual".[2] Religion was no longer just an exterior ritual confirmation of the perpetual tribal order, the upholding of which required every sacrifice, even human sacrifice, so as to placate the needs of vengeful gods; rather, the transcendent God, who had no needs, demanded one's individual, very personal, and free ethical choice. He demanded something interior. At the end of time, all would stand before the judgment of this God. From now on, man was alone, alone before God. From now on, this injunction held true: you must obey God more than man. Moreover, with time, it became clear to man that he was free, free to decide, and that he had to take responsibility for his decisions, in the sense that he would stand before God's judgment seat and *respond*. This is how man broke free from the mental prison of tribal religion, which did not recognize any religious freedom. He had to learn tolerance. Since God himself wants man to follow him interiorly, forcing someone to follow God is, they now saw, pointless. Thus, monotheism, which required a voluntary conversion, carried the seed of what people today understand as the freedom and self-determination of man. Of course, not all of this was explicitly present immediately, but rather unfolded over the course of the centuries. It was the prophets of Israel and the Greek philosophers who—long freed from polytheism—steered this development away from exterior forms of religion: in Israel, toward a "culture of the heart" and in Greece, toward a "culture of the mind".[3]

2. To Hell with the Nobility: How Global Society Was Invented

As a result of monotheism, people not only noticed man's freedom, but could see the equality of all men before this single God. The fifth commandment—"You shall not kill!"—applied not only to the lives of tribe members, but ultimately to the whole world. For the first time, standing in the presence of this one God, it makes sense to speak of something like mankind and world history. Christianity alone makes this exceedingly clear. Christ does not send Christians to one chosen people alone, but to all nations. This is something Peter, the Jew, also eventually understands: "Truly I perceive that God shows no partiality, but in every nation any one who fears him and does what is right is acceptable to him" (Acts 10:34f.). Christianity opted for the equal treatment of all nations. The brilliant sociologist Niklas Luhmann observes that world religions "anticipate global society, so to speak." That is why we could say about Ancient Greece that nothing yet existed there "which came close to legal regulation or to humanization in the sense of modern international law." But Jesus goes even further. He demands: "Love your enemies!" Not only to do without killing one's enemies, but even to love them—this must have seemed to people of his day like a totally crazy, unrealistic provocation.

In earlier times, everything had revolved primarily around family relations, clans, tribes, and races. Christianity, however, gathered into the Christian Church people of various nations and endowed them with equal rights. For Christians, then, there was no longer just one chosen people. Rather, the chosen were all those who believed in Jesus Christ, and these came from all nations. Thus, Christianity from the beginning was aimed at the entire inhabited world—or, in today's language, at the global community. Bishop Agobard of Lyon (ca. 769–840) declared for Charlemagne's empire that there would "no longer be Aquitani, Lombards, Burgundians, or Alemanni". There were religious grounds for this decision, perhaps even some undertones of social revolution: "Since all have become brethren, they all invoke the one Father-God—the servant and the master, the poor and the rich, the unschooled and the learned, the weak and the strong, the lowly worker and the lofty emperor".[4] To bring about this universality, there emerged very early on a Christian training program, in which coexistence with foreigners was actually something to be worked at and practiced. The second-century Epistle to Diognetus, for example, says of Christians: "Every foreign territory is a homeland for them, every homeland foreign territory."[5] Monasticism—which explicitly conceived of itself as the spiritual implementation of God's biblical command to Abraham "Go from your country and your kindred and your father's house" (Gen 12:1)— had a catalyzing effect in this regard. In the Christian "ethics of brotherhood", which embraces all of mankind, the Frankfurt sociologist Karl O. Hondrich sees "an enormous achievement of the prophetic religion of salvation and a monstrous affront against all known morality", which had always given "preference to one's own tribe".[6] Modern nationalism once again promoted national blood and with this nourished its national chauvinism. In contrast, the Letter to the Colossians says that there will no longer be "Greek and Jew, circumcised and uncircumcised, Barbarian, Scythian, slave, free man" (Col 3:11)—all these barriers are overcome in the Christian faith. There is a provocative reason for this in the Gospel of John: Christians are all equally children of God, because they are born "not of blood nor of the will of the flesh nor of the will of man, but of God" (Jn 1:13). These words that sound so familiar to Christians today were "a moral revolution" back then.[7]

Indeed, there are not many things the New Testament rejects as strongly as the claim of blood, the idea that privileges in salvation derive from a person's descent. When Jesus was informed that his mother and his relatives were waiting for him outside, he responded brusquely: "Who is my mother, and who are my brethren? ... For whoever does the will of my Father in heaven is my brother, and sister, and mother" (Mt 12:48). By contrast, from a socio-historical perspective, it is natural for societies to define themselves by the blood of their birth and to divide themselves up accordingly. Underpinning this social structure is an idea of a divinely begotten ancestor, in whose superior blood all members of his nation participate by descent—to varying degrees, of course: the pure carriers of his blood on the one hand, and the lesser ones, the commoners, on the other. In comparison, Christianity's attitude seems almost to militate against the family, since it has called for equality from the very beginning. Saint Luke writes in the Acts of the Apostles: "The company of those who believed were of one heart and soul, and no one said that any of the things which he possessed was his own, but they had everything in common" (Acts 4:32). To Otto G. Oexle of the Max Planck Institute for History in Göttingen, these are the "most momentous sentences ever written", because they gave rise to a commitment to the common good, which included social equality.[8] The ancient historian Jochen Martin concludes: "With the victory of Christianity, the family as a cultural unit generally diminished."[9] The Canadian philosopher and political scientist Charles Taylor contrasts this reality with families in India, where it is difficult to make any decisions independently of the family.

The New Testament knows no nobility. But already in the early Middle Ages, during Christianity's slow saturation of Germanic estate-based society, aristocratic institutions, which were originally entirely foreign to Christianity, began to play a special role in the Church as well. Time and again, liberation movements rose up against these institutions, under the motto: "When Adam was digging and Eve was weaving, where was the nobleman then?" (*Als Adam grub und*

Eva spann, wo war denn da der Edelmann?). Later on, Luther once again opened up the perspective onto the original egalitarian nature of Christianity, emphasizing the "freedom of a Christian". However, he radically reversed this stance after the frightening events of the peasant wars: he subjected the Protestant churches to territorial lords, though this did not prevent Protestant theologians from eventually resisting this lordship, as happened in Saxony. With this reinstitution, the nobility regained de facto its rightful position. Lutheran theologian Heinz E. Tödt explains: "From that point forward, confessionalist Protestantism has been oriented toward authority, to the divine right of the monarch, to the Christian—or at least ethical—authoritarian state; in other words, it has been anti-democratic."[10] Thus the privileges of the aristocracy, which are completely alien to the Christian message, survived in different ways in the Catholic and Protestant realms up until the twentieth century.

On this point, a fundamental change had already occurred in the Old Testament. While the Greeks still recognized several primordial forms of the human race, the Israelites saw in Adam the sole ancient father of all mankind. The story of Adam and Eve—too often misunderstood in the conflict between science and theology—proves to be a fundamental statement of political theology asserting that no man or nation is of a privileged descent; rather, all descend from a single pair of parents and are equal in terms of origin. This was already nothing short of a revolutionary transformation. In the eighteenth century, the biblical story of Creation was subjected to scholarly criticism, and many discussed the idea that humans are descended from different tribes. As a result, the universalist ideal of humanity was jeopardized, and now the "enslavement of negroes" was legitimized by a theory of race. In the struggle between the Nazi Party and the Church, the Christian view of the unity of mankind remained a thorn in the side of the ruling powers.

Tribal religions proceeded on the basic assumption that human beings were by nature unequal—not only in this life, but also in the next. This eternal inequality legitimated divisions here on earth: the king remained king even in heaven, and the slave remained a slave. Monotheism, by contrast, laid the groundwork for really considering all human beings equal and attributing to them the same dignity. Jan Assmann agrees.

Monotheism carried yet another seed. In prehistoric cosmological religions, man usually corresponded to the sun and woman to the moon, which caused the latter to be a mere reflection of the former and never obtain equal rights. Monotheism, however, accords her the same human dignity. As a result, the nature of marriage, for example, also changed, becoming, over time, consensual, based on partnership between spouses.

Freedom, equality, and human dignity became the order of the day in world history only through monotheism. The modern constitutional state rests on these spiritual foundations: in its effort to maintain law and justice, it relies on the interior assent of its citizens and thereby contributes significantly to the decrease of violence.

Monotheism was innovative and revolutionary, whereas tribal religions continually reaffirmed the status quo. Only monotheism could produce the "Magnificat", Mary's song of praise in Luke's Gospel: "He has put down the mighty from their thrones, and exalted those of low degree" (Lk 1:52). For Christians, God's judgment primarily meant hope for the oppressed, the weak, the victims of life—hope that, in the end, divine justice would prevail.

All of this has to be taken into consideration when we speak of the price of monotheism. Jan Assmann is certainly right in saying that there is the temptation for people to believe they are in sole possession of the truth. Theoretical as well as practical intolerance and violence have occurred among fanatical representatives of monotheistic religions. But the crucial question is a historical one: would the alternative, a world without monotheism, have been more peaceful and humane? The most recent scholarly studies have been unequivocal on this point: definitely *not*! Even Assmann himself, who reconsidered his original thesis in 2015, admitted in the end that although the monotheistic turn had "manifest[ed] itself in countless acts of violence and bloodshed", the previous tribal religions had been full of that, too, and many of these forms of violence were "domesticated, civilized, or even eliminated altogether by the monotheistic religions as they rose to power".[11] No wonder, then, that Assmann writes in summary in the end: "Nothing is further from my mind than to accuse monotheism of bringing violence into the world. On the contrary, monotheism—with its prohibition to kill, its revulsion to human sacrifice and oppression, its argument for the equality of all men before the One God—has done everything to decrease this violence."[12]

3. Theory and Practice: Is Islam the Most Tolerant Religion, Logically Speaking?

Of the three monotheistic world religions, Islam is the most tolerant one. In theory. There is a logical reason for this. Each of the three monotheistic religions understood itself to be definitive and thus rejected its respective younger offshoots. This resulted in Judaism's rejection of both Christianity and Islam. Christianity rejected the younger Islam, but had partially to acknowledge the elder Judaism, from which it descended. Islam adopted some material from both the Old and New Testaments and therefore had partially to acknowledge both Judaism and Christianity. This latter acknowledgment was due to the fact that Islam wanted to include free religious consent, which in turn meant that alternatives to Islam had to be tolerated. However, because all three monotheistic religions claimed to have the only truth and, on top of that, understood themselves as universal, these acknowledgments were never at eye level, so to speak. Thus, Islam allowed Judaism and Christianity internally to practice their cults and granted them basic civil rights, but at the same time imposed certain limitations, especially higher taxation. Christianity issued similar regulations for Jews.

Judaism understood itself as having come first, as unique, and consequently it saw no reason to tolerate the other Islam and Christianity as "permitted religions". Of course, one reason for this was also that—with the exception of the special case of a mythical Khazar empire in the Far East—it never rose to the status of dominant religion anywhere and thus was never in a position to tolerate others. Throughout its common history with Christianity and Islam, Judaism remained a powerless minority: oppressed, repudiated, banished, and often even murdered—a two-thousand-year "valley of tears", of which Jewish historiography still speaks to this day. Even though Jewish existence was always a stricken one, it was still spared one challenge: granting tolerance to other religions. While Judaism was not at any point less absolute than the other two monotheisms, it never had actively to define the boundaries of a "permitted religion". American political scientist Gary Remer even thinks that if a Jewish state had existed in the Middle Ages, some gentiles might have been subjected to persecution.[13] Only today is the state of Israel beginning to face the task of regulating religious diversity.

The situation was very different for Christianity. The question of Judaism presented itself as soon as the Church gained state power in the Roman Empire. Christian emperors adopted the institution of "permitted religions", with which they were familiar from their pagan predecessors, and which was granted exclusively to Jews at the time. When the Western empire fell, the Church took up the legal protection of Jews. It was Pope Gregory the Great (ca. 540–604) who laid the foundation for a "very balanced Jewish policy",[14] as Judaism scholar Günter Sternberger puts it—a policy that, according to Hebrew University's Michael Toch, "proved extraordinarily enduring, even under the varying circumstances of later periods, right up into Modernity".[15]

"Permitted religion" reached its broadest significance in Islam, which was spread over vast regions often inhabited by Christians. At the time of the first expansion in the eighth century, a small number of Muslims—some 10 percent of the general populace— were ruling over a 90 percent non-Muslim population. Only in the twelfth and thirteenth centuries could North Africa be considered largely Islamized; Asia Minor did not follow until the fifteenth and sixteenth centuries. In Islamic lands, the "book religions" Judaism and Christianity were "protected", though of course their faithful were required to be loyal, to pay special fees, and even to label their clothes. The result was a relative freedom of religion and cult, but only within the proper cult spaces, and only if the works did not attract public attention. Minarets had to remain the tallest structures. At the same time, different religious communities had autonomy and their own jurisdiction, including guaranteed property and income.

For Christians, it was not possible to grant the followers of the Qur'an the status of a "permitted religion" in their territory, because Muslims were known as false latecomers. For this reason, they could not grant to Muslims what they could indeed grant to Jews. In this respect, Christian tolerance remained limited in practice. It was at least attempted when Spain was recaptured by Christians: in the twelfth century, the Muslims of Valencia obtained the right to attend mosques undisturbed, a guarantee on their dwelling places and property, autonomous jurisdiction, and relative self-government, as well as the assurance of not being obligated to accept non-Islamic legal decisions.

However, on the whole, such mixed zones were rare and were ultimately eliminated—from both sides. On the Christian side, for example, take the re-Christianization of a string of Mediterranean islands and of parts of Spain; on the Islamic, there was the complete Islamization of North Africa and Asia Minor. There is another special problem in Islam: in the case of Christian rule, Islamic jurists considered "emigration ... at the very least recommended and in most cases obligatory", as British-American historian Bernard Lewis notes. Those who voluntarily remained under Christian rule were "despised by both the emigrants and the unconquered", because the worst Muslim rule was preferable to the best rule of unbelievers.[16] Against this background, we can understand how the current emigration of Muslims to non-Muslim countries poses a problem to Islam that it has never known before.

The system of "permitted religions" naturally gave rise to a two-class society that, through many disadvantages, always exerted a certain amount of pressure on the members of the religion that was merely being tolerated. This could lead to the strange phenomenon of a double religion, with crypto-Jews, crypto-Christians, and crypto-Muslims. When in fifteenth-century Spain ten thousand Jews had themselves baptized Christian, in many places a double practice emerged, whether out of habit or out of ignorance. On the Sabbath people went to the synagogue, and on Sunday to Mass; they ate kosher at home, and pork outside of the home. Similar practices emerged among baptized Muslims. There were crypto-Christians in Albania, for example, where men lived as Muslims and women as Christians; they were Christians in their families, Muslims in public. Christian Lenten commandments were observed at home, and Ramadan at the mosque; when a person died, he received Christian sacramental last rites and yet was buried with Muslim rites. When taxes were collected, the heads of households declared themselves Muslim—in order to escape higher taxation as Christians—and when they were recruited for military service, they declared themselves Christian—in order to claim exemption. Even today, they often share pilgrimage sites and holy tombs in common.

In point of fact, all these regulations prevented the three monotheistic religions from becoming entangled through the centuries in perpetual war over their respective claims to absoluteness. Yet it is clear that the new age, Modernity, really did bring something new, namely equal religious freedom in all places, for all people.

II

The First Thousand Years

A Religion of Love Encounters Violence

Tolerance is a Christian invention. While the classical Latin *toleran-tia* meant enduring physical burdens and labors, injustice, torture, and violence, but never enduring other people or their opinions, Christians took care to change the word's meaning. From now on, it would be understood as loving respect for other men and forbearance toward those who think differently. This change had to do with the twofold commandment at the center of the Christian faith:

" 'You shall love the Lord your God with all your heart, and with all your soul, and with all your mind, and with all your strength.' The second is this, 'You shall love your neighbor as yourself.' There is no other commandment greater than these" (Mk 12:30–31). From this statement of Jesus, Paul draws out the injunction: "Let all that you do be done in love" (1 Cor 16:14). This had immediate consequences for tolerance. It meant, "Love the man, but detest his misdeeds." Such was the new Christian concept of tolerance. Despite his sins, the other should retain his right to live, and even be loved. The great Western Church Father Augustine of Hippo (354–430) explains this very practically: "Love sinners, not as sinners but as people."[1] Eight hundred years later, Thomas Aquinas (1225–1274) puts it the same way: "For it is our duty to hate, in the sinner, his being a sinner, and to love in him, his being a man."[2] Nothing like this existed in other religions, where every sin was an offense to God and all offenses to God had to be punished and that was the end of the story.

31

1. What to Do with the Weeds? A Parable
Changes Religious History

To love God "with all your mind"—this commandment marks the birth of theology, the pondering of God. The earliest Christian theology had already made a case for tolerance. In clear terms, the great north African jurist and theologian Tertullian (after 150–after 220) fought religious coercion, which "takes away a man's freedom of religion and forbids him the free choice of his god, so that he is no longer free to worship whom he will, but is forced to worship one he does not want to worship. Surely, no one, not even God, wants to be worshipped by someone who does not do so willingly."[3] Tertullian explicitly calls this freedom a "human right".[4] This was new.

For Christians, to be sure, faith in Jesus Christ, the incarnate Son of God, was not just some arbitrary opinion; he was divine truth, whom they confessed and for whom, if necessary, they died without violent resistance. Thus, the apostle Paul had already warned of believing in any different gospel and urged that false teachers and false brothers be expelled from the community. He pronounced a curse on them and consigned them to divine judgment at the end of time. But he did not write a single word in support of any form of violence against these deviant teachers. This, too, was new.

In contrast, paganism had not demanded a profession of faith in its innumerable gods with one's heart and mind, but rather required exterior subjection, through the performance of certain rites. Whoever rejected these rites could be punished by death, something the Christians of the first centuries repeatedly experienced first-hand during waves of persecution. One thing that held true across all pre-modern religions was that whoever made himself an enemy of God was to be eliminated. Otherwise, divine wrath would be poured out not only on him and those around him, but on society and the state as well. The notion that all offenses invoked the wrath of God or the gods is undoubtedly one of the most potent religious mechanisms there is. All cultures took it for granted that in order to forestall the deity's wrath, the governing entity must promote the worship of the gods in the interest of the common good, and use every necessary means of preventing offenses, sacrilege, and hostility toward the gods—since there loomed the threat of devastating divine

punishments that would imperil the existence of absolutely everyone. Enemies of the gods were punished with decapitation, burning,
or crucifixion. Already in the Babylonian legal code of King Hammurabi (1792–1750 B.C.), there stood the death penalty. In Greece,
Socrates (469–399 B.C.) is the best-known victim of a charge of godlessness, and curiously enough, even his student Plato (ca. 428–347
B.C.) pleaded in favor of the death penalty for those who deny the
existence of the gods. Later, even classical penal law retained such
provisions. When, in the first century A.D., a member of the Flavian
imperial household converted to the Jewish or the Christian faith,
he was punished by decapitation. The situation was no different in
ancient Israel: even the Christian Stephen was cast out of the city and
stoned (see Acts 7:58) for the same reason.

Only once we have gotten all this straight can we understand what
a tremendous religious-historical novelty was Christianity's radical
break with the standard religious practice of physically obliterating the
enemies of God. When the disciples wanted to call down "fire from
the heavens" onto the Samaritans, whom the Jews thought godless,
Jesus rebuked them. And in the Sermon on the Mount, he prohibited
all violence: "Love your enemies and pray for those who persecute
you, so that you may be sons of your Father who is in heaven; for
he makes his sun rise on the evil and on the good, and sends rain
on the just and on the unjust" (Mt 5:44–45). The only thing left for
Christians was to work at converting those who had gone astray and
to pray for their salvation. Killing was forbidden.

Instead, Christians debated, using arguments and counter-
arguments—and they did this with vigor. In one dramatic example,
the apostle Paul contradicted Peter to his face. In the end, they came
to an agreement at the Council of Jerusalem around 48 A.D., using the
solemn formula: "For it has seemed good to the Holy Spirit and to
us ..." (Acts 15:28). Later councils of the first millennium, too, saw
passionate debates: in the interest of the truth of the faith, teachings were condemned, bishops were deposed, entire groups were
excluded from the Church, but in the end no one had to fear for
life or limb. Divergent teaching, heresy, means believing only a part
of the whole and thus not being catholic—i.e., all-encompassing—
which is the adjective that the Creed uses to describe the Church.
But there remained the fundamental principle that curses could only

be laid on the heresies themselves, not on the heretics. These had to be spared and their salvation prayed for.

This radical nonviolence rested upon a famous text. Over the centuries, this text has saved thousands of lives. It can be found in chapter thirteen of Matthew's Gospel:

> Another parable he put before them, saying, "The kingdom of heaven may be compared to a man who sowed good seed in his field; but while men were sleeping, his enemy came and sowed weeds among the wheat, and went away. So when the plants came up and bore grain, then the weeds appeared also. And the servants of the householder came and said to him, 'Sir, did you not sow good seed in your field? How then has it weeds?' He said to them, 'An enemy has done this.' The servants said to him, 'Then do you want us to go and gather them?' But he said, 'No; lest in gathering the weeds you root up the wheat along with them. Let both grow together until the harvest; and at harvest time I will tell the reapers, Gather the weeds first and bind them in bundles to be burned, but gather the wheat into my barn'" ... And his disciples came to him, saying, "Explain to us the parable of the weeds of the field." He answered, "He who sows the good seed is the Son of man; the field is the world, and the good seed means the sons of the kingdom; the weeds are the sons of the evil one, and the enemy who sowed them is the devil; the harvest is the close of the age, and the reapers are angels. Just as the weeds are gathered and burned with fire, so will it be at the close of the age. The Son of man will send his angels, and they will gather out of his kingdom all causes of sin and all evildoers, and throw them into the furnace of fire, where there will be weeping and gnashing of teeth. Then the righteous will shine like the sun in the kingdom of their Father." (Mt 13:24–30, 36–43)

Even if these depictions of hell sound foreign to our ears, the meaning is still clear. The judgment of false teachers and the wicked is to be handed over to God on the Last Day. Until then, the apostle Paul's admonition holds: *caritas tolerat omnia*—love bears all things. The parable of weeds among the wheat was the unequivocal demand to end all religious violence; it was the Magna Carta of tolerance. One could not count the number of times this parable was textually cited during the first Christian millennium and even beyond. The parable of the weeds and the wheat is primal Christian material.

In fact, this parable ensured that in the first Christian millennium not a single false teacher or heretic was killed for his deviation with the approval of the worldwide Church. When in 385 A.D., at the insistence of some imperial dignitaries at the court in Trier, Germany, the false teacher Priscillian from Spain was condemned by an episcopal synod and slated for execution, the great archbishops of Milan and Tours, Saints Ambrose and Martin, personally made the arduous journey to Trier two times, rushing there to prevent this misdeed from happening. When an imperial decision on the matter was requested and Priscillian was nevertheless executed, Pope Siricius solemnly excluded from the Church all bishops in Trier who were involved in the killing. This scandal had its repercussions: there were no executions of heretics until 1000 A.D. In the Eastern Church, this held true all the way until the end of the Byzantine Empire in 1453.

To combat deviant teachers, Christians were armed with nothing but theology. This also meant that the Church had to steer a middle course. On the one hand, she had to struggle ever anew against spiritual and moral decline with new movements of reform. On the other hand, she also had to confront the opposite problem, since false teachings tended to be hyper-moralistic, elitist, and hostile to the body. In contrast to this, Christianity, which believed in the Incarnation of God and the resurrection of the body, was almost provocatively sensual [*sinnlich*, related to the senses]; Jesus treated sinners with compassion, and prideful elitism was completely alien to early Christians. Christianity's humanity and urbanity had to be defended against fanatical ideologies. This was not always easy.

For example, with great eloquence, the great Church Father Augustine (354–430 A.D.) threw himself into the debate with the Donatists. They supported the view that sinful priests could not relay God's grace. Augustine saw immediately that this theory would have meant the death of the Christian faith: since no one can judge the personal worthiness of a priest, the common faithful would be left without the certainty of really experiencing God's love. For the theologian Augustine, this was an all-or-nothing debate. And yet, he pleaded for nonviolence. After all, faith was a matter of free will. Besides, one had to be tolerant because all people are sinners and therefore all dependent on their neighbors' own tolerance. The same was true for false teachers, he said: "They should not be deemed lost in a physical sense, but instead, we should approach them spiritually and do what serves the correction of evil."[5] This sentence of Augustine's was included in medieval canon law. False teachings, it was said, even have their benefits: "Many matters of importance to the Catholic faith are canvassed by the feverish restlessness of heretics, and the result is that they are more carefully examined, more clearly understood, and more earnestly propounded, with a view to defending them against heretical attack, and thus an argument aroused by an adversary turns out to be an opportunity for instruction."[6] False teaching as an occasion for lifelong learning—that is a rather modern notion. For Augustine, too, the parable of the weeds plays a decisive role. This, in the end, is why the Church "tolerate[s] those whom she cannot correct";[7] the sinner and the heretic, too, have to be met with love, "because in this life it is always uncertain whether or not they are likely to experience a change of heart."[8] In a religious dispute in 411 A.D., Augustine brilliantly proved the Donatists wrong, thus decreasing their influence.

But eventually, when a branch of the Donatist movement, the Circumcellions, became violent and began to rove across the land plundering and murdering, this religious terror prompted even Augustine to endorse state pressure on the followers of this heresy, in order to bring them back into the Church. He invoked the parable of the wedding banquet (Mt 22:1–14), in which the invited guests snub the host and he goes out into the roads and lanes to impel people to come to his home (Latin: *compelle intrare*). Augustine continued, however, to reject violence, torture, and above all killing of false teachers, just as John Chrysostom (c. 349–407) had done in the East. For the next six hundred years—that is, for the entire first Christian millennium—people understood Augustine in this light. Only later was this principle misused. However, the principle of his that had a more enduring effect than any other was the one included in the authoritative *Decretum Gratiani*, the jurist Gratian's collection of canon law compiled around 1140: "No one is to be forced into the faith."[9] The Middle Ages' most eminent theologian, Thomas Aquinas, cites this principle when he states that no one is to be compelled to believe, "because to believe depends on the will."[10] This principle holds true in the Church to this day.

The rapid spread of Christianity in the ancient world has always been a cause for amazement. Perhaps even more astonishingly, it all happened without planning or strategizing, without institutions, and without a host of specially trained missionaries. The Church worked through its "mere existence", as the great Lutheran theologian Adolf von Harnack incisively put it in his still-foundational work *The Expansion of Christianity in the First Three Centuries*.[11] According to historian Norbert Brox, fundamental pronouncements about evangelizing the world did not enter into the ordinary theology of the early Christians. They "did not express a concern for evangelization, for example, the necessity to convert all non-Christians and a corresponding general Christian duty to evangelize. They did not feel compelled to embark on missionary campaigns."[12] In any event, neither did they bank on the whole world coming to believe, since as the Second Letter to the Thessalonians says, "Not all accept the faith." Consequently, Augustine could be of the opinion that not all "may believe, for God promised all the *nations*, but not all the *human beings* of all the nations".[13] The nations, not the individuals, were the object of Christian mission.

Sacrileges—including, later on, the practices of pagan cults—were combated by government authorities in order to hold off the divine wrath, but never through the death penalty. During the Carolingian dynasty, intellectual heretics were threatened rather with monastic imprisonment. In a focused study of "public anger in the early middle ages", the Swiss medieval historian Monica Blöcker has shown just how quickly the public could demand condemnation and exclusion from the community, and even lynching, driven by the archaic fear of supernatural punishment. In this phenomenon, one can see at work both "the public's anger against the victim, and the clergy's mitigating influence."[14] Christian tolerance and the Christian renunciation of violence shaped the writing of leading theologians in the first millennium, such as Venerable Bede (672–735) and Rabanus Maurus (780–856), the abbot and archbishop of Mainz celebrated as "Germany's teacher".

No wonder, then, that Rainer Forst, a student of respected German philosopher Jürgen Habermas, holds that even into Modernity, the New Testament is "of central importance ... for the entire European discourse of toleration.... [T]he word is the sole weapon of Christians, not earthly coercion or violence."[15]

2. Tensions: Christian Nonviolence and State Authority

When the people of Israel seized the land of Palestine, it was with violence, and enemy nations were threatened with annihilation. The humanizing effects of monotheism prevailed only very slowly. The earliest ages of Islam, too, are marked by militant expansion. The prophet Muhammad himself rode into war on a horse. Then within a hundred years, all of North Africa—including Spain—had fallen, and Muslim troops reached the south of France. It is hard to imagine a greater contrast to this expansion than that of Christianity: Jesus of Nazareth rode into Jerusalem on a donkey, not in order to prevail militarily, but in order to suffer; not in order to kill, but in order to let himself be killed; not in order to win land, but to lose everything, down to the clothes on his back. And the first Christians followed suit. The Israelites knew holy wars, "Yahweh Wars", and for Muslims, too, "holy war" was later to become key in spreading Islamic rule, so that, as scholar of Islam Tilman Nagel writes, "The standard relationship between Islamic and other territories was war".[16] By contrast, Christians renounced all military force from the outset. For this reason, they did not participate in the Jewish revolt of 66/70 A.D., which was one of the reasons for their separation from Judaism, as historian Johann Maier states. Thus, Christians were radically nonviolent. Many were complete pacifists, refusing military service, not defending themselves when they were attacked, and even rejoicing when, in public spectacles, they could follow their Lord into death as martyrs. This went on for centuries. And when it came to dealing with the state, Jesus' words gave the rule: "Render therefore to Caesar the things that are Caesar's, and to God the things that are God's" (Mt 22:21).

The Christians' problems all began with an apparent stroke of luck for the Church. The Roman state ended the persecution of Christians, and Emperor Constantine eventually became a Christian. What now? The emperor did what all Roman emperors have always done: he also looked after religion.

Emperor Constantine had to battle with a particular problem. On the one hand, he wanted to practice the nonviolence of Christianity, but on the other hand, as emperor—according to policy from time immemorial—he had to eliminate sacrilege against God so that the community did not suffer damage. And deviation from the true faith was seen as sacrilege. To be sure, in the first millennium, early Christian nonviolence did have an effect on the implementation of state regulations. After all, it was Emperor Constantine who, when theological discord arose between Christians, convened a council, the Council of Nicea, which conveniently held its meetings not far from his residence. For this, the Church was quite grateful to the emperor. But when Constantine's Christian successors started to interfere willy-nilly with ecclesial matters, there came to light an issue that concerns the Church to this day: How should the Christian Church deal with a Christian state, and how should a Christian ruler behave toward the Church? Up to now, for Christians, violence had always been violence from others. But now the state power was Christian, and for a situation such as this, Holy Scripture, the New Testament, had no answers at all. After all, the state in itself was nothing bad; it civilized the original unreflecting domination of the stronger over the weak. Still, the Church wanted to be free in the Christian state, too, and yet the Christian emperor saw himself first and foremost as Roman emperor and not as a mere aid to the Church. There was no ideal solution to this problem.

To all those who see this flirtation with the Roman state as the fall of the Church, the obvious reply is this: the Church had no choice but to take on the challenge posed by the Christianization of the Roman Empire if she did not want to back out of history. In doing so, the Church contributed to the humanization of the state. The pagan enemies of Christianity in the Roman Empire, the old, still-powerful elites, accused the Christians of making the state into a weakling and thus at fault for the eventual conquest of Rome by the Barbarian Visigoths under Alaric in the year 410, which shook the whole empire. It was in answer to this accusation that Augustine wrote his principal work, the *City of God*. He distinguished the worldly kingdom from the kingdom of God—a kingdom that germinates in the heart of man.

It was also Augustine who drew out the consequences of this fact that Christians now had to take over state responsibility. No state could be built on total pacifism. Thus, he created something entirely new. Against the thousand-year-old Roman military tradition that understood war as a legitimate means for Romans to "bring peace" to a region at any time—a euphemism for conquest—he promulgated the teaching on "just war", which remains the basis of international politics to this day. According to Augustine, wars of conquest are always forbidden. Only wars of defense are justifiable, and only under strict conditions: in the event of attacks by an enemy or as resistance against injustice. Even then, one can respond only with proportionate means, so that the damage is not excessive. In addition, wars had to be conducted with ethically spotless intentions. They were never to be justified by mere pugnaciousness or greed for spoils, and they had to be conducted by a legitimate authority—no one should act on his own initiative. The following points constitute Augustine's "teachings on peace":

1. State violence and especially war are only ever justified as a reaction to an overt and serious disturbance of outward justice and of the social order.
2. The identification of a certain people or a country as specially chosen by God shall be rejected.
3. Holy wars for the sake of achieving personal sanctity shall be ruled out.
4. Limits to the use of violence have to be respected. Augustine vehemently rejects torture and the death penalty.[17]

If we find all these points rather obvious, perhaps this is because we simply do not realize how profoundly we are the heirs of a Christian tradition, even if we no longer see ourselves as Christians.

The Christianization of the Roman Empire was a bumpy process. Again and again, there arose tensions between the emperors and the Church. To the Christian emperors, Saint Augustine's ethics of peace seemed rather distant from their Roman tradition, and his "one can only believe voluntarily" maxim was alien to some. Though the pagan emperors had incorporated the gods of conquered peoples into the Roman pantheon, they did so only on the condition that from then on the conquered would also worship the Roman gods, especially the divine emperor. Otherwise, one qualified as an enemy of the constitution and was eligible to be killed. Only the Jews were exempt from this, because of their official status as a "permitted religion". When the empire became Christian, the emperors expected subjugated peoples to worship the Lord of heaven and earth, Jesus

Christ, rather than the divine emperor. An imperial religious policy developed that included coercing people into baptism. As a result, in a move completely foreign to Christianity, compulsory baptisms started to take place. Even though Christians eventually approved of the prohibition of pagan cults and the destruction of temples, they had little missionary incentive, and in the fourth century, only about 15 percent of the empire's population was Christian. However, these few set the tone for the rest, and paganism dwindled more and more. Within the empire, paganism was increasingly discriminated against by the state until finally, under Emperor Justinian, pagans had practically no rights at all. However, ancient historian Johannes Hahn points out that in spite of all the state coercion, one cannot generally speak of an age of religious violence: "The decline of paganism and its displacement by Christianity mostly takes place in a much less spectacular way—peacefully."[18]

The close link between Church and state remained alien to Christianity and repeatedly led to conflicts. Against this background, Jesus' famous dictum gained relevance: "Render to Caesar the things that are Caesar's, and to God the things that are God's." At the turn from Antiquity to the Middle Ages, Pope Gelasius (492–496) drew some unambiguous conclusions that became famous: state power, "knowing that their sphere of competence granted only the jurisdiction of human affairs, does not include the charge of divine affairs.... Mindful of human weakness, as befits [Christ's] care for his own, he has made a distinction between the two roles, assigning each its sphere of operation and its due respect.... Christian emperors were to depend on priests for their eternal life, priests were to profit from imperial government for their historical existence."[19]

This was a bombshell. Such a clear separation between Church and state was an absolute novelty in world history. In all other religions, separation between the two was inconceivable and to this day still presents tremendous problems. However, this principle that would later be implemented more broadly in the Enlightenment first had to be chiseled out in a struggle that lasted centuries. And it was never the state that wanted to free itself from the Church; it was always the Christian Church that had to fight for its freedom from the state. But by what means? Whoever maintains today that the Church of those days should have fought on a purely argumentative basis misunderstands the circumstances of the age. One could only escape state authority by having power in the first place. Especially in Germany, rulers availed themselves of the bishops as loyal subjects. Since these men had no children, the king did not have to worry about any egotistical family agendas. But of course, he also wanted the authority to appoint these bishops himself. This, in turn, brought on the so-called investiture controversy, a fierce debate that lasted hundreds of years, wherein the popes eventually won for the Church her autonomy in episcopal appointments, though of course with only partial success. Scarcely had they struggled out from under the power of the German emperor and wrestled down the Staufer dynasty than they lay completely exposed under the power of the French kings in Avignon. Only in this light does it become clear why today even a tiny state such as the Vatican is for the pope a guarantee of the freedom of the Church—a fact that had very real consequences during the Second World War. Even, by the way, under Otto von Bismarck's rule, when the state upheld the Protestant policy of unity between throne and altar, Catholics were reproached for the old battles of the popes against medieval imperial rule, and for this reason, the Catholic Church was tyrannically subjugated by the new German state in the *Kulturkampf* of the late nineteenth century. All this despite the historical fact—unearthed through the work of medieval historian Gerd Althoff—that Holy Roman Emperor Henry IV (1050–1106) himself was a violent tyrant and a rapist. By contrast, his adversary Pope Gregory VII (ca. 1025–1085), who lifted Henry's excommunication in Canossa, proved to be a significant man of the Church. After the emperor's subsequent betrayal, Gregory died in exile in Salerno and asked for the following distressing inscription on his tomb: "I loved justice and hated injustice; therefore I die in exile." Protestants, of course, in many ways subjected themselves to the state. Luther, frightened by the atrocities of the peasant wars, called the princes of the Holy Roman Empire to his aid. And from the earliest times, Eastern Orthodox Christians, too, had the habit of unreserved loyalty to rulers, which was not even diminished during the Second World War by the reign of Josef Stalin, to whom the patriarch of Moscow continually demonstrated his loyalty.

3. Cultivating Barbarians: Christianity and the Germanic Tribes

Christianity had hardly Christianized the Roman Empire, when the empire's—and the Church's—next big problem reared its head: the Germanic peoples. The Germanic tribes were pagans who glorified violence and occasionally dwelled "like the Vandals" in enemy territory. Tolerance was entirely unknown to them. There was basically constant war, and everyone outside of the peace agreed upon between certain clans was an enemy. Peace constituted an exception and had to be declared by contract. Religious historian Hans-Peter Hasenfratz relates some astonishing stories: "At the age of seven, the Icelandic boy Egil—to his mother's great pride—slays his playmate with a bearded axe after losing to him in a ball game. The Danish lad Vagn might hold the record, though, for having already slain three men by the age of nine."[20]

It wasn't easy to fill these people with enthusiasm for the radically nonviolent Christian message. And their conversion did not exactly take place in the way one might wish for today. The Frankish king Clovis I had himself baptized after winning a battle in the name of Christ, and subsequently all Franks had themselves baptized, or more precisely, the king had them baptized.

Was this mere politics? Did Clovis become Catholic simply to ally himself with the Catholic population of the former Roman Empire against the other—non-Catholic—Germanic peoples? Some have suspected this to be the case. What speaks against it, however, is that with this step, Clovis ran a great risk. His hereditary kingship depended solely on his descent from Merovech, the demigod founding ancestor whose blood flowed in all Franks, but which was purest in the royal clan. But Christianity could endorse neither a founding ancestor nor a special quality of blood, because according to the biblical Creation narrative, all men are descended from Adam and Eve and so everyone is equal and is of the same blood. By his baptism, Clovis risked losing his privileged blood ancestry. Legal historian Hans Hattenhauer formulates the king's problem dramatically: he had "committed a constitutional infringement" and for this reason "any Frankish person could deny him obedience and call him a lawbreaker and a harbinger of calamity."[21] In sum, Clovis' and the Franks' baptism may not have been mere politics.

The baptism of entire peoples sounds curious to us today, because individual conversion is now a requirement for baptism. But with the appearance of the Germanic peoples, the understanding of religion once again became more tribally motivated and consequently the Christian mission changed as well. Individuals did not convert; rather, entire tribes did. Anything else would have seemed very strange to the Germanic tribes. This is why historian Hans-Dietrich Kahl calls for "exercising greater caution than we have before when we use the terms 'mission by force [Gewaltmission]' and 'coercive Christianization.' "[22] How else could such religious groups, who judged the pantheon of gods by their strength in war and victory, have been converted?

At the same time, the contrast between Christianity—something new—and Germanic religion was the greatest imaginable. The Germanic tribes considered themselves subject to a blind fate, and their gods acted in a manner that was as warlike as that of the warrior aristocracy on earth. Even the afterlife, Valhalla, was a battleground where heroes continued to fight. The only difference was that the slain rose again on the next day and rejoined the combat. No wonder, then, that in their language there was no word for "interiority" or "cordiality", for "compassion" or "conscience"; no wonder the spiritual state we call "love" was not a concept for the Germanic tribes. Conveying to such people that a person should love God with all his heart and all his soul, with all his mind and all his strength, was a true challenge. But the Christian mission succeeded, and this had very practical consequences. For example, Germanic jurisdiction knew only liability based on deed: one was liable for one's actions, irrespective of one's intention. In contrast, the New Testament said clearly that if you desire something in your heart, the deed has already been done. The modern notion of liability for intentions emerged from this, which is to say that when considering a deed committed, intention and motive have to be considered as well. The Christian practice of confession and penance was the first to take man seriously as a psychological creature. People were now being asked for their motivations, in an effort to bring about healing and change. The great sociologist Max Weber wrote that by virtue of the system of confession and penance, which was unmatched throughout the world, "the Catholic church in the Occident carried through the Christianization of Western Europe with unparalleled force."[23]

In reality, the Christianization of Germanic and Slavic tribes was also a difficult process, thanks to the clash between high culture and folk culture. These two worlds had completely different standards. On one side, there were philosophers, jurists, laws, and courts, and on the other, Germanic folk traditions and brute single combat; on one side, schools of high culture centered on reading and writing, and on the other, there were Germanic tribal myths and ritual magic. Christianity actually called for high cultural conditions, since it had a body of sacred scripture and spiritual liturgical practices. But the ancient literary world north of the Alps had largely collapsed. Christianity thus found itself confronted with the question of whether to be or not to be: either give up on literacy, textuality, and spirituality, and lose its character as a book religion, or else create anew those civilizational and cultural preconditions required by such a religion of the book.

How, then, was the book of the Bible supposed to be conveyed to an illiterate people? Through schools? But how could schools be introduced into the forests east of the Rhine, where there were only a handful of people per square mile? Not until the fifteenth century did literacy, it seems, become a bit more widespread again, particularly with the emergence of printing. Before then, one had to make do with the resources available, namely oral sermons and the *biblia pauperum*—the "Bible of the poor" found in churches in the form of sculptures, frescoes, and stained glass, allowing the message of Scripture to take on a visible shape for everyone. Still, it was obviously not possible to do without written language. Those of a more educated class could learn Latin in monasteries, which opened up an understanding not only of Christian liturgy, but also of the great Latin literature.

There was, however, an even bigger problem facing the missions: the Germanic languages were not adapted for conveying the Christian faith. German literature scholar Hans Eggers describes this dramatic situation:

For the Our Father to be understood at all, a revolution of the entire Germanic imagination was necessary. The prayer begins with the image of a Father in heaven, which can be expressed with Germanic words, but which hardly has an equivalent in the pagan Germanic imagination. Then how ought a young church community understand the phrase "Hallowed be thy name; thy kingdom come"? Further, how should it understand the Christian terms of guilt and forgiveness, of temptation and salvation? But if the simple Lord's Prayer already poses such difficulty, how immeasurably difficult must it have been to understand the Creed, laden as it is with dogmatic terminology in the spirit of the theologians of early Christianity? And how much other Christian thought had to be absorbed! Christian thought and imagination must have appeared strange at first, unheard of. Hundreds and thousands of concepts from Christian doctrine and, what's more, from philosophical abstraction had now to be acquired for which the native language had no expressions at all.[24]

Metaphors were important in the interpretation of the Bible and the liturgy, expressing the spiritual through the material. But that did not really work for the Germanic peoples. Peter's receiving the keys of the kingdom of heaven from Jesus was originally supposed to mean that he was endowed with *spiritual* authority. But the Anglo-Saxons could not quite understand this, which is why at a council in north England's Whitby in 664, they very "realistically" declared that Peter was standing before the gates of heaven and would only unlock it for his friends. This gave the Anglo-Saxon church a big push to join the Roman Church of Peter.

To pagan Germanic peoples as well as the Slavs, human sacrifice was a very normal and very real part of life. The bog bodies[25] bear witness to this, and the last human sacrifice took place on the island of Rügen in 1150. In contrast, Christianity demanded a spiritual, bloodless sacrifice: to offer oneself for truth and love of one's neighbor. The old Germanic notion that real blood was an obligatory part of the sacrifice might explain the medieval desire to see real, bleeding hosts. The Germanic difficulty with metaphors is evident throughout the Middle Ages. For example, in some reliquary collections, there are feathers that supposedly come from the Holy Spirit as a dove. All of this, however, is due less to "stupidity" than to poor education stemming from a lack of linguistic resources. One can understand that for these peoples, well thought-out theology was, from a linguistic standpoint, simply beyond the realm of possibility. That is why early on, theology only worked in Latin.

It was first and foremost Christian theology that, nourished by the spirit of the gospel, made a stand against the newly converted Germanic peoples' relapse into the old tribal religion. The Anglo-Saxon monk Venerable Bede (ca. 672–735), who stood out in his time for his astonishing learnedness, paints a picture that defies the ethnocentrism of the German peoples. A recent study states: "In Bede's work, the nation does not represent itself as a chosen people, but as a nation integrated into the world of nations. The movement of expansion in which it takes part is the movement of the 'Church of nations,' which grows with each successive conversion."[26] The basic idea is this: a people in the Church of peoples, which is the Church of Christ. For Bede, the awareness of being one people includes the idea of internationality. And in the case of conversion, Bede calls for something that was taken as given in the first centuries, and still is today: conscious acceptance with individual consent of the Christian faith. The Anglo-Saxon missionary spirit consciously trained itself to be international, for instance in the missionary school in Utrecht founded by the Northumbrian Willibrord (ca. 658–739). We can read in the *Vita Gregorii* from 790:

> The students did not come from a single people, but were gathered from the blood of all neighboring peoples. They were animated by such trust, such friendliness and spiritual joy, that they were easily recognized in their unity as the sons of the one spiritual Father and of the Mother of all, which is love. Some came from the noble tribe of the Franks, some from the pious nation of the Angles, some from the new shoot that God had planted only in our days among the Frisians and the Saxons. Others came from the Bavarians and the Swabians, who had the same religion, or from whichever nation or tribe God happened to send them.[27]

In this way, the Christianization of the Germanic peoples was also a cultural mission.

However, when the Germanic people were baptized, they did not immediately cast off their tendency for cruelty. That is why the remaining centuries of the first millennium saw an arduous struggle for the Christianization and humanization of the Germanic Barbarians, one that often threw Christians backward, beyond the spiritual depths achieved in the first centuries. But Christianity was so successful in its endeavor that even someone like the polemical poet Heinrich Heine could write almost prophetically in 1834:

> Christianity—and this is its greatest merit—has somewhat mitigated the brutal German love of war, but it could not destroy it. Should the subduing talisman, the cross, be shattered, the frenzied madness of the ancient warriors, that insane berserker rage of which Nordic bards have so often spoken and sung, will blaze up once more. This talisman is fragile, and the day will come when it will collapse miserably. The ancient stony gods will then rise from the forgotten debris and rub the dust of a thousand years from their eyes, and Thor with his giant hammer will finally leap up and shatter the Gothic cathedrals to pieces. When you hear a crashing such as has never been heard in the history of the world, know that the German thunder has finally reached its destination. There shall be a performance staged in Germany, compared to which the French Revolution will appear like a harmless idyll.[28]

The recently Christianized Germanic peoples were certainly tamed by Christianity, but these powerful Christian rulers of the early Middle Ages were by no means as nonviolent as one might expect of Christians, and certainly not as nonviolent as those exemplary Christians of the first century. Augustine's old idea of just warfare almost collapsed during this period. Instead there broadly prevailed a kind of "natural war"—the perennial state of affairs, as it were, between Germanic peoples—or else an entirely un-Christian "holy war" that wrestled down all other peoples or tribes in the name of one's own folk or tribal god, only now this deity happened to be the God of the Christians. It was no longer possible to do all this very openly, since the Christian Scriptures, the Christian monks, and the Christian Church in general spoke a whole different language. But for a long time, beneath a Christian veneer, sometimes a rather thin one, the volcanic Germanic violence lay dormant—the same violence that would be admired much later by those neo-pagans who glorified the Germanic race, the violence that so repulsed Heinrich Heine.

4. Charlemagne: The Saxon Slaughterer
as a European Role Model

To Europeans who know their history, there is perhaps something comical in the fact that year after year, pious, peace-loving European elites gather in Aachen, Germany, in honor of Charlemagne (ca. 747–814), awarding the Charlemagne Prize to a person distinguished only by the fact that, ideally, he has absolutely nothing in common with the person after whom this prize is named. Charlemagne, literally Charles the Great, is great mostly because he reigned for a long time, and because he usually won the cruel, permanent wars he waged. At the very least, he forced the core of Europe to draw together into one as his battle spoils. Historian Thomas Scharff notes: "During the reign of Charlemagne and of his successors there was hardly a year without war. In this period, the omnipresence of war and violence was very high, even by medieval standards."[29]

Charlemagne was a tall man, proud and power conscious, and unscrupulous in achieving his goals when he needed to be, which possibly cost his underage nephews their lives. His sex life bore a striking resemblance to Mick Jagger's. Mixing the Old Testament idea of a chosen people—here, the Franks—with Roman imperialism, he resolutely and confidently claimed hegemony over other peoples. Thus, just as in the religious warfare of tribal societies, he not only thought his own empire better, but he also destroyed the pagan sanctuaries of "other gods". His renowned Saxon Wars began in 772 with the destruction of the Irminsul, the Saxons' sacred tree, which was worshipped as a pillar of the world. The Saxon Wars were to drag on for thirty years, waged on both sides with the utmost brutality. When the Saxons vowed to convert to Christianity in 777 and the masses had themselves baptized, the goal—later indicated by Einhard, Charlemagne's biographer—seemed already achieved: the Saxons "join[ed] the Franks as one people" by means of the sacraments of the Christian faith.[30] But when they broke their word in 782 and destroyed a Frankish army under the leadership of Widukind, Charlemagne responded mercilessly. In the legal code of the Saxon Capitularies, which was forced on the Saxons, he threatened: "If any of the race of the Saxons hereafter should conceal himself unbaptized among his people, scorn baptism, and wish to remain pagan, let him be punished by death."[31] This contradicted all Christian principles. Most notably, Charlemagne set a warning example at Verden. This event, the Massacre of Verden, which went down in history as a scandal, still triggers disagreements among scholars. Four thousand five hundred Saxon ringleaders are supposed to have been decapitated in a single day, as the Royal Carolingian Annals proudly state. Spreading terror was back then a method for securing state authority.

But current scholarship tends to consider this number a major exaggeration. Dieter Hägermann, historian of the Middle Ages, has voiced his opinion on this issue in the most detail. Common sense forbids us to think that there were four thousand five hundred conspirators or ringleaders, he says. One can assume, rather, that it was a group of several dozen who were extradited by the Saxons themselves. To be able to execute four thousand five hundred people presupposes enormous concentrations of troops on both sides, whereas the Carolingian armies numbered perhaps between five and ten thousand men. Also, it is doubtful that the capacities and the skills for the execution of such a great number of people were available:

> The *Annales Petaviani* seem to have passed on the events quite accurately, reporting: "The Franks slayed a number of Saxons, and they led many defeated Saxons to the Francia." A very small portion of the rebels, the instigators and the leaders, were thus executed; a much greater portion was deported and released in the Frankish parts of the country. Moreover, all other sources, including the letters from Charlemagne's circle, remain silent on this matter, even Alcuin's writings, which commented on Charlemagne's Saxon mission quite critically and would not simply have accepted a blood orgy. This criminal court, which had the purpose of establishing an example and which has been associated with the town of Verden ever since, remains an exception [in the Carolingian campaign] and served exclusively as a deterrent. Its success was not long in coming either, since Widukind, the Saxon adversary par excellence, submitted to the king in 785.[32]

Horst Fuhrmann, one of the most prominent scholars of medieval German history, describes the "myth of the Saxon Slaughterer" in similar terms.[33] Still, this event at Verden apparently gave Charlemagne a reason for contrition. This is believed to be the reason why he had the portrait of his predecessor, Arnulf of Metz, altered so that he was dressed not as a bishop but as a penitent. The pagan slogan "baptism or death" was also replaced by a milder regulation. Later sources show that the pressure to get baptized cannot have been very strong in practice at all. As a matter of fact, the death penalty was commonplace in Saxon law. Even the theft of horses or bees, the Saxons punished by death.

Yet it would be a mistake to reduce Charlemagne to politics, especially to military politics. For all the alarm of today over the violence factor in the Frankish empire, a pure military-historical perspective is too narrow, as British historian Robert Bartlett confirms: "It would be easy to concentrate a strictly military eye on this expansionary movement, but as important is the process of cultural change."[34] Even though the Frankish king's "mission by sword" was un-Christian, Charlemagne did much to civilize and cultivate his empire, and he achieved this mostly by vigorously supporting Christianity. What Charlemagne initiated was no less than a religious and cultural revolution. In the areas along the Rhine and beyond, there developed ecclesial centers of culture and writing: Sankt Gallen and Reichenau in the south, Fulda and Corvey in the east. Alcuin, Charlemagne's "state minister of education and culture", prescribed the Roman liturgy for the entire empire in order to secure its unity. However, Alcuin also contradicted his lord, especially regarding the important question of forced conversions. He declared frankly: "Faith, as St. Augustine says, is a matter of will, not necessity. A man can be attracted into faith, not forced. He can be forced to be baptised, but that is useless for faith except in infancy. A grown man should answer for himself about his beliefs and desires. If he professes faith falsely, he will not have true salvation."[35] This had been the Christian understanding, and it remains so to this day, but medieval Germanic princes and even Charlemagne had to be continually reminded of it by the Church.

Later, in the ninth century, two translations of the Bible emerged from the Germanic-speaking part of the empire: the *Heliand* and the *Christ*. Of course these were not simply "translations". Rather, as mentioned before, a new language had to be created, in a sense, in order to make the Bible understandable. East of the Rhine, the language was still Barbarian, as medieval historian Johannes Fried observes: "Every sort of elevated thought, of theological speculation, of scholarship was still beyond the reach of its linguistic scope. Even the adoption of the Latin alphabet already represented great obstacles, due to its different phonology."[36] Germanic languages were missing the necessary religious and interior expressive ability. The translation of the key Christian term "compassion" alone took no fewer than seven attempts.

Even if the wars were rooted in the un-Christian idea of the Franks' being the "chosen people", Charlemagne still achieved the consolidation of his rule through the Christian idea of one unified Church of all nations. Carolingian imperial thinkers expanded the Pauline imperative "neither Jew nor Greek" to include their own circumstances: "neither Aquitanian nor Lombard, Burgundian nor Alemanni". The theologian Rabanus Maurus declared programmatically that there should be no difference among the various nations, because the Catholic Church existed as a unity spread over the entire world. It is really thanks to Charlemagne's empire that Europe—despite all the wars—still kept one common foundation: Christianity.[37] Noting the exchange of the basic tribal-religious structure of society for a Christianity's universal-religious structure, historian Hans-Dietrich Kahl considers this an epochal achievement that, in fact, originally brought forth Europe—an "event of truly world-historical importance".[38] The most significant achievement, then, was not military imperialism, but rather Christianization.

On Christmas Day of 800, Charlemagne had himself crowned Holy Roman Emperor by Pope Leo III at Saint Peter's Basilica in Rome. This event is widely considered to mark the beginning of the Middle Ages. Here in this brief moment, the two great powers of the medieval period appear unified. But the papacy, more than imperial rule, was to define this epoch. It was the papacy that proved itself an international force for cohesion in Europe, capable of reaching even the remotest regions. The administrative centralization of the individual churches by the popes was only possible because of a broad faithful veneration of Saint Peter's successor and the idea of Holy Rome, "an expression of the unity of the Church on earth like no other", as historian Gerd Tellenbach emphasizes.[39] British research today speaks of a "papal revolution" (Karl Leyser) that really allowed Europe to emerge in the first place.[40]

In the end, it must be said: for secular Europe, whose constitution—among other things—has failed because many wanted to prevent all references to God and Christianity from being included in the text, Charlemagne is the wrong person of reference—unless one wants to follow his example and block all exit from the European community through a carefully measured dose of massacres, as Charlemagne did with the contract-breaking Saxons. Every convincing reason for attributing greatness to Charlemagne from today's perspective has to do with his intensive and truly enduring efforts to Christianize his empire, which actually founded European civilization.

Charlemagne's reputation today is a powerful instance of psychological "splitting", wherein something partly bad or partly good gets viewed as entirely bad or entirely good—either/or. The first Holy Roman Emperor is conveniently used by Europeans as an excuse for attributing all that is bad in their history to Christianity—that religion from which, at the same time, they distance themselves: it would never occur to Charlemagne's political successors across Europe to apologize for his *political* misdeeds. At any rate, the Catholic Church is never credited for the great feat of Christianizing and humanizing Charlemagne's empire, but rather must justify herself time and again for his so-called "mission by sword" among the Saxons, which in reality was a brutal, political act of violence. And if Charlemagne's canonization is lamented as a scandal, the Catholic Church shouldn't be blamed for that, either, because it was an illegal act, a deliberate provocation of the Church by the antipope, who was appointed by Frederick Barbarossa and was completely dependent on the emperor. The one to apologize would be rather, to make an analogy, the German president—or his chaplain, if he had one.

5. Sensationalism: Pope Joan and the End of the World

Every now and then, the ZDF [*Das Zweite Deutsche Fernsehen*, a public television station in Germany] produces excellent documentaries. But it apparently has a weakness for church histories that are opulently staged but unfortunately false. Not that there is anything wrong with this per se. After all, fictional stories can be quite entertaining.

Most movies are based on fiction. But sometimes, a work of fiction serves a false cliché, and this can have some unjust consequences.

It has long been common knowledge, thanks to the work of Protestant church historian David Blondel (1590–1655), that there never existed a female pope called Joan, and even today, her nonexistence has been secured by scholars beyond doubt. This story was only invented in the mid-thirteenth century and then projected back into the ninth century. Even back then, it was already rather unlikely, but following the Italian motto *"se non è vero è ben trovato"* [even if it is not true, it is well conceived], the idea that a woman could have stolen in as a pope is simply too good not to be invented.

In order to create a certain sensational atmosphere, there has to be at least some murmur that perhaps it is true after all. And that is what ZDF did. But they didn't content themselves with murmuring. In fact, ZDF publicly claimed that it was the story of "a smart woman, hungry for knowledge, who did not allow herself to be intimidated by the Church's teaching that women are inferior creatures." Petra Gerster, host of the news program *Heute* and thus eminently believable, proceeded to illuminate audiences on this subject: "According to the Church, she does not exist, even though five hundred chronicles tell her story. Many traces were certainly falsified or destroyed, because history is always written by the powerful." Finally, Gerster presents the hypothesis that under the rule of a female pope, there would never have been a sexual abuse scandal. This hypothesis is not really worth commenting on. One does, however, gloomily wonder how a public broadcaster like Gerster could not afford the expertise of one single knowledgeable historian who could have prevented this demonstrably absurd nonsense. In that case, it would have been possible to discover that such a "Church teaching" on female inferiority never existed, that the "five hundred chronicles" are all based on a single source, namely Martin of Opava, and that this particular period in Rome was not misogynistic whatsoever: the renowned "senatoress" Marozia is supposed to have ruled tyrannically over no less than four popes from 914 to 932.

To summarize: the scandal about the female pope Joan was never real. ZDF, however, is very real indeed.

Shortly after Marozia was taken prisoner by her son in 932 and disappeared from the stage of history, Otto the Great ascended to the throne in Germany. He followed in Charlemagne's footsteps by being crowned Holy Roman Emperor in Rome in 962, where, while passing through, he set in order the chaos of the Roman Curia. The so-called "Ottonian Renaissance", however, lagged far behind the Carolingian "cultural revolution". It was Otto who endowed the bishops with worldly powers, which later on would bring the above-mentioned investiture controversy upon the Middle Ages. American historian Thomas A. Brady calls the rule of prince-archbishops, the foundation of which was laid at this time, "an unparalleled anomaly in the world of Catholicism"—one that nevertheless was to last almost a thousand years.[41]

What is most surprising, however, is that with Otto the Great, a *Saxon*—a member of that people so fiercely chastised by Charlemagne little more than a century before—rises to royal and imperial dignity. This testifies to the success of the process of integration. Already in Antiquity, the peoples left of the Rhine had taken up the lifestyle, language, and culture of their conquerors with surprising velocity, and the Saxons followed suit. They did so even with the religion that had been forced on them, taking it as their own. Even more than that, under the Ottonian dynasty, they continued exactly the same aggressive policy of conquest and Christianization east of the river Elbe that they themselves had so painfully suffered under Charlemagne. The Ottonian policy of expansion and mission, then, continued to carry on the violent spreading of the empire while simultaneously disseminating Christianity—Charlemagne's own modus operandi. But the identification of national expansion with Christian conversion also led to problems. In the late Middle Ages, the Teutonic Order [an order of consecrated knights that fought Islamic and barbarian troops in Asia Minor and what is now Eastern Europe] was still failing in its efforts in Slavic regions, because the Christian God was perceived by the Slavs as a "German god". Was, then, the violent expansion of Christianity to the north and to the east a mistake? Surely a method like this cannot be called Christian, since Christianity stands for nonviolence. However, as historian of the Middle Ages Johannes Fried says, we must set the record straight on this point: "Without the Roman legions and without the Christian missionaries, there would have been no alignment with the rich tradition and the superior culture of the Mediterranean world, no higher civilization in the budding land of Germany."[42] And it must be added: there would have been no higher religion, either—nor Christianity, the religion of peace.

In 1000, the young, enthusiastic German Holy Roman Emperor Otto III, grandson of Otto the Great, came to Rome to await the end of the world—which was expected at the turn of the millennium— in the company of the highly educated Pope Sylvester II. If the end of the world had actually taken place then, we would not have to dwell on the everyday run of scandals, since they would not exist. During the first thousand years of Christianity, there were neither crusades, nor inquisitions, nor witch hunts. There were no pogroms, either, or lasting schisms with the Eastern Church. Humanizing the barbarian cultures was a major achievement, and by the end of the first millennium, slavery was all but abolished in the Christian realm—unlike anywhere else in the world.

Looking at all the mess of the second millennium, one can note the places where things got off track. Again and again, people wish to go back to these good origins of Christianity. This is called reform. It was not only Francis of Assisi who wanted reform, but also Jan Hus; not only Martin Luther, but also the Council of Trent; not only the ecumenical movement, but also the Second Vatican Council. Yet it is not possible simply to slide back into the past. If one radically insisted on going back, this would be a denial of the value of human history, which amounts to fundamentalist totalitarianism—a phenomenon that Navid Kermani, the German-Iranian laureate of the German Book Trade's Peace Prize, warns against. Much that was possible in the first millennium was no longer possible in the second, but at the same time, the second overcame the burdens of the first. The second millennium offered new opportunities and new risks. If we understand this, then reforms can succeed—reforms that recall Christianity's originary desires and bring them to life in new historical situations.

III

The Middle Ages and the Crusades

From the Invention of the New Human
Being to the End of a Monstrosity

1. When Men Give Birth without Women
and Women Invent Things without Men:
How the West Was Created

The world did not end in 1000 A.D. New churches were built in the
Romanesque style. And soon, the papacy was to ascend to new heights
as well. During the first millennium, in the upheavals of the migra-
tion period, this institution had not only defended Christianity, but
also more or less civilized Roman behavior and culture; it stood
up to the Huns under Leo the Great in the fifth century, and again
under Gregory the Great around 600, then later on repeatedly
against the Langobards. Finally, it was able to ally itself with the
Carolingians, to determine the fate of Europe together with Pepin,
Charlemagne, and his successors—with great success. In his book
Why Europe?, which was awarded the Deutscher Historiker prize
in 2004, Viennese social historian Michael Mitterauer praises the
papacy as "a unique phenomenon in religious history", one that
understood itself as an office for all peoples. Much that makes up
Europe today has its "origins in the papal church".[1] Europe was
never unified under political rule, but as a Church community, it
was unified indeed, thanks to the unique position of the bishop of
Rome. Harvard historian Harold J. Berman could not be clearer
in his assessment: for many centuries, Western Christianity could

be equated with the papacy, as a community of peoples "in their common allegiance to a single spiritual authority, the Church of Rome." Of all the revolutions on record in the Western world, the papal revolution was the first, and in its effect it could be compared only to the splitting of the atom: "The overthrow of the preexisting *law as order* was justified as the reestablishment of a more fundamental *law as justice*." The Church produced the first modern Western governmental and judicial system, a "structure governed by a single system of law, the canon law. Being the church and constituting, therefore, the spiritual sphere, it was supposed to be as close as humankind could come, in this world, to the divinity."[2]

Medieval universities had a universalizing effect similar to that of the papacy, overcoming barriers of ideology as much as those of blood. In the eleventh century of all times—after every sort of revelation-independent philosophical scholarship disappeared from eastern Islamic countries and Islamic learning thus lost its long-standing claim as the world's leader—Europe experienced an intellectual awakening. In the twelfth century, for the first time since Antiquity, conditions were right once again for the development of an argumentative Christian theology, and a new awakening and deepening of Christian sensibility took place. Cities had once again developed; the economy produced enough surplus to finance schools and to support teachers as well as students. The first universities were founded, one for law in Bologna, another for theology in Paris. The universities represented a new kind of institution, one that, as medieval historian Michael Borgolte writes,

> produced a different form of scholarship—study in the community of the university—and virtually a new type of human being: the intellectual, in his two manifestations—both inside and outside of learned establishments. Compared to the Byzantines, who held fast to their traditional canon of texts and their traditional teaching methods, and to the Muslims, who kept the challenges of the Greek inheritance away from the core of their school system, and also to the Jews, who focused on the interpretation of the Bible and the Talmud, the innovations of the Western system of education seem almost revolutionary. There can be no doubt that in the high Middle Ages the "occident" gained a historically decisive advantage over other cultures. In Byzantium and in Islam, all attempts to integrate

rationalism into the core of the educational system had failed at that time.[3]

The apparatuses of culture multiplied explosively. There were ever more books, first on parchment, and then, in the thirteenth century, on paper, and finally, beginning in the fifteenth century, in print.

It was the women mystics of the high Middle Ages of the thirteenth century who first created an expanded German vocabulary capable of describing religious, spiritual, and interior matters. These women knew spiritual experiences of a higher nature and wanted to describe them, but they could not speak Latin. In this respect, one can say that the German language is to a considerable degree the invention of devout women, a product of the Bible and of mysticism. This new interior life made itself evident in prayer, too. While a "piety of numbers" was practiced during much of the early Middle Ages—monks had to pray as many as 150 psalms a day, with innumerable Masses offered—Meister Eckhart (1260–1328) said that a single Hail Mary prayed with devotion is better than thousands of recited ones. Also, there emerged in the fourteenth century so-called *devotio moderna*, which promoted a personal, interior following of Christ in daily life, even among laypeople, and grew into a larger movement. Then in the late Middle Ages, a pious devotion to the Passion developed, which urged the faithful to place themselves in Jesus' Passion and death spiritually and emotionally, with their whole hearts, living this reality with him. One can find artistic traces of this movement in the German "Vesperbilden", or pietàs, depictions of the Mother of God holding the body of Jesus in her lap. Eventually, through Passion piety and the mysticism connected with it, a new kind of interior man was born: the compassionate man—an important precondition for tolerance.

Finally, by about 1500, the circumstances were right for Christianity fully to unfold, just as it had done once before in Antiquity. This gave the period a religious dynamism. Then in a tragic twist, right at this moment, Christianity divided itself.

It was Christianity that brought forth European culture. Surgically to remove the religious factor from European history in order, supposedly, to arrive at a pure culture—one that, it is said, developed directly into its current secular form without Christianity—would be impossible. Historian Michael Borgolte says, "Monotheism's victory over pantheism and myth was never perfect, but it distinguished Europe from pre-Christian Antiquity as well as from the pluralism of the Far East; in this sense, it made Europe."[4]

2. A Sly Fox and a Hesitant Shepherd: The Smoldering Wick

The year 1000 not only brought new beginnings. It also heralded some problems. Until then, Islamic rulers had always made it possible for Christians to make pilgrimages to their sacred sites in the Holy Land. But suddenly, Islam became radicalized. Already in 966, the Muslim inhabitants of Jerusalem had burned the Christian patriarch John VII at the stake. Then the Fatimid Caliph Al Hakim, whom the Druze people venerate as God incarnate to this day, launched a de facto persecution of Christians; he had crucifixes burned and churches demolished, so that in the end, thirty thousand churches were plundered and reduced to ashes. And then, Caliph Al Hakim committed an outrageous act: in 1009, he had the Church of the Holy Sepulchre in Jerusalem destroyed, with hateful precision. He even had Jesus' holy tomb ground down, quite literally leveling it to the earth, so that the site of Jesus' Resurrection venerated today is more or less a reproduction from the time of the Crusades. This event shook all of Christendom. Yet their response remained mere helpless anger. For it was impossible to think of helping the beset Christians in the East: the sub-empires of France and Germany, which had grown out of the great Carolingian Empire, were only just beginning to consolidate themselves, and with great difficulty. The threat of Hungarian invasions had just passed, and the Normans were no longer troubling Europe's coasts, but there was still a lack of practicable unifying structures.

At the same time, the old Christian Byzantine Empire in the east remained, unlike the recently Christianized Germanic West, "an empire reluctant to wage war", as Hans-Georg Beck writes.[5] It was seldom adequately armed, would only bring itself to launch war efforts at the very last minute, did not invent new weapons, never led wars of aggression, always preferred to seek peace by diplomatic means, pursued a defensive kind of imperialism, and essentially considered war "a last resort". The Byzantine Empire had long settled matters with the Fatimids, but was embroiled in interminable interior conflicts. Yet even here, the Byzantines did not consider war. For centuries, Byzantium had continuously remained a Christian empire. Constantinople was by far the largest city in Europe and still shone in its old splendor, since it had never been overrun by those barbarian Germanic tribes who brought their savage conceptions of combat and honor to the West. Saint Basil the Great, a leading Church Father of the East, even punished soldiers who had killed in wars with a three-year ban from the reception of Holy Communion. Thus, the soldierly profession was not very well respected; dying in the battlefield was not viewed as glorious, and death in battle against infidels was not considered martyrdom. Byzantium rather did all it could to avoid the spilling of blood. In this respect, this ancient empire was significantly closer to its Christian origins than the wild west of Christendom. Steven Runciman writes in his classic work *The History of the Crusades*: "Princess Anna Comnena, one of the most typical of Byzantines, makes it clear in her history that ... she considered war a shameful thing, a last resort when all else had failed, indeed in itself a confession of failure."[6] In contrast, the Church in the West was still struggling just to teach German warriors about the Christian love of peace.

The Christians of the East were highly cultivated and felt more at home in the equally cultivated cities of Baghdad and Damascus than in Goslar or Worms. They mostly lived in peace with their Muslim neighbors, trading with them. Thus, at bottom, Islam troubled the West much more than it did the East. Muslims had already landed all over the western Mediterranean coasts, robbing and murdering everyone. Then, suddenly, the Turkish Seljuqs appeared on the eastern border of the Byzantine Empire, and the situation fundamentally changed: in 1071, they dealt a crushing defeat to the Byzantine emperor's army, and later, they even conquered Jerusalem. These events made Christian pilgrimages to the Holy Land considerably harder or even halted them completely.

In this situation, the Byzantine emperor Alexios (1048–1118), the father of that highly educated princess Anna, put out a dramatic call for help to Western Christendom. But who could answer it? The controversial Holy Roman Emperor Henry IV was in constant conflict with the princes of his empire and had fallen out with the Church, to the point of getting excommunicated. No one else was in a position to exercise authority over the West—that is, except for one man: the pope. So Byzantine envoys appeared at the Council of Piacenza in 1095 and desperately begged Pope Urban II and all the bishops present for their assistance. To that end, they probably exaggerated a little, and painted the affliction of Christians in the Holy Land in the gloomiest tones possible, appealing to Christian solidarity. At the same time, though, this was a peace offering in the conflict between the Eastern and Western Churches, which had been setting these two Christian regions of the world against each other since 1054. In this case, the Byzantine emperor was hoping for no more than some western mercenaries, some of whom were already fighting under his banner anyway.

Alexios was a typical Byzantine diplomat, and he was a sly fox. In his court, he tolerated all sorts of adversaries, other former imperial families, and even the families of deposed usurpers, and through all the possible intrigues, he somehow skillfully managed never to lose track of them. When it came to foreign affairs, he was pressured from all sides and for this reason entered into risky coalitions—at one time even asking the Turkish Seljuks for help against the wild Catholic Normans, who were attacking. Alexios did not want a crusade. He wanted help, help that was under his own control.

Pope Urban II (1035–1099) also wanted control—control over the violence that was the order of the day in Western Europe. For almost two hundred years, the Church had been laboring to contain this violence, especially among the lower nobility, through the *Pax Dei* movement. Through negotiation, she established periods of time when all military force was prohibited. This may sound strange to us today, but it was a real blessing for the people at the time, who were constantly under threat of violence. The Church assembled an ecclesiastical peace militia to secure this peace and prevent or punish robberies. Yet this movement did not meet with resounding success. Thus, a relief expedition to the Holy Land would offer an opportunity to channel the unruly powers of the land's perpetually armed knights toward "higher" goals than plunder and honor. To fight for Christ, to free the Holy City and the Holy Land from destructive infidels—this "noble purpose" far outdid the self-serving aims of knightly raids. It was a period of religious turmoil anyway; the impending end of the world was on people's minds much more than it is for us today, who think we know better. People flocked into religious orders in droves, chasing the promise of a life pleasing to God. But now there was to be an opportunity for laypeople, too, to qualify for eternal life through extraordinary deeds.

Already shortly after 1000, when Muslims in Spain were threatening the existence of small Christian realms in the north of the Iberian Peninsula, the pope had been the only universally accepted representative of Western Europe entrusted with organizing a resistance—which he did successfully. The pope did not simply absolve the soldiers who came to the Christians' aid, forgiving them of all the sins they had accumulated over the course of their lives; this could happen by the grace of God alone, after a sincere confession of sins, and even then only if there was sincere contrition and a serious resolution not to commit the sin anymore. However, the pope did allow military tours in the defense of Spanish Christians to be carried out as *penance* for sins, standing in for traditional pilgrimages.

But even more was at stake in the military campaign to the Holy Land. A military tour for the liberation of holy sites in Jerusalem was at the same time a pilgrimage, and of course, it was an incomparably riskier undertaking. Whoever decided to embark on it had to put his whole preexisting life behind him, leaving behind his wife and children for an unpredictable future and placing himself in mortal danger for the love of God. Presumably, it would only be possible to do so with a religious motivation. But still, the pope hesitated. First, he moved from Piacenza to France and conferred with a number of people, including Bishop Le Puy, who had already made a pilgrimage to Jerusalem and knew the situation first hand. Only then did Urban II head to Clermont, where he had convened a council of bishops.

3. Loss of Control: Jews Murdered and a Bloodbath—Did God Really Want That?

There were evidently rumors that something very extraordinary was about to happen. Thousands of people had gathered in Clermont, and the cathedral could no longer contain the crowd, which is why the emperor's throne was placed on a podium before the city's eastern gate. The event that was to take place there on November 27, 1095, became one of world historical import. Pope Urban II was French and, as Steven Runciman writes, "an impressive man, tall, with a handsome, bearded face, courteously mannered and persuasive in his speech.... He could be stern and relentless, but he preferred to be gentle; he preferred to avoid controversy that might arouse bitterness and strife."[7] And his eloquence came in handy now, seated before thousands of expectant people who were pushing and shoving before his throne at the eastern gate of Clermont. Urban II began his speech by saying that it was necessary to help the Christian brothers in the east. They were under threat from the Turks, who had penetrated into the heart of Christian lands, abused their inhabitants, and desecrated their sacred sites. Then he firmly emphasized the holiness of Jerusalem and the manifold sufferings of pilgrims who traveled there. Finally, the great moment came: Pope Urban II called on the crowd present—indeed, he called on all of Christendom— to save the East. Rich and poor alike were to set out. They were to leave off slaying one another and, in its place, go wage a just war. In all this, they would be doing God's work, and God would lead them in it. The pope spoke impressively and with enthusiasm, and the people's answer was even more exuberant than he had expected. "Deus le volt"—it is God's will—rang back in response.

After this speech, many declared instantly that they would enlist to set out for Jerusalem. Now, one could do effective penance through chivalric battles, on crusade, and this, as historian Jonathan Riley-Smith notes, was "truly revolutionary. For the faithful, fighting for the forgiveness of one's own sins was a completely new way of waging war."[8] To justify this, many made reference to the last two books of the Old Testament, First and Second Maccabees, which tell the story of the Maccabee brothers in their fight for the liberation and sanctification of Jerusalem's sacred sites. The popes invoked the Maccabees, and the laity responded with enthusiasm. The religious scholar Christoph Auffarth remarks: "The choice of the Maccabees as an example to the crusaders has to be understood as a shift—effected by lay people, demanded by their own religious needs—toward a path to salvation attainable even for the laity."[9] However, to light this path, there was only the one reference in the Old Testament. The New Testament remained silent.

Lay enthusiasm led to an unexpected dynamic. Israeli historian Benjamin Z. Kedar observes that for the theologians, a crusade could only be a war of defense—a just war as Saint Augustine understood it, helping the threatened Christians of the East, rather than a "holy war".[10] Does a just war become religious just because it is accompanied by prayers and rites? Or because it is commanded by a pope, a bishop, or even God himself? Of course not, for as long as a war has no other goal than justice, it remains a *secular* just war, no matter how many religious factors are involved.

But the laymen, the knights, and the other warriors got carried away by their emotions. It was all about winning back the Christian heritage, and there arose ideas about vengeance and retribution, which were not supported by Christian teaching. Theologians disagreed with this approach, at times even vehemently so. The learned Englishman Radolphus Niger (before 1146–ca. 1200) wrote an entire anti-crusade tract: God had no need of retribution carried out by men. If he indeed wanted one, he could send twelve legions of angels. If the pope as a representative of God recommended pilgrimages to Jerusalem as penance, then temperance and fairness had to be safeguarded at the same time, because God only accepted such penance if sins had already been repented of and atoned for. After all, Niger continued, random bloodshed did not represent reparation: "I do not know with what right one can take up arms in order to kill Muslims."[11] Such criticism had to strike at the heart of the crusader mentality. And this criticism was still echoing in 1217, in Wolfram von Eschenbach's *Willehalm*: "Is it sin if people never learned about Christianity? I call it sin to slay them like cattle. Everyone is made by God's hand."

Though most professed religious motives for fighting, this did not mean that no socio-economic reasons were in play. In some areas, such as in the north of France, many ill-off younger sons set out simply because they had no inheritance. Besides, it was finally possible to skip monetary donations to monasteries as penance, since laypeople could now make their own acts of penance in the crusade.

According to the pope's wishes, the whole endeavor was to take place under ordered circumstances. Precise regulations were made regarding the protection of property belonging to armed pilgrims. Before setting out, every crusader was to speak with his spiritual director to ensure that his motives for going were sincere. The crusade was decidedly not to be a war of conquest. In all cities that were wrested from the infidels, the churches of the East were to be given back their rights and their property.

But what followed then surprised even the pope. Urban II had counted on organizing an army of maybe a few hundred or a few thousand knights. Instead, people gathered together in disorderly masses. Jonathan Riley-Smith supposes that there were about one hundred twenty thousand of them, only 10 percent military professionals (i.e., aristocrats or knights); of these, only about five thousand may have arrived in the Holy Land. A certain Peter the Hermit, a zealous, bizarre fellow, magically attracted thousands of people, among them even women and children, and convinced them not to wait for the day appointed by the pope, August 15, 1096, but rather to head out immediately.

One sub-group of this so-called People's Crusade, under the leadership of the notorious robber baron count Emicho of Leiningen, committed terrible atrocities against Jews along the Rhine, who—although protected by the bishops who opened their palaces to them all over the land—were massacred in droves by the mob. In a special study, historian Friedrich Lotter has described how the bishops of Trier, Cologne, Mainz, Worms, and Speyer tried to protect their Jewish communities, some even risking their lives in the process, but with only limited success. The violent mob was beyond control. Aside from one incident under the rule of the Visigoths in Spain, this was the first European persecution of Jewish people, and it contradicted all the customary relations between Jews and Christians in the first millennium, as well as the Church's own position. According to medieval historian Rudolf Hiestand, throughout the twelfth century, the papacy resolutely adhered to the two key principles of canon law regarding Jews: the prohibition against killing Jews and the prohibition against forced baptisms. "The uniform stance of the papacy and the episcopacy," Hiestand writes, "proves that there was no theologically or canonically supported turn against the Jews with the aim of physically destroying them. Neither anti-Jewish propaganda nor the baptism-or-death alternative originated from the high church.

The pope's homily on the crusade contained no words to this effect, nor did bishops receive any such order, nor were these bishops involved in the emergence of the Jewish persecutions."[12] And the American professor of Jewish Studies Robert Chazan emphasizes: "The papacy ... nearly eliminated major anti-Jewish violence in the ensuing great crusades."[13] Thus, during the later crusades, anti-Jewish violence was blocked from the outset. Even the outbreak of anti-Jewish violence at the beginning of the First Crusade was apparently "very limited". During Frederick Barbarossa's crusade, the Jews had excellent protection through the Holy Roman Empire.

But back to the "People's Crusade": on their way through the Balkans, all the various chaotic military detachments kept running into trouble. When they arrived in Constantinople on August 1, 1096, the sensitive Byzantine emperor Alexios was appalled and hastened to pass these raucous barbarians along to Asia, where— inexperienced at war—they were quickly cut down en masse by the Turkish army. "To most good Christians," Steven Runciman writes, "it appeared as a punishment meted out from on high to the murderers of the Jews."[14]

The "People's Crusade" was actually not even a crusade, since the pope had proclaimed that the real one would begin on August 15, 1096. Peter and his followers, then, were rather more like a wandering riot, and a portent of bad things to come. It was already becoming evident that the masses set in motion could not really be controlled. Could anyone have reckoned on this? The pope, in any case, had not accounted for it. What he had had in mind was a noble endeavor, not a chaotic mass movement, and certainly not a platoon of marauders. And Emperor Alexios had not wanted a crusade at all, but just a few competent mercenaries.

The rest of the story can be told quickly. Even though the army of knights arriving in Constantinople on December 23, 1096, was more disciplined than the one mentioned above, Emperor Alexios, erring on the side of caution, had these unruly people swear an oath of allegiance before ferrying them across the Bosporus. In Anatolia, the Turkish Seljuqs were defeated and Antioch was conquered after a long siege. There, the papal legate, who had had a pacifying influence on the crusaders, died, and the army was left without a real leader, since the aristocrats on crusade were in rivalry with one another. Thus the conquest of Jerusalem on July 15, 1099, turned into a fiasco, a bloodbath that harmed the reputation of Christians throughout the whole Islamic world. The Second Crusade in 1148 proceeded under the de facto leadership of the German and French kings and failed completely. Then the Third Crusade in 1187, which rose up after the Muslims recaptured Jerusalem, was also mostly an endeavor of secular European powers. It was led by Holy Roman Emperor Frederick Barbarossa, who, however, died unexpectedly in Anatolia on the way to Jerusalem. He was succeeded in his command by the English king, Richard the Lionheart, and the French king, Phillip II. For self-serving reasons, the Venetians redirected the Fourth Crusade to Constantinople, which was conquered and plundered in 1204. Among some Greek Orthodox Christians, a bitterness over the wickedness of the "Latins" persists almost unmitigated to this day. In 1291, the Muslim conquest of Acre, the last crusader fortress, put an end to the crusades.

Unlike in Christendom, the Crusades did not cause any outrage in the Islamic world. They were a rather peripheral phenomenon, and there was "an overwhelming lack of interest in dealing with" this issue, notes Islam scholar Albrecht Noth.[15] The British-American historian Bernard Lewis points out that the words "crusade" and "crusader" are not even mentioned in Arabic historiography. In contrast, on the Christian side, the Crusades are "a long-delayed, very limited and finally ineffectual response to the jihad"—with a lag of over three hundred years. The word "crusade" was of course used not only to denote crusades to the Holy Land, but also to indicate other ecclesial and secular action, for example against heretics or for the liberation of slaves.

The darkest chapter of the Crusades is the aforementioned conquest of Jerusalem in 1099. There were only five thousand crusaders left when they arrived at the walls of Jerusalem; more than one hundred thousand of them had been butchered, had starved, or had died of diseases. And now, the worn-out remnant encountered another brutal reality: in the outskirts of the city, the Jerusalem garrison had rendered the watering places unusable, destroyed everything that was edible, and chopped down all the trees. There was a blazing summer heat, and to top it all off, as the crusaders processed around the walls, they were mocked by the city's defenders.

The situation was desperate; many starved or died of thirst. But eventually they managed to bring wood from far off and build siege towers, which allowed them to storm the city. Reports abound of the massacre the crusaders then committed. Not only Muslims, but also Christians and Jews, were slaughtered by the thousands. Not a single person survived, they say. Jerusalem had already seen many terrible bloodbaths—for example, when the Shiite Fatimids conquered in 979 and slayed not only Christians and Jews, but also Sunni Muslims, and then again in 1076, when the Seljuqs raged among the Shiites and killed three thousand of them. Nevertheless, the crusader massacre is legendary, because it was Christians, pilgrims, who carried it out, and they did it at their holiest sites.

However, the scholarly debate surrounding this event remains unsettled to this day, because the surviving accounts are distorted by both propaganda and counter-propaganda. British historian John France observes: "However horrible the massacre at Jerusalem, it was not far beyond what common practice of the day meted out to any place which resisted."[16] It is by no means true that all were killed, whether Muslim or Jew, since the very next day the crusaders asked survivors to bury the dead and then released prisoners on ransom. France clarifies that the Jewish community had already been seriously diminished in Jerusalem, and according to Jewish sources, the crusaders, unlike the Muslims, took no women or children as prisoners; most significantly, there is no evidence of Jews commemorating victims after the siege.

From a literary standpoint, the conquest of 1099 "is described with the images and words provided by the literary tradition"—as is always the case in war chronicles.[17] Since the reports were supposed to emphasize the purgation of the Holy Land from pagan defilement, they used especially "bloody language". Recent French research interprets the conquest of Jerusalem—though without trying to whitewash the blood-lust—"in the sense of a reclaiming and cleansing of sacred sites."[18] If, as German historian Ernst-Dieter Hehl notes, no Christian chroniclers sought to cover up the massacre, this was in order to invoke and even to outdo the Old Testament parallels with the Maccabean wars. For instance, Judas Maccabeus "destroyed every male by the edge of the sword, and razed and plundered the city. Then he passed through the city over the slain" (1 Mac 5:51).

Elsewhere, it is written that they "slaughtered untold numbers, so that the adjoining lake, a quarter of a mile wide, appeared to be running over with blood" (2 Mac 12:16). The reports about the conquest of Jerusalem by the crusaders themselves sometimes literally repeat these texts. It is true that primitive concepts of cleansing might have been a determining factor, with Jerusalem seen as the defiled Bride of Christ who was to be absolved through avenged blood. Even the chancellor of the Kindgdom of Jerusalem William of Tyre (ca. 1130–1186), of all people, confirms this: "Certainly, all this happened according to God's righteous judgement, that those who had desecrated the sanctuary of the Lord with superstitious rites and had alienated faithful peoples from them, should cleanse it with the spilling of their own blood and atone for their punishable, disgraceful deeds by their death."[19] Already at the beginning of the crusade, the Maccabees, those heroic Jewish freedom fighters who confronted the superior pagans, had been held up as examples, and this is why the crusade's end in Jerusalem was told with the words of the Old Testament. However, it is significant that not a word from the New Testament was found to justify the Crusades, nor did anyone cite Jesus for the battle cry, "It is God's will!"

As for the Islamic sources, the tremendous number of victims mentioned there cannot be accurate, because Jerusalem did not even have that many inhabitants at the time. Besides, almost all Christians were expelled from the city before the siege, since they were not trusted, and the accommodations arranged in Damascus for surviving Jerusalem Muslims speaks against any obliteration.

4. Taking Stock: What the European Commission Has to Do with the Crusades and Why We Should Love the Turks

The Crusades raise serious questions. For a thousand years, Christianity had stood out as a religion of peace. Wherever it was not able to prevent wars, it at least endeavored to alleviate their impact and curb belligerent mentalities—a practice continued by the Byzantine Empire. But now the highest representative of Western Christianity had called Christians to arms. So, first, the question of holy war presents itself. Were the Crusades holy wars, like the ones the prophet

Muhammad had prescribed to the Muslims? That would indeed be a scandal.

Islam scholar Tilman Nagel explains that holy war in Islam serves the purpose of "approaching the goal of all human history: the expansion of the realm of Islam over the entire inhabited world."[20] This war is first of all about an interior struggle, but then it is also the "enthusiastic participation in campaigns against the dissenters." British-American historian Bernard Lewis sees the term "jihad" as being used primarily in a military sense since the time of the prophet. Hans Küng explains that Islam "has from its origins a militant character that includes fighting for God, and in this sense, it is closer to early Judaism with its 'Yahweh-wars' than to early Christianity."[21] Islam considers itself under an obligation to fight. Even the great intellectual spokesmen of medieval Islam, such as Al-Farabi, Avicenna, and Averroes, endorsed war "much more radically than common, unphilosophical Islamic practice" did.[22] There was no criticism of a "holy war" on the part of Muslim theologians to correspond to the "Deus non vult" (It is *not* God's will) of many Christian critics of the Crusades.

Christianity, by contrast, had always been a religion of peace that did not know holy warfare. And thus, the call to a crusade found Christian critics, too, especially among canon law experts, who supported the view that "if the Saracens live in peace with the Christians, they must not be attacked or killed."[23] For this reason, Israeli historian Benjamin Z. Kedar stresses that Christians must not be accused of general hatred against Islam. Most of all, it was the Church herself who was hostile to warfare. The Second Council of the Lateran in 1139 condemned "that murderous art of crossbowmen and archers, which is hateful to God."[24] Erasmus of Rotterdam later voiced his sheer horror at destructive firearms, which caused the death of twenty thousand at the Battle of Marignano (1515); they were machines from hell, more refined and terrible than anything ever invented by barbarians or pagans. For him, war in general was "an ocean of every harm", and he called for Christian pacifism: "Whoever of the sacred writers announces Christ, announces peace on earth.... How can you say our Father, addressing the universal parent, while you are thrusting the sharp steel into the bowels of your brother?"[25] According to Luther, too, Adam would have "died from grief" if he had seen the new artillery.[26]

However, Christians at the time did not live in a vacuum, and modern international law did not yet exist. One had to be able to defend one's rights, and the Church was no exception. The pope was aware of this, too. Pope Leo the Great had repelled the Huns in the fifth century, and Pope Gregory the Great had to defend himself 150 years later against the warring Langobards. To be sure, the eventual Donation of Pepin [in 756] had made it possible for the papacy to be more independent of worldly powers, since now it more or less disposed over its own territory. Yet in practice, the representative of Christianity—the religion of peace—was obliged to face military conflicts. When in 846 the Arabs came up from the sea, ravaged Rome, and plundered Saint Peter's Basilica, Pope Leo IV only fended off the enemy after an intense struggle—a great military struggle, of course. In those ages, that was the inevitable cost of freedom, even for the pope.

The love of peace was more than just a mission that Christians received from Jesus Christ. It also had roots in the positive Christian view of human nature. Thus, in preparation for the Third Crusade, the Englishman Radolphus Niger warned that the Muslims were "of the same nature as we are", just as the pagans in general "are men, albeit unbelieving."[27] William of Tyre declared that "Muslims, too, are in full possession of the right of man", grounding this on their common "worship of the one and identical God, the God of Abraham, Isaac, and Jacob."[28]

The notion that rights followed from human nature was missing in Islam, which only knew divine law. This alone can explain why at the siege of Vienna in 1683, the Turkish sultan Mehmed IV (1642–1693), who as caliph also considered himself the spiritual leader of Muslims, publicly addressed the Holy Roman Emperor with the following words:

> This army will trample your little country underfoot with horseshoes, without mercy or compassion. Most of all, we command you to await us in your royal capital, Vienna, so that we can behead you. We are going to destroy you along with your followers, and wipe every last creature of God, every mere infidel, from the face of the earth. We will expose the old and young alike to the most cruel agony and then leave them to die a most disgraceful death. I will take from you your little empire and sweep its people altogether from the earth.[29]

A further question is whether or not the Crusades aimed to spread the Christian faith by violence. If so, that, too, would be a scandal. On this point, one might be surprised to learn that the idea of conversion is completely missing from the Crusades. Of the numerous extant reports about Pope Urban's summons, not a single one claims that he called for the converting of Muslims, and never do the later summons of various churchmen call for the conversion of unbelievers, as Benjamin Z. Kedar has discovered.[30]

This conformed entirely to the Christian approach to missionary work in general. While even Bernard of Clairvaux—admittedly, the age's only significant theologian—at times saw violence during missionary work as justifiable, Gratian's definitive decree in 1140 declared with Augustine: "No one is to be forced to accept the faith."[31] Thomas Aquinas adopted Augustine's teaching about just warfare, holding that wars were only permitted if "they defended the poor and the entire state from the attacks of the enemy." Moreover, he learned from Aristotle that even pagan state orders, which were organized in accordance with human nature, were to be respected. Hence, it was forbidden to wage wars against pagans simply because they were not Christians. He, too, emphasized that conversion had to take place voluntarily. Pope Innocent IV (1195–1254) also confirmed this: every lordship that followed the measure of human nature—even pagan ones, which had their own legitimacy despite being non-Christian— was to be acknowledged and therefore not simply attacked, especially not with the goal of a forced baptism. Jonathan Riley-Smith emphasizes that war against pagans or for the sake of missions was never a prevailing concept in the Middle Ages:

> The opinions that vengeance for such injuries as the mere denial of the Christian faith or the refusal to accept Christian government, and the opportunity for conversion by force constituted just causes, were those of minorities and were never held by most reputable Christian thinkers, among whom it was generally agreed that non-Christians could not be made to accept baptism nor could they be physically attacked simply because they were of a different faith.[32]

There were also practically no conversions from Islam to Christianity worth mentioning. The only person to undertake a relevant missionary effort in the Christian spirit of nonviolence was Francis of Assisi. In 1219, he went to Egypt with the crusaders in order to preach before the sultan Al-Kamil. The sultan is said to have been impressed, but that was all. By his nonviolence, Francis of Assisi showed himself to be a worthy representative of Christianity.

The religious historian Carsten Colpe also writes:

> Life in the orient at the time of the Crusades, that is, from 1098 to 1291, should not be imagined as a permanent state of war. Already the Frankish colonists of the second generation considered war only a necessary evil. And the Frankish princes in Syria often pursued an extraordinarily sympathetic and liberal policy. Truce—almost always extended on both sides by implicit agreement—was the normal condition during the crusades and counter-crusades. Between the castles of the Frankish barons and the neighboring Arab emirs, relationships of high chivalry were maintained, as western chroniclers and Arabic annalists broadly attest.[33]

Canon law, too, supported such peaceful circumstances. A collection of laws from 1160 states concisely: "If they are unruly, whether they be Muslims or Jews, we must pursue them. However, once we have subjected them, they must not be killed or forced into baptism."[34] And historian Marie-Louise Favreau-Lilie confirms: "The Franks had neither extermination nor forced conversion in mind."[35] Ernst-Dieter Hehl explains that in the Holy Land, "living conditions could develop that completely contradict the popular image of the fundamental contrast between Christians and Muslims."[36] As a striking example, he cites the historical account of a Muslim prince who, thanks to some members of the Knights Templar, was able to pray in his Muslim way at the Al-Aqsa Mosque, which had been turned into a church. What William of Tyre writes is especially impressive, and William is not just anyone. He was born in the Holy Land, studied for twenty years in Paris and Bologna, and became a leading politician and jurist in the court of the Christian king of Jerusalem, eventually being appointed archbishop of Tyre and participating in the Third Lateran Council. This man, highly educated in theology, implemented what he had learned at the most significant universities of the West: Muslims were men just like Christians, because they shared the same creator God, and there were devout and just men among them, too. Since those who served God with reverence and justice were acceptable to him, Muslims were neighbors to Christianity and close to salvation. Humanity dictated it, said William. And according to him, it was not only individual Muslims who deserved acknowledgment, but also the Islamic states with their people as well as their rulers: Islamic rulers waged just wars, if necessary, even against Christians. Moreover, he asserted, the contracts signed with them must be kept and never arbitrarily broken—not even on account of their alleged paganism. This course taken by the chancellor of the kingdom of Jerusalem did not remain without consequences.

Today, it is often historians—rather than churchmen—who encourage others to understand the people of the past. One of the most knowledgeable among them, the often-cited Jonathan Riley-Smith, at the end of his life made a case for giving up conventional prejudices about the Crusades: "I have always believed that objectivity and empathy demand that we abandon them, because otherwise we will never understand a movement which touched the lives of the ancestors of everyone of European descent."[37] And British historian Norman Housley mentions Pope John Paul II's confession in 2000:

> There is a further problem with denouncing the Crusades as unchristian .... Painful though it is to accept, a movement which was responsible for terrible atrocities cannot be disentangled from one of the great spiritual revivals of the Christian past.... The answer for the Catholic who wants to respond positively to the Pope's challenge of "purification of memory", and for non-Catholics who want to establish an ethical perspective on the crusading experience, must surely lie in precision: repudiating the massacres while celebrating the human achievement, in every sphere, to which the movement gave rise.[38]

The Crusades were not holy wars such as jihad is in Islam, which is meant to expand the territory of Islam over the entire world in the name of Allah. Neither were they missionary efforts by fire and sword. To the Crusaders themselves, these were not wars of aggression, but rather wars of defense for the protection of Christians in the Holy Land. Above all, however, the Crusades represented something unique: they were armed pilgrimages with an originally religious motivation. Even though they were led by unified European powers—the forerunners to today's European Union—rather than the popes, the popes launched and supported them. Nevertheless, they contradicted everything the early Christians had represented; they were the deformed offspring of violent Teutonism and peace-loving Christianity. But perhaps even this verdict is too harsh. Historian Egon Flaig writes:

> Had Constantinople already fallen in 1100, the enormous military power of the Turkish armies would have fallen upon central Europe four hundred years earlier; in that case, there probably never would have emerged a versatile European culture, no free urban constitutions, no debates about the constitution, no cathedrals, no Renaissance, and no rise of the sciences. For in Islamic regions, free—Greek!—thought was disappearing during that period. Jacob Burckhardt's verdict that "it is fortunate that Europe as a whole was able to resist Islam" also means that we owe thanksgiving as much to the Crusades as to the Greeks for their victories repelling the Persians.[39]

At the end of the age of the Crusades, there stood the Spaniard Juan Luis Vives (1493–1540). At that time, the Turks were considered the scourge of God; with indescribable cruelty, they had made a bloody conquest of Constantinople in 1453, and in 1529, they were threatening Vienna. Nevertheless, Vives writes:

> We have to love the Turks because they are indeed human beings; they must be loved by those who seek to follow the directive, "Love your enemies". We will desire the good for them—a sign of true love—and specifically desire that true and unique Good: the recognition of the truth. This we will never attain by abuses and curses, but only by the means through which we ourselves, with the help and blessing of the Apostles, attained it: that is, in accordance with natural and human insights, by leading pure lives in humility, temperance, integrity, and impeccable conduct, in order that by our deeds we might first prove what we believe and bid others to believe, so that the Turks might not be deterred through our deviant way of life from giving credence to our words.[40]

IV

Sins

The Medieval Persecution of Heretics and, Finally, the Borgias

Let us return once again to the year 1000. What was the intellectual situation of Christianity at that time? For a thousand years, there had been discussions and public controversies, to be sure, and at times people had been excluded from the community of the Church. But around 1000, Christendom was facing a crisis. In the year 1000, many—among them Holy Roman Emperor Otto III and Pope Sylvester II—were expecting the end of the world. For this reason, the churches had ceased to be renovated and there developed a tense atmosphere full of apocalyptic omens. The papacy was weak. In the tenth century, it had fallen into the hands of urban Roman noble families locked in ferocious feuds with one another, and only the German king Otto the Great was able to remedy this ugly situation. But by the mid-eleventh century, things in Rome were already frantic again. There were three self-proclaimed popes competing against one another, and during and after the Council of Sutri in 1046, Holy Roman Emperor Henry III, in a spectacular move, deposed all three of them and appointed a German as the successor of Peter. Owing to these circumstances, the papacy now had to bow before the emperor, which caused much concern among those who defended the freedom of the Church. This is how the Gregorian Reform came about, which was initiated by Pope Gregory VII and led to the protracted investiture controversy between the emperor and the bishop of Rome.

To top it all off, in 1054, Christendom split into east and west, and the impending conflict in the Holy Land loomed on the horizon. In other words, the eleventh century was a time of unrest. In order to accommodate the growing population, cities were now starting to develop once again, fostering a more lively intellectual life. For this reason, the fight over fundamental questions was never more fierce than in the eleventh and twelfth centuries. Yet for the time being, deviant theological opinions were treated leniently. For example, in keeping with the parable of the weeds among the wheat, several bishops' councils grappled with the teachings of Berengar of Tours, who claimed that transubstantiation during Holy Mass did not apply to the substance of bread and wine, but rather was to be understood in an intellectual and spiritual sense. Though he was condemned several times for his false teachings, he never had to fear for his life, and he died in 1088 at the old age of almost ninety.

1. Under Pressure: A King Has People Burned

But then, suddenly, followers of a certain strange teaching appeared in various parts in Europe. While Christianity believed in a single, all-powerful God, who had become flesh in Jesus Christ, was visible in the Church through the Holy Spirit, and remained present in the sacraments, these people believed that there existed de facto two equally powerful forces, one good and one bad, with an eternal battle going on between them. This is what we call "dualism". Some even believed in two gods: an evil one, who had created the sensory world, and a good one, who ruled over the realm of pure spirit. The consequences of this dualist perspective differed slightly among its followers, but they amounted to a strict hostility toward the body, a rejection of matrimony and sexuality, a contempt for women, a prohibition against conceiving children, a condemnation of meat eating, and a rejection of the visible Church—thus, an entirely spiritual faith, which they followed fanatically. Needless to say, with all these ideas, they threatened to overthrow the existing social order. The Church hardly seemed ready to face this phenomenon. Right after the turn of the millennium, she herself was still weak, and so were the worldly rulers, who saw heretics as blasphemers of God and—egged on by the people—sought to eliminate them. The people, for their part, feared God's wrath and staged wild riots in their attempts to hang these enemies of God. As we saw in chapter I, in pre-Christian times it had already been common practice for worldly rulers to call blasphemers to account, with the hope of diverting God's anger away from state and society.

And this is how, in 1022, the inconceivable happened. Something Christianity had consistently rejected for a thousand years as utterly un-Christian finally came to pass in Orleans. Accompanied by a few bishops, the French king Robert commanded that the priests of the city's cathedral chapter, supposedly convicted of teaching and refusing to renounce certain dualist doctrines, were burned as heretics. Some say that a general uproar among the townspeople is what pressured the king into doing the deed.

Orleans broke the dam. In Germany, Duke Godfrey of Lorraine also had heretics seized and hanged, during Holy Roman Emperor Henry III's stay in Goslar. But Bishop Wazo of Liège [in modern-day Belgium] (985–1048) gave an impassioned warning against the escalating killing of heathens, using the arguments of the early Christians: in the parable of the weeds among the wheat, the Lord had preached patience; those who were in error today could be converted tomorrow; there must be no premature separation, for God does not desire the death of sinners. Bishops, he insisted, should remember that they had not been given the sword of the worldly order and were therefore called not to kill, but to awaken to life. He raised the horrifying prospect that there had certainly been sincere Catholics among the victims. Thus Wazo ultimately cries out: human judgment must retreat, halt, stand down, wait for God's judgment at the end of time!

The heretics' appearance on the scene seemed systematic. They sprung up in various places all over Europe, but their teachings were similar. With this, an entirely new problem presented itself: how could one determine if something was heresy, and who had the right to condemn or even to execute heretics? For a long time, people were simply at a loss in this regard. Instead of holding trials based on canon law, they supposed that God would establish a person's innocence through ordeals by water or fire. The ordeal by water determined a person's guilt or innocence based on whether the water "accepted" the person immersed in it as innocent, or "rejected" him as guilty. In the ordeal by fire, it came down to whether—or how fast—a burn inflicted by a fiery iron would heal, or whether it would fester for an extended period. It was not uncommon for things to devolve into lynch law, because often "the people's rage already dragged heretics to the stake while bishops and synods were still deliberating."[1] In England, the king took the initiative. Henry II (1133–1189) issued the first anti-heresy decree by a secular legislator since Antiquity. Once again, the reason for this measure was the traditional fear that enmity with God was a threat to the common good—precisely the thing that kept driving the common people to set upon heretics. In 1184, the two major powers, imperial rule and the papacy, agreed on a code of procedure.

A decree by Pope Lucius III, coordinated with Holy Roman Emperor Frederick Barbarossa, assigned special responsibilities to both powers in dealing with heresy: the Church would track down and condemn heretics, and the ruler—if necessary—would execute them. Not only state rulers, but even rulers of cities in Germany and Italy made such a stand against the enemies of God. This system was explicitly confirmed by the Fourth Council of the Lateran under Pope Innocent III (ca. 1160–1216). The Church condemned heretics and delivered them, when necessary, to the so-called "secular arm" for punishment. However, Innocent III still called for utmost caution: an experienced farmer, as well as a skillful vintner, he would know how to avoid uprooting the wheat along with the weeds or to avoid damaging the vineyard when pests are removed: "The innocent must not be condemned, nor the guilty acquitted."[2] The *Sachsenspiegel* of 1230 lays the foundation for the relationship between secular and ecclesial rule: "Any [entity] resisting the pope in a way that he cannot control by ecclesiastical jurisdiction needs to be compelled by the emperor and his use of secular law to obey the pope. So, too, shall the spiritual jurisdiction assist the secular power when necessary."[3]

In this way, heresy in the Middle Ages was "a matter both of high politics and of the common people; it was both a mass movement and something restricted merely to esoteric circles; it was the subject both of ecumenical councils and of locally limited lynch law; it captured the imagination of both poets and notaries, preachers and legal scholars", as historian Alexander Patschovsky writes.[4]

Traditionally, passing judgment on heresy had been the task of bishops, who to this end often convened a small assembly of bishops called a metropolitan council. Later, expert circles of specialized theologians would gather together to counsel the bishops. Ever since the Gregorian Reform of the eleventh century, the pope had claimed for himself the power to decide all important matters. It was not uncommon for these different responsible authorities to get into disputes over their competencies. In the end, an episcopal or papal verdict would be passed, and the accused would have to recant the condemned errors, sometimes at a public cathedral Mass in the presence of the clergy and the people.

It had to be determined above all how far one could deviate from dogma and maliciously persist in one's views before being truly guilty of erroneous belief. It was not very easy to declare someone a heretic, as specialist on the Middle Ages Heinrich Fichtenau shows: "A man could only be called a heretic, in the strict canon-legal sense of the word, if he continued to stand by his errors after a complaint, a legal process, and an admonition to teach the right doctrine."[5] Whoever recanted was theoretically out of danger. After all, this struggle was more about Christian life than about theological questions. However, it was not always possible to make such sharp distinctions, and orthodoxy and heresy were often close to each other. There was, for example, the question of poverty, which stirred up the entire Middle Ages and which Umberto Eco impressively dramatized in his novel *The Name of the Rose*. Francis of Assisi (ca. 1181–1226) was canonized just two years after his death and was of course therefore considered a shining example of orthodoxy. But if one looks more closely, he represents doctrines that are by no means thoroughly common. Biographer Helmut Feld even claims that his radical ideal of poverty "only partly agrees with the corresponding biblical terms."[6] For him, money amounted to "filth", and he forbade his friars even to touch it. And Francis desired a pure Church, just like many heretics did. He wanted to convert ecclesial authorities, though not a single member of the high clergy joined his movement. Still, Francis of Assisi and his teachings were officially accepted by the Church by his canonization. But where did tolerance end and heresy begin?

According to sociologist Walter Rüegg, the universities that emerged in the twelfth century called for "the recognition of the scientific achievements of dissenters, people of different faiths, and people of lower social status, as well as for the readiness to allow one's errors to be corrected by persuasive insights, whatever their provenance."[7] Within these new universities, there took place a veritable explosion of exceedingly heady and controversial discussions. Georges Minois, an expert on atheism and himself an atheist, emphasizes: "Contrary to an assumption that has too long prevailed, the intellectuals of the Middle Ages were wild about reason."[8] Extreme positions were defended with argumentative brilliance and disproved with equal argumentative brilliance. The culture of disputation was exemplary. Before someone was allowed to criticize an attitude, he had to be able to present it in such a persuasive manner that even his opponent could recognize his own arguments in the presentation. Only then came the intellectual counter-attack. But there were also "fouls" in this game. A person could make an attempt to put an opponent under suspicion of heresy and to indict him accordingly. However, only about fifty such heresy proceedings against professors can be identified in the entire period of the Middle Ages, most of which of course came to nothing. Bernard of Clairvaux (1090–1153) brought lawsuits against two theologians: the University of Paris' star theologian, Peter Abelard (1079–1142), and later the bishop Gilbert of Poitiers (ca. 1080–1154). Abelard immediately appealed to the pope, and even though some of his teachings were declared heretical in Rome and his books were thrown into the fire, nothing more was done; he even found favorable acceptance at Cluny, the most famous monastery of the West, and was eventually able to reconcile with Bernard as well as with the pope. Gilbert of Poitiers likewise had to accept a burning of his books, but he was able to return to his bishop's seat in Poitiers with all due respect. The writings of both continued to circulate, and Gilbert was even given a highly positive report on his character by one of Bernard's religious brothers.

In general, the Middle Ages remembered the old Christian principle of condemning heretical opinions without personally prosecuting heretics. One prime example of this is the famous abbot Joachim of Fiore (ca. 1130–1202), some of whose teachings were even condemned by the Fourth Council of the Lateran, but who was never considered a heretic by the Church. This example represents a clear distinction between a man and his teachings. Censorship emerged in this way in the thirteenth century. It meant that even though specific sentences by an author may have been designated "heretical", "dangerous", "foolish," or "offensive to pious ears", the person himself was not condemned. In these cases, all that was demanded was a retraction of specific passages, without any further personal burden on the author. Convictions of this kind were only made after obtaining an expert theological assessment, which often did not even focus on detecting the presence of heresy; rather, their comments pertained to wrong ideas listeners or readers might derive from their interpretation of a passage. If a defendant accepted that his statements or writings gave reason to be misunderstood, he remained in his office, kept his good name, and was neither condemned nor stigmatized.

If one doesn't take into account this significant difference, one arrives at misleading conclusions. For example, the historian of philosophy Kurt Flasch claims that the Church at that time condemned Meister Eckhart (ca. 1260–1328), but he is wrong.[9] In a heresy trial before the archbishop of Cologne—brought against him by his own brother Dominicans—Eckhart appealed to the pope. Legal historian Winfried Trusen considers the results of the trial typical of the new censorship: twenty-six statements by Eckhart were censored, meaning only that they were marked as "discordant sounding", "bold", or "suspicious of heresy". But he himself was not condemned, nor for that matter were his teachings. Trusen says: "What was actually condemned was not what Meister Eckhart had really said, but what the judges, and many others along with them, had imagined and understood" as they were reading his texts, which was "in no way" a condemnation of the "the person Eckhart."[10] By the way, Lutheran Church historian Martin Brecht has pointed out that many years later, in Luther's case, the papal commission first worked on a decree against Luther's writings while sparing him personally.[11] American historian William J. Courtenay summarizes his research on the medieval theologian trials in three points:

> First of all, the university community allowed a considerable range of debatable propositions, even ones which on the surface might seem blasphemous or heretical.... Second, censure had little serious effect on subsequent careers even for the obstreperous.... Finally, the right of masters of theology to evaluate and censure the opinions of members of the university community was ultimately more durable than either episcopal or papal control.[12]

That being said, not all heresy trials had such happy endings. William of Ockham (ca. 1288–1347) was sentenced to temporary imprisonment, but the sentence was never imposed. And the remains of John Wycliffe (ca. 1330–1384), who by the way had declared that a true heretic must be punished by death, were burned after a posthumous conviction. Jan Hus' burning at the Council of Constance, after Holy Roman Emperor Sigismund's breach of promise, was a grave injustice and, what's more, an ecclesial and political disaster.

For centuries, the parable of the weeds and the wheat had reminded Christians to be patient with deviant teachers. But the sin of proud medieval theology was in presuming to have at its own command the intellectual means to separate accurately the weeds from the wheat, in order to eradicate the weeds before they caused any trouble. Still, the old Christian call for nonviolence had a mitigating effect on this development. Thomas Aquinas (ca. 1225–1274) was the most prominent supporter of a theology of this kind. He cites four reasons for tolerance: (1) the good are made stronger by the bad; (2) in this way, tolerance helps to make theology clearer; (3) whoever is bad today could, like Paul, be converted tomorrow; and (4) last but not least, when heretic authorities are excluded from the Church, their gullible followers are exposed to danger. But this same peace-loving Dominican monk Thomas also supported violence when it came to countering persistent heretics, though this endorsement was made in hindsight, fifty years after the massacres of the Cathars in southern France. He utilized Augustine's "*Compelle intrare*"—Compel them to enter!—which in eight hundred years had never been so interpreted, in such a way that would eventually be used to justify even the death penalty. Augustine himself had explicitly countered such an interpretation. But Thomas argued that if the state could sentence coin counterfeiters to death, then the killing of heretics, who falsified for everyone the salvific truth, was even more justified. For the time, such a perspective seemed open-minded and progressive. But in reality, with views like this, the high medieval theology returned to what had always been the norm for the other two monotheisms, Judaism and Islam: accepting followers if their conversion was based on reasoned consent and free decision, but punishing those who have fallen away by expulsion or even destruction. By contrast, the early Christian decision sounded downright "tolerant": the elimination of deviant teachers must never be a personal, physical one, but rather remain God's own prerogative at the end of time. And in the Middle Ages, too, people were reminded ever again of the tolerant vision in the parable of the weeds as the true Christian vision.

To discuss certain aspects of ecclesial jurisdiction, it is necessary to keep in view the reality of secular trial and punishment procedures. What took place back then—much of which remained common practice into the nineteenth century—would make us shudder today. Legal historian Wolfgang Schild speaks of an almost unimaginable cruelty: "People were simply slaughtered and dismembered in the style of a butcher, their remains hung on or nailed to the gallows, burned, or boiled; they were torn to pieces by animals or pinched to death with glowing tongs. When they were wheeled, their bones were brutally broken. Oh, how people could look on with the excitement of a festival as human beings were being burned or hanging half-charred on stakes!"[13] Next to hanging or beheading, the most common punishment was "wheeling", which still took place up to the nineteenth century and which some legal historians interpret as an ancient sacrifice to the sun god; in any case, it was already in use among the early medieval Franks. One can still hear the shock effect today in the German saying "to feel absolutely wheeled", even though this does not convey anything about the nature of the original ordeal. In an illustrated book, Schild provides a picture of what it was like: the convict was thrown to the ground or tied to beams with pointed knobs, then run over with a wheel so that his bones were crushed; afterward, if necessary, they beat him to a pulp so that he could be braided into the spokes of the wheel, where some continued to survive for days. The modern historian Richard van Dülmen confirms and actually intensifies this image in his book *Theater des Schreckens* [*Theater of Horror*]: wheeling, burning, beheading, hanging, and burying alive were all standard practice, and on top of that they held such an attraction that they not only lured many common folk, but were often staged by the authorities at festivals, often with tens of thousands of spectators; the last such episode in Vienna came in 1868, with "gallows beer" and "poor sinner's sausages" served as concessions. In addition, there was, to our modern eyes, "an unbelievably high number of executions", carried out for offenses that harmed the social order, such as murder, stealing, or arson, and also for ethical and moral crimes such as adultery, fornication, and incest. Van Dülmen says that torture was "a means used by public institutions for investigating the truth."

None of this strove for the betterment of the delinquent, and "prison sentences were unknown." For a long time, because of a lack of jails, authorities practiced physical punishment such as mutilation. In the case of perjury or theft, this might entail the amputation of hands or fingers in public on a butcher's block and often, especially in the case of women, the removal of an ear—the origin of the German expression *Schlitzohr* (a devious person who spreads lies, literally, "a slit-eared person")—or even the removal, or at least the slashing, of the tongue; and finally, the chopping off of the nose. An essential part of the punishment was always to "injure and destroy a person's honor", hence the scold's bridle, the pillory, public whippings, and public mockery: "Although the pillory spared the condemned man's physical life, it destroyed his social life."[14] In this gruesome, hardly "Christianized" environment, there stood a Church convinced that obtaining eternal salvation for the souls of as many people as possible was far more important than worldly justice. This was a dilemma.

2. An Ill-Fated Judicial Reform: Fiction and Truth about the Medieval Inquisition

A Concise Defense of the Holy Inquisition: this is the title of a small, entertaining booklet by journalist Hans Conrad Zander, wherein he reveals amazing things that diametrically oppose the common conceptions about the institution in question. Zander simply did his research very thoroughly—an exemplary instance of clearing things up.

Hardly any institution in history has fallen into such terrible disrepute as the Inquisition. Brutal stories, terrifying statistics, inhumane practices—everyone has heard at least something about it at some time. The Inquisition—a scandal like no other. But what is true here, and what is not? Recently, using source materials just lately made available, scholars have provided us with some surprisingly clear answers.

The Inquisition was first a judicial and legal reform, and a good one at that. Legal historian Winfried Trusen states that "the inquisitorial trial with its investigation of the truth was a great step forward."[15] First of all, this means the purely juridical procedure of an official investigation. Though this procedure was introduced by

Pope Innocent III, this did not change anything about its secular juridical character. It was about finding facts, and that is just what *inquisitio* means: "investigation". The Inquisition was actually introduced not to judge heretics, but to punish offenses within the Church, for example in the case of bishops, who, as supreme judges of their dioceses, simply refused to open a trial if it might unearth certain suspicious facts regarding themselves. For this reason, the investigation was given a second instrument. Whenever there were seriously questionable facts in play, officials were to be appointed to conduct the investigation, and press charges if necessary, taking on the task of modern prosecutors. The Inquisition was a step forward because it allowed pre-rational methods, such as ordeals by water or fire, to be phased out and even become explicitly prohibited by the Church. Official investigations would penetrate into the matter so thoroughly that the accusation could—through confession or through concordant testimonies—be either confirmed or refuted. The interests of the defendant were to be especially guaranteed. For according to Trusen, "the accused under investigation had to be present for the procedure to be valid. The *capitula*—the statue or bit of law driving the investigation—had to be laid before the accused, so that he had an opportunity to defend himself. He had to be given the names of witnesses along with the 'what' and the 'by whom' of the accusation." In the end, there was supposed to be "condemnation only in the event of total proof, typically through a confession but at least through two agreeing witness statements."[16]The process of the Inquisition, with its fact-finding and official indictment, was soon adopted by secular law as well, since it so obviously represented an advancement. By the Middle Ages, France had already adopted the office of a publicly appointed prosecutor and further developed it, although Germany lagged behind in this regard. The introduction of a truly independent prosecuting authority only took place after the revolution of 1848.

But of course, there is more to the matter than this mere formal aspect. In order to understand what followed, we have first to learn about an uncanny phenomenon: that of the Cathars, the *katharoi* in Greek. The name itself does not tell us much: in Greek, it means "the pure ones", and the German word *Ketzer* ("heretic") was later derived from it. But who were the Cathars? We do not know exactly. Essentially, by all appearances, they supported the dualist teachings of eleventh-century heretics, who may have in fact been the first Cathars. But what distinguished the Cathar movement of the twelfth and thirteenth centuries was its massive scale. Nothing like it had been seen before. These teachings spread at a furious pace. They seized the Netherlands, Germany, England, Italy, and—with particular force—the south of France. In earlier times, the Church had only had to deal with individual heretics or with deviant theological opinions. Now suddenly there was a whole radical movement gaining ground, on the verge of destroying the existing order. The Cathars criticized the wealth and luxury of rulers, especially of the high clergy—which made them popular—while personally living what seemed like radically frugal lives—which made them attractive and admirable. But that was only the surface, and without examining the movement more closely, today one might think that the Cathars were a left-wing social-revolutionary grassroots movement, fighting against a Church that was concerned only with its own power; one might think that it was a case of liberal Christians being cowed by the strict finger-wagging of the institutional Church. However, new scholarly insights about the Cathars tell a different story. They came from all social classes and evidently their beliefs varied somewhat. But fundamentally they were dualists, who believed in a good spiritual God and a bad creator of the horrible world. The consequences of this were terrible. The Cathars strictly rejected sexuality and despised women, who were "fearfully avoided, as downright evil", reports medieval historian Arno Borst.[17] Procreation was the work of the Devil. If a pregnant woman died, the Cathars believed she would go directly to hell. Marriage was considered harlotry. Some did not eat anything that was a product of procreation, and at the end of their lives, the so-called *perfecti*, the Cathar elite, had a kind of spiritual baptism administered to them, the *consolamentum*; after, they could eat no more food and so starved themselves to death. As Gerhard Rottenwöhrer has observed, they murdered their enemies and fiercely cursed and branded each other as heretics. Thus, the Cathars were a grim, life-hating sect whose followers held on fanatically to its teachings and way of life. At the same time—and this is what made them so dangerous—they were perfectly organized. They possessed a nimble power structure with so-called bishops at the top; they were well connected with secular rulers in the south of France, who wanted the Cathars' help in maintaining their independence from the Crown. In 1167, they even held a council there.

If a group such as this existed today, it would certainly not be considered left-wing or liberal. In fact, the Cathars seemed to have had more in common with the Church of Scientology or other cults whose members stand ready to dedicate their entire lives to an elite group, sometimes even to the point of death. One might also say the Cathars had a lot of the traits that people tend to wrongly attribute to the Church: they were misogynistic, hostile to the body, detached from the world, fanatical, elitist, devil-obsessed, and driven by fear. All in all, they were daunting. And it was the Church who had to take them on.

How did she respond? Helplessly. But we should not pretend to be complete strangers today to such helplessness in the face of fanatical religious movements. The bishops were weak; the priests— often uneducated and lacking spiritual depth—frequently lived in objectionable situations. The religious orders, who could perhaps have provided a spiritual example, were bound to their monasteries, while the Cathars traveled around the country preaching and collecting followers.

What was to be done? Catholic theologians emphasized the goodness of the world; matrimony was made one of the seven sacraments and declared a means for achieving salvation. This was important, but how could all of it be conveyed to the people, who were fascinated by the radical new movement of self-proclaimed "perfect ones"? Pope Innocent III especially counted on the conversion of heretics through substantial homilies and persuasive examples. That is why he particularly supported the new orders: the Franciscans, who enthusiastically exemplified the ideal of poverty, and the theologically hyper-trained Dominicans, who, like the Cathars, were now able to travel around as preachers since they were not bound to a monastery. The founder of the Dominicans was a Spaniard, Domingo de Guzmán Garcés (1170–1221), Dominikus in Latin, and on a trip through the south of France, he had experienced the desperate situation brought on by the Cathars. In response, he founded the Order of Preachers, which stood poised first and foremost to face intellectual debates but at the same time was persuasive because of its frugal lifestyle. As for the Franciscans, Innocent III took the wise and courageous step of officially recognizing Francis of Assisi's movement of radical poverty, thus freeing it from a reputation of heresy. This allowed him to utilize it for the Church reform that he was launching, which reached its peak at the Fourth Council of the Lateran, convened in 1215.

But all that was not enough. The Church tried to resist the Cathars with preaching and failed. Saint Augustine in the fourth and fifth century, despite his vigorous support for tolerance, had already almost lost his cool with the rampant Donatist movement. Cathars, too, were undoubtedly a mass phenomenon with unprecedented momentum. Until then, fighting heresy had been a more sporadic challenge. But now, the pope decided to apply the newly developed Inquisition to heretics more generally. Legal historian Hans Hattenhauer emphasizes that Inquisition trials were now to be broadened to include heretics, but were still supposed to remain "scientifically conducted procedures".[18] Not only that. Innocent III went one problematic step further. He decided to apply classical imperial law to heresy, since heresy was directed against the divine majesty. This law was originally a sort of summary procedure for rebellions against a ruler, and they generally stipulated severe punishments. However, when it came to punishment, Innocent did not have the death penalty in mind. It was only Pope Gregory IX (1167–1241) who granted the Dominicans the right to exercise justice independently, which made it possible for the death penalty to be imposed. This marked the ill-fated transition from pastoral services to judicial responsibilities, where Dominican inquisitors began to function simultaneously as investigators, prosecutors, and judges. The goal of these trials was still confession, and that is commendable. The Synod of Narbonne determined in 1227: "Never proceed to sentencing anyone without transparent and open evidence or a personal confession."[19] Great as this sounds, the insistence on confession had one dreadful consequence: torture. Classical law had already used torture to obtain confessions, and this continued to be the case with secular law in the early Middle Ages; the burgeoning cities of the twelfth century simply took it as a given. Ecclesial law alone had always rejected torture. Then in 1252, Pope Innocent IV issued a decree permitting the use of torture in heresy trials, albeit with certain limitations: torture was only allowed to take place once, and it had to be halted if it would result in mutilation or death; also, clerics were not permitted to carry it out. Strange, however, that all the many sources French historian Emmanuel Le Roy Ladurie was able to assess, hardly yield anything regarding the actual practice of torture. Indeed, there have been scholarly arguments over whether or not torture was really employed, because it is not possible to provide any direct evidence about its actual use. Still, a dam had been breached, and even just the threat of torture must have had a torturing effect.

Of course, torture and the death penalty in no way ever formed the center of the Inquisition trial: they started with sermons calling for conversion and for a voluntary confession within a certain "grace period", where traditional secret confession resulted in a definitive acquittal. If a person was not yet prepared to do it but made a voluntary confession within thirty days, only a mild penance was imposed. In case of refusal, there was eventually an ultimate, solemn verdict of heresy as *actus fidei generalis*, from which the Spanish *auto-da-fé* (or *auto-de-fé*) is derived. The transfer to the secular arm followed, where the old commandment that the Church shall not exert high justice remained in force. This transfer, however, measured by concepts of the early Church, was un-Christian.

3. Fact Check on *The Name of the Rose*: The Victory of Heart and Reason

The Inquisition systematically began combating heresy in 1240, in the south of France. Since the bishops first in charge of it continued to fail, papal representatives, mostly Dominicans, were sent as inquisitors, in order to track down heretics and, when necessary, sentence them. Taken as the whole, the actual findings hardly allow us to identify any system. With prison sentences, there were both brutality and leniency, not to mention corruption among guards. Bishops, in turn, often mitigated punishments imposed by the Inquisition, for example reversing confiscations, expropriations, and impoundments. It would be impossible to get a definitive overview of all the trials that took place; we can only rely on examples. For instance, there was an inquisitor named Petrus Seila. He sentenced 650 people in nine places in 1241 and 1242, but he neither sentenced anyone to death nor imposed prison terms or confiscations; rather, he punished people with pilgrimages to Constantinople, with military service in the Holy Land, or with a cross sewn onto their clothes. On the whole, "it was more a kind of confession that Seila heard", as historian of the Middle Ages Lothar Kolmer summarized in his seminal research on the subject.[20] Inquisition registers for subsequent years, 1245–1256, have been partially preserved. In the years 1245 and 1246 alone, there were 5,605 witness statements. This kind of questioning was unprecedented: entire populations were summoned for it, and everything was recorded. In the summer of 1246, inquisitor Bernard of Caux pronounced 207 sentences: 23 incarcerations and 184 mandates to wear a cross, but not a single person to the stake. For the years of 1249 to 1257, there is a list with 306 sentences, 239 of which are prison and 21 are death sentences. The registry by Bernhard Gui (ca. 1261–1331), who also plays a role in Umberto Eco's novel *The Name of the Rose*, is considered the richest source. Spanning March 3, 1308 to June 19, 1323, his list counts a total of 907 "proceedings" with 633 penalties, 2.7 percent of which are pilgrimages, 21.5 percent the wearing of one or more yellow sewn-on cloth crosses, 48.7 percent prison time, 6.5 percent death by burning, and 14.1 percent posthumous sentences. Overall, the French historian and expert on the Inquisition Yves Dossat observes: "The inquisitors did not mechanically and blindly punish all guilty parties, and there is nothing to prove that they abused their power. Bernhard of Caux only imposed prison sentences in one out of nine cases and his successors only sent guilty parties to the stake in one out of a hundred cases."[21] This number of 1 percent is mentioned again and again, though it does not provide a reliable total number.

During the investigations into the sins of the Church initiated by Pope John Paul II on occasion of the Great Jubilee in 2000, new figures emerged on the Inquisition in Languedoc, France. The Cathar movement is estimated to have made up 5 to 8 percent of cases; in Albi, between 1286 and 1329 (43 years), of 250 known Cathars, 58 received a penalty—about 0.7 percent of the total population of 8,000 to 10,000 inhabitants. On the whole, French medievalist Jean-Louis Biget notes: "The Inquisition is far from having perpetrated mass persecutions. Over the course of a century, potentially 15,000 to 20,000 people were subject to special attention by the Inquisition, which represents no more than 1.5 percent of the total population of Languedoc."[22] However, we also have to note that the severest critic of the Inquisition came from its own ranks, the Franciscan Bernhard Délicieux (ca. 1265–1320). Together with the townspeople of Carcassonne, he kindled a rebellion against the Inquisition, sought the support of the French and Aragonese king, appeared in papal court, and ended up in custody.

And then there was also the Cathar Crusade. At some point, as reports about the unbridled spread of the Cathars were arriving almost daily, Pope Innocent III was completely at a loss about what to do, and in 1209, as a last resort, he called a crusade against the Cathars. That was a serious mistake. For immediately, the same thing happened as in the First Crusade: marauding soldiers went wild and raged in the conquered Cathar fortresses, hungry for spoils; they butchered thousands in the process, and the stories of these horrors were topped off with exaggerations that have come to be partly doubted by most recent research. The bloodbath at Béziers, in southern France, marked the climax of all the terror, with innumerable Cathars and Catholics randomly slain right at the outset. From the beginning, this crusade was dominated by political interests. The king welcomed the opportunity to realize his brutal quest for power under the guise of piety. By the end of the Cathar Crusade, all his enemies in southern France had been eliminated, and the French Crown had subjugated every region all the way to the Mediterranean. The Cathar Crusade was a desperate measure, but also a terrible mistake. Its goal, the destruction of the Cathar movement, was not achieved, even after twenty years of fighting. Ultimately, the Cathars were overcome not by force, but rather by the convincing monastic communities of the Franciscans and of the Dominicans, who led exemplary lives as mendicant friars and who again passed on the Christian faith to the people by heart and mind. The opinion of the great historian of the Middle Ages, Arno Borst, is as follows: "To oppose this new way of fighting, of theoretical refutation and practical example, the Cathars had nothing but imitation, and this sealed their defeat."[23] The last known arrest of a Cathar was documented in Florence in 1342.

In the period that followed, the Inquisition developed more and more into a state affair. Secular state courts not only adopted the Inquisition's methods, which were in themselves progressive, but also broadened their own competencies to include religious issues. This was already obvious in the proceedings against the Knights Templar, wherein the king ruthlessly enforced his own interests. The ecclesial Inquisition remained ineffective, and it was to be revived no more. The future belonged to the University of Paris, which was soon regarded as an unassailable authority in decisions relating to heresy. The process that prevailed was one with which we are already acquainted: certain theological positions were scientifically assessed and sentences were pronounced where necessary, though this did not always mean that delinquents were delivered to the secular arm.

Nevertheless, the final balance is still disturbing. For the first time in the history of Christianity, a heretic was executed. To be sure, this did not happen arbitrarily, but only after an "inquisition." Still, it ended in violence.

What especially jars us today is the Inquisition's claim that it had to limit people's freedom in the interest of their salvation. Yet this concept is not entirely unknown to us. In our own legal system, there is a certain sphere wherein citizens' freedom is limited in the interest of their own well-being, wherein people are even punished if they continue to try to harm themselves: drug use. Here, it truly is astonishing that the liberal constitutional state, by threat of punishment, prevents free, adult citizens from voluntarily harming themselves. In certain southeast Asian states, drug use is even punished by death. The assumption, of course, is that drugs in the long run rob men of their freedom. So it goes, too, with anti-constitutional groups as well as certain cults: many hold the opinion that a well-defended democracy should prevent such people from harming the general public through their radical, anti-constitutional ideas and getting others addicted. Only once we understand this can we comprehend why even the fiercely anti-Catholic Inquisition historian Henry Charles Lea acknowledges it as an eternal merit of the Inquisition to have suppressed the dangerous teachings of the Cathars. Combating the Cathars was not just about suppressing some liberal forces, but a desperate defense against rampant fanaticism—though by disastrous means.

Germany was much less affected by all this than France was. In the first case brought before the Inquisition—the trial of Friedrich Minneke, provost of the Neuwerk monastery at Halle—historian of the Middle Ages Dietrich Kurze notes "the thoroughness, the variety of authorities, and the formal fairness" at play.[24] Yet the Inquisition's ruin began shortly after its initiation. The brutal inquisitor Konrad von Marburg (ca. 1185–1233) raged against heretics on his own authority, met the unified resistance of the bishops, and made himself hated so rapidly that he was eventually murdered, with some even wanting to burn his dead body. Pope Gregory IX expressed his horror not only at the murder, but at the murdered person's own actions, which had been reported to him. The number of victims cannot even be estimated, according to the current state of research.

After this disaster, multiple attempts to reactivate the Inquisition could not help it back on its feet. After 1300, some Beguines were tried, and Emperor Charles IV also worked to revive the Inquisition. However, it was to no avail, because "the bishops, as usual, gave ... the cold shoulder", according to Henry Charles Lea.[25] Later, the Inquisition continued to work in Austria and Bohemia against the wayward penance-and-poverty movement of the Waldensians; in the period between 1335 and 1350, a total of 4,400 people were prosecuted, 5 percent of whom were burned at the stake.[26] At the end of the century, there was another persecution of Waldensians in Germany, where a mass trial in 1399 in Freiburg ended inconclusively and other individual trials after 1430 similarly resulted in no sentence. Eventually, in the late Middle Ages, heretical groups in Germany became insignificant; the word "heretic" became no more than a polemical term used within the Church, notes Alexander Patschovsky, who has written numerous works on medieval heresy.[27]

In German lands, just as in France, the evaluation of whether or not something was orthodox devolved de facto upon the theology faculties. The universities in Vienna and Cologne deserve particular mention. As in France, secular rulers took the persecution of the enemies of God out of the Church's hands, citing the old reason that it is the state's task to deflect God's wrath. Already during the Great Plague in 1348, the Church's recommendations for appeasing God's wrath were apparently considered insufficient, and there arose more and more attempts by laypeople to find their own way outside of official channels.

Now secular courts were handling religious offenses. First, starting in the fourteenth century, the cities issued special prohibitions against blasphemy and thus became "pioneers of criminalization", as crime historian Gerd Schwerhoff puts it.[28] Even if the numbers are low in terms of percentage, they are still considerably high: in Basel, between 1376 and 1455, there were easily ninety-nine offenders; in Konstanz, between 1430 and 1460, there were fifty-seven. For the most part they were punished by having their tongues cut out, by the pillory, by expulsion from the city, or by a monetary fine, but sometimes they were killed. At the same time, in the late Middle Ages, authorities made another attempt at legislation on the level of the Holy Roman Empire, instituting a special law against blasphemy under Emperor Maximilian (1459–1519).

Much has been said and written about the creativity of heresy. Certainly, some information has been lost in the persecutions, but not all heresy was creative; some of it was simply anarchic, or even violent. Patschovsky summarizes it thus:

> The contribution of heretics to medieval society must be regarded as extraordinarily minimal. One wonders just what it concretely changed, what new things it created. Aside from the worker cooperatives of the Upper Italian Umiliati and the Waldensians, as well as the Bohemian Brethren, or the Bohemian Church more generally in post-Hussite times, there is no sign that heretics developed any special social forms or left any special mark on society.[29]

At any rate, having arrived now at the end of the Middle Ages, we have to note that this age was not one of continuous warfare against heretics. For centuries, there were no significant heresies, and in the case of certain countries, such as England and Scandinavia, the whole land remained entirely free of them, at least until the late Middle Ages.

4. Pope Alexander IV: Borgia and German Television—How Germany Defeated Spain

In 1864, the German diplomat Kurd von Schlözer found a box in a storeroom at the Church of Santa Maria in Monserrato degli Spagnoli in Rome containing some rather eerie items. They were the bones of two people, with a small, old piece of paper revealing whose mortal remains they were. The bones belonged to two popes who had been lying in this storeroom awaiting the resurrection of the dead: Popes Callixtus III and Alexander VI. But how on earth did the bones of two servants of God, two successors of the apostle Peter, two representatives of Christ on earth, end up in this shabby store-room? The story is quite simple. Both these Borgia popes had actually been buried in Saint Peter's Basilica, as so many popes are. But when Saint Peter's was rebuilt, space needed to be cleared, and some papal tombs had to move. The remains from almost all these tombs were set aside, and then buried in the same place later. But in the case of these two renowned Borgia popes, some took the opportunity to dis-pose of them discreetly. The ancient Romans already had experience in blotting out memories, and no one saw much value in keeping the memory of the pontificates of Callixtus III and Alexander VI alive. Thus, the old bones eventually ended up in the storeroom of the Spanish national church Santa Maria in Monserrato, on the Via Giulia in Rome.

In 2011, ZDF, a German national television station, along with several other major European TV networks, aired a six-part mini-series called *Borgia*. Just as in its American HBO counterpart *The Borgias*, almost the entire script was false and unhistorical, and abso-lutely everything in it was salacious, cruel, and bloody. A scandalous story at its finest, where "blood, poison, and sperm flow unchecked", as a commentator at the newspaper *Die Welt* vividly expressed it.[30] High audience ratings were expected, and this led to the production of further seasons—an endeavor comes all the more easily the less one is concerned with historical truth and the more free rein one gives to the imagination. Besides, there is perhaps no pope more surrounded by spicy rumors and dark legends than Pope Alexander VI. The series was broadcast in forty countries. It was just the sensational block-buster ZDF had been waiting for. All this, however, presumably took place under one condition: that producers first got rid of the set's lead historical consultant—in classic Borgia style.

But what is behind this scandal? Why is the counterfeiting of his-tory so unrestrained on this point? Why was this pope so embar-rassing to his successors? Why did even defenders of the Catholic Church sit back and do nothing when it came to Alexander VI? Why did images of the immoral papal court focus exclusively on Pope Alexander VI? Certainly, he had children, and that was not right. But why does no one know that his predecessor, Innocent VIII

(Giovanni Battista Cibo) possibly had more children than Alexander VI did, with his son, Franceschetto Cibo, holding a magnificent wedding at the Vatican? Why is his successor, Pope Julius II, still highly praised in all travel guides as the patron of Michelangelo, though he, too, had children and in reality brought almost nothing but trouble to Michelangelo, and was constantly waging personal wars?

The answer is clear and simple: Pope Alexander VI was a Spaniard! Indeed, he and his uncle Pope Callixtus III were the first non-Italians on the papal throne since the depressing exile in Avignon, which no one liked to remember anymore. Since then, a new Italy had come into being, with an Italian culture and an Italian sense of national identity. With Francesco Petrarca and others, the Italian language had developed into a language of high culture. Through the work of many brilliant Italians, there sprouted a new art, what was later to be called the Renaissance. Italians were rightfully proud of leading the new age. Rome was in the process of becoming the most splendid cultural center of the country, alongside Florence. After the alarm of the Western Schism of 1378, the papacy had slowly worked its way up again and taken back Rome, restoring bit by bit the churches and the whole city. The Romans now also lured great artists to the Eternal City. Aspirations were high, the rebuilding of Saint Peter's Basilica was in order, but despite all this, the popes remained tied down by the day-to-day politics in their central Italian microstate. They had to be not only pious, but as smart and politically savvy as possible, not to mention well connected, ideally with the other players in this Renaissance Italy—mostly ruthless power seekers who knew every trick in the book. Thus, even though there were some great humanists elected pope, such as Nicholas V and Pius II, there were also cunning politicians like Sixtus IV and Innocent VIII— all of them Italians, of course. But in reality, the papacy is actually a worldwide institution and could not afford to get tangled up in Italian turmoil. In 1453, Constantinople was cruelly conquered by the Turks, but the far-ranging sea adventures of the great powers of Spain and Portugal demanded the attention of the single accepted supranational institution of Christianity. Just as, later, the immediate reaction to the Reformation would be the election of a German pope, Hadrian VI of Utrecht, the election of the Spanish popes was definitely not least a reaction to the world's situation in the fifteenth

century. Two years after the conquest of Constantinople, Callixtus III was elected, eventually followed by his nephew, Rodrigo
Borgia, who took the name Alexander VI, in 1492, the year when
America was discovered. But just as with Hadrian VI in the sixteenth
century, the Italians, proud of their nation, did not like these foreigners, and that is how the trouble began.

Callixtus III was a pious, smart, and cosmopolitan man. There are
probably few people who have successfully negotiated as many significant peace settlements in their lives as this Alonso Borja. He was
the man who, as canon of Valencia and vice chancellor of the king of
Aragon, finally settled the Western Schism—because it is not entirely
true that the disastrous spiritual division of the West ended with the
election of Pope Martin V at the Council of Constance in 1417. At
Peniscola, a wild and romantic fortress on the Spanish Mediterranean
coast, the power-conscious antipope Pedro de Luna, as Benedict
XIII, was defying almost all of Christianity with his ghostlike court
of self-appointed cardinals. After his death in 1423, these cardinals
even elected a successor, Clement VIII, in the subterranean conclave
room. All of Europe gave a sigh of relief when Alonso Borja, in a
bold endeavor, surprisingly managed to have Clement VIII formally
abdicate in his presence there at Peniscola on July 26, 1429. Alonso
had already negotiated an important peace treaty in 1419 between the
Spanish kingdoms of Aragon, Castile, and Navarre, whose renewal he
also helped bring about in 1436. When Pope Eugene IV offered him
the position of cardinal during his peace negotiations between King
Alfonso of Aragon and the Holy Father, he declined, only accepting
the appointment after he had successfully negotiated the peace of
Terracina in 1442, which, among other things, made it possible for
the pope to return to Rome.

In his three-year pontificate, Callixtus III tried to motivate the
Christians of the West to go on another crusade to save the Christians
of the East, who were being cruelly persecuted by the Turks. His
efforts remained without success. To this day, the Greek Orthodox
reproach Roman Catholics for letting concern for good trade relationships with the Turks deter them from a costly war against a brutal
enemy. This sealed the fate of the Greeks, who were thus robbed of
their freedom for almost four hundred years. At least the pope, by his
untiring efforts, managed to overcome the incredible self-absorption

of the European powers in the face of distress and prevent the Turks from advancing farther into central Europe. Callixtus III was morally pure, exceedingly humble, and above reproach. When he made his nephew Rodrigo Borgia a cardinal, and when he procured offices in Rome for other family members in order to have trusted supporters of his government in an Italian environment riven by party disputes, he was doing something that had been common practice among Italian popes since at least the thirteenth century: "family-friendliness." A pope, such as the later Hadrian VI, who did not behave in this way was literally considered "antisocial" by the Italians.

This young nephew, Rodrigo Borgia, really showed his mettle. For thirty-five years, he served not only his uncle but four more popes as vice chancellor. This had never happened before and was in itself regarded as a feat—one for which his outstanding abilities are the only possible explanation. "Highly gifted" is what the famous Swiss cultural historian Jacob Burckhardt calls him.[31] Rodrigo was incredibly diligent and did his job so well that he rose continually higher in the ranks. During an exceedingly delicate diplomatic mission to Spain, he also succeeded in bringing peace to that unsettled area. It was he who had the marriage between Isabella of Castile and Ferdinand of Aragon legitimized, ending a ten-year battle for Barcelona. Thus, Rodrigo unified Spain. The unbridled debauchee of television's *Borgia* would never have been able to accomplish something like that.

Of course, the (then) modern rulers of Italy, the Renaissance princes, cultivated a rather lax morality. It was common for them to have concubines and numerous illegitimate children, so-called "bastards". People knew that such behavior was not good, but they were not really troubled by it, either. Cardinals and popes, too, were Renaissance princes (though unmarried because of priestly celibacy), so they, too, permitted themselves to lead a lifestyle that the world considered modern. They did not hide their actions, but conducted this lifestyle openly, demonstrating quite a sense of family and of responsibility. Rodrigo Cardinal Borgia was true to his lover, Vannozza de Cattaneis, for many years, having four children by her and ensuring that they were well educated. When he became pope, his election was marked by more or less the same intrigues and pacts that had already been the norm among his Italian predecessors and continued to be the norm among his Italian successors after his death, to the annoyance of Church reformers.

His pontificate from 1492 to 1503 differed from that of his predecessors and successors mostly in the simple lack of preoccupation with Italian affairs and the adoption of global political perspectives. Pope Alexander VI mediated the famous Treaty of Tordesillas, which divided the world between the sea powers of Spain and Portugal after the pope's decision. Without going into the contested details, we can safely say that it is one of the great peace treaties in the history of mankind. It did not end a war, but instead prevented from the outset what might have been a 100-year war between the two greatest maritime powers of the time. Through shrewd policies, Alexander brought peace to the Basque country, one that lasted up until his death. In addition, he managed to brave the massive military aggression of the French king, which forced him to defend himself in great hardship at Castel Sant'Angelo.

The high Renaissance was beginning in Rome at this time. Bramante, the great architect, built his first work in the city, the Tempietto at San Pietro in Montorio, and the young Michelangelo sculpted the Pietà for Saint Peter's Basilica. Under Alexander, a thoroughly liberal atmosphere prevailed in Rome; when Copernicus appeared at the university, the pope invited people who had most crudely taunted the young man earlier, to be his guests. He advocated for virtually limitless freedom of opinion. For a long time, in the case of the fanatical Dominican monk Savonarola in Florence, who had established a hyper-moralist regime in that city and who from the chancel was calling on people to lop off the heads of his enemies, Pope Alexander pleaded for leniency toward the man, until the city of Florence itself wanted to get rid of the tyrannical zealot. This pope was certainly not a saint. He was, however, deeply pious. The petition in the Hail Mary, "Holy Mary, Mother of God, pray for us sinners, now and at the hour of our death", is attributed to Pope Alexander VI, which reminds Christians of the two most important moments in life. He celebrated the Jubilee in 1500 with dignity, and it was only after his death that the fateful sale of indulgences began, under Pope Julius II. Against the fierce opposition of the Spanish king, he welcomed into the Papal States those Jews and Moors who had been banished from Spain. In addition, he internationalized the College of Cardinals. At the same time, there was an inner disunity in him, one that, according to Johan Huizinga, characterized many in the "autumn of the Middle Ages", such as Philipp the Good of Burgundy and later Martin Luther.[32] Despite his deep piety, he was capable of reacting suddenly with violence and injustice. In these moments, he was definitely aware of his sinfulness, and afterward he often sank into self-doubt. After the brutal murder of his son Juan by unknown assailants, he was contrite and promised improvement; he convened a commission of cardinals, who were supposed to develop suggestions for reforming the Church. Soon, however, these efforts petered out.

It was perhaps above all his great love for his children that cast a shadow on his pontificate. However, this accusation, which is woven through all historical accounts of him and to many critics is the key to his pontificate, may be too hasty. The situation of the Papal States at the time was exceedingly precarious. Unscrupulous power politics reigned in Italy, the coalitions changed in quick succession, and in the bat of an eye, yesterday's ally could be tomorrow's deadly enemy. No one cared that the French king was well on his way to subjugating Italy, and aside from Venice, which was attacked directly, no one was concerned that the Turks in the north had already entered Italian ground. Alexander alone was tirelessly active in keeping the French out of Italy and in pulling together a coalition against the Turks. He had only limited success in this. For Rodrigo Borgia, the Spaniard, seemed the only one who wanted to fight for Italy's freedom. He repeatedly implored the representatives of the Italian powers on this issue, to which they responded with nothing more than a cynical smile. Alexander's motto, "Italy to the Italians", simply did not meet with any interest among the Italians themselves. In the end, the pope had to watch helplessly as the French king, Charles VIII, who had been summoned by the Italians, occupied Rome and extorted concessions from it, although the pope bravely resisted the king's most important demand, to enfeoff him with the kingdom of Naples. In this ceaseless political turmoil, the pope realized that he could not rely on his own vassals, the unruly barons of the Papal States, who actually repeatedly conspired against him. The cardinals were of no help either. Giuliano Cardinal della Rovere, the later Pope Julius II, was the pope's fiercest enemy; he wanted to have him deposed, to convene a council against him, and in fact, it was he who lured the French king to Italy. Finally, the "Roman king" Maximilian of Austria was far away and occupied with other matters than the protection of the *Patrimonium Petri*, which would actually have been his responsibility. The pope was alone.

Thus, Alexander's relatives were the only people he could really rely on. And once that became clear, the entire Spanish family met the unbridled hatred of the Italians, who until now had conducted all their power battles among themselves. Juan, one of the pope's sons, was murdered, and his son Cesare and his daughter Lucrezia were subjected to defamation. Hardly any serious historian today believes what everyone was talking about at the time, namely, that Cesare had murdered his own brother and Lucrezia had committed incest with her father. But there was literally no story too perverse for the slanderers. Alexander had made Cesare a cardinal—just as the Italian popes had done with their relatives. But in reality, Cesare was most unsuitable for a clerical profession. So he soon put down the office of cardinal and stood his ground as an assertive man of power, whom Machiavelli admired, Leonardo da Vinci readily served, and the people loved and feared. He was glamorous, and he could certainly be brutal and sly, no different from the other Renaissance rulers of his time. In fact, he tried to set up for himself a dukedom in Romagna, which was part of the Papal States. But Pope Julius II would do exactly the same for his family in Urbino. Although for the Holy See, a peaceful Romagna would certainly have been better than its current condition—a disorganized collection of cities, each with its own little tyrant who shared one thing above all in common with his "colleagues": a disregard for the supremacy of the pope. In the end, Alexander managed to do the impossible. The tyrants were banished, the barons were tamed, France was kept out of Italy. Lack of sufficient means of power had made it impossible to prevent Spain's establishing itself in Naples. It was on these achievements that Pope Julius II was able to build when he consolidated the Papal States.

Even when reading texts on Catholic Church history from the nineteenth century, one can only learn all this in the footnotes, if anywhere. Because on the one hand, Alexander had the misfortune never to care about malicious gossip and for this reason was at the mercy of his Italian contemporaries' imaginative hatred, which was eagerly exploited in show trials after his death by his energetic

successor, Julius II. Moreover, nineteenth-century historiography
was so dominated by the obsession with sexuality that the promiscu-
ity of the Borgia pope was in itself enough to render a fair assessment
by leading historians very difficult. We know today that Alexander's
daughter, Lucrezia, did not commit any of the atrocities she was
accused of. She was highly intelligent and thoroughly educated and
ended up as duchess of Ferrara, beloved by the people. Serious studies
on the matter agree that nothing gives evidence to her alleged inces-
tuous affair with her father. And the famed Borgia poison, which
supposedly was able to work days after having been taken, never
existed either. Pharmacologically, such a thing is not possible.

And so we come now to the inventors of the Borgia myth. To
be fair, it was not the ZDF. Most of the people who wrote the
"script" for the German television fairytale have long since passed
away. These were the Italian enemies of the Spanish pope, but there
was also one German, supposedly bribed by these Italians: Johannes
Burckard from Strasbourg [in modern-day France]. To this day, the
Largo Argentina in Rome is named after his home that once stood
there; Argentoratum was the ancient Roman name of Strasbourg.
This man, who had to flee his city for forging documents, was the
pope's master of ceremonies; he was fastidious, as MCs can sometimes be, and petty-minded to boot. To such a man, the dynamic and
spontaneous Alexander must have been a nightmare. In addition, the
pope simply struck a man like Burckard as too modern. Burckard, by
contrast, believed firmly in witches and gossiped in his diary, which
was only published about a hundred years ago but whose stories he
certainly made public at the time. He did so in graphic and sensual
detail, but of course full of disgust at the Holy Father's consorting
with witches, amusing himself with his daughter at sexual orgies,
and being terribly disordered in general. The sexual fantasies cooked
up by this prudish man are, from a psychological perspective, quite
remarkable. And his stories were taken seriously by many. The diary
of Johannes Burckard roughly corresponds to yellow journalism
today. For it was exactly what people wanted to hear. This Spaniard must have been a monster, a fiend, in league with the Devil, a
greedy lecher who did not even shy away from lying with his own
daughter. Under normal circumstances, everyone would immediately doubt such horror stories. But to the Spaniard's enemies, the

tales spun by this bigoted German cleric and others came just at the right time. And thus, together with the Italians' hatred of Spaniards, an insignificant little German desk criminal [*Schreibtischtäter*] and many others succeeded at destroying a pope who, although not holy, was not unimportant, and they persecuted his bones all the way to that store room at the Church of Santa Maria in Monserrato. There was never again a Spanish pope, and even the greatest defenders of the Catholic Church in the nineteenth and twentieth centuries found the Borgias simply embarrassing. It was only when more recent historical research began attending to the Borgias that the situation changed. Historian Susanne Schüller-Piroli for instance published her detailed work on the Borgia popes in 1979, which confronted common myths about them, and the period following her work yielded studies that provided a new, more nuanced picture.

When in 1864 it became clear that the bones really did belong to the Borgia popes, piety prevailed in the end, and they were buried in Santa Maria in Monserrato, in the first side chapel on the right. But even there, as the Devil would have it, the two were mixed up, so that a portrait of the pomp-loving nephew Alexander was hung above humble Callixtus' name, and the image of the kind-hearted uncle appeared above the name of Alexander.

V

Modernity

Old Problems, New Solutions

1. The World Stage: Martin Luther and Indulgences

Fourteen years after the death of Pope Alexander VI came the Reformation. Just as had been the case around the year 1000, the period around 1500 was religiously agitated. The new spirituality of *devotio moderna* had moved many people deep in their souls and had brought about a profound personal piety. The printing press made it possible to spread spiritual literature, and art provided devotional images that moved the senses. But a widespread fear of the supposedly imminent end of the world came in handy for frivolous wheeler-dealers looking to make a quick profit. The most famous among them was to be the Dominican Johann Tetzel.

Johann Tetzel was evidently a sketchy fellow. There circulated a story that one of the prince-electors of the Holy Roman Emperor, Frederick of Saxony—the later advocate of Luther—once had to pay a ransom for Tetzel when he had been sentenced to death by drowning for adultery and game fraud. However, this was only a rumor that Luther himself spread. At any rate, in 1504, Tetzel briskly started selling indulgences, which he promoted using arguments that contradicted Church teaching. One slogan on his money collection boxes is a good example: "As soon as the gold in the coffer rings, the rescued soul to heaven springs." In other words, Tetzel claimed that with money, one could make sure that dead people would rise from purgatory to heaven. This was complete nonsense,

of course, but a very lucrative business for him. The Augustin-
ian monk Martin Luther was justified in his protest against him,
as the Catholic Church affirms today. Luther found it outrageous
that another authority should be allowed to impose itself between
Christians and God. God gave his mercy completely without any
merit on the part of the recipient, he said, and this gift of mercy
made man free and whole. Yet this was no innovation on Luther's
part; rather, it was already the common Catholic perspective. Still,
through misunderstandings, political intrigues, and tragic events,
this indulgence controversy became the departure point for the
schism in Western Christendom.

But are not indulgences already scandalous in themselves? What
is an indulgence, really?[1] It has nothing to do with the forgiveness
of sins, because only God can forgive sins, if one goes to confession,
admits one's sins, repents, and makes a resolution never to commit
them again. Forgiveness of sins is pure mercy from God, and even
Luther saw it that way. However, sins are never just personal, a matter
exclusively between God and an individual person; sins always also
affect the community. And that is why a person should do penance
for the suffering he has caused, not only later, when he is purified in
purgatory, but even in this world—for example, by helping people
in need or by making a burdensome pilgrimage. Through so-called
indulgences, the Church only mitigated this penance, in the event
that certain prerequisites had been met. The selling of indulgences,
which arose in Luther's time, was an abuse that the Council of Trent
eventually explicitly forbade and that Pope Pius V even punished
by excommunication in 1570.

But by then it was too late. In 1517, Luther published his 95 Theses
and thus unleashed a storm. By that point, it was no longer just about
indulgences. Even though Luther did not want a new Church, he
very decisively wanted a reform of the old one. This temperamental
man campaigned primarily against abuses in the Church, not least in
Rome. And it became abundantly clear that he was completely justified in doing so. Just six years after the 95 Theses, the pope himself
to a great extent already agreed with Luther. But that was no longer
Pope Leo X, the Medici Pope and art lover who had excommunicated Luther without really knowing the situation in Germany and
had written the whole issue off as "monks' squabble".

Instead, this new pope was a highly educated German humanist, Adriaan Floriszoon, born in Utrecht, which was then part of the Holy Roman Empire. He had just been elected pope after serving as Emperor Charles V's tutor, and had already made himself unpopular among the Romans by not tolerating nepotism and by rejecting the amusements of courtly life. He had chosen the name Adrian VI, and he sent a papal legate to the Diet of Nuremberg in 1523 to pronounce the following text:

> We know that for some years now in this Holy See there have been many abominable abuses in spiritual matters, offenses against the divine commandments—indeed, that everything has been perverted. Thus, it is no wonder that the disease has descended from the head to the members, from the popes to the prelates of lower rank. We all, prelates and priests, have strayed off the path; each went after his own way (see Is 53:6), and it has long been the case that no good man is left, not even one (see Ps 14:3). For this reason, we must all glorify God and humble ourselves before him; each one of us must acknowledge his own fall and judge himself, lest he be judged by God with the rod of his wrath (see 1 Cor 11:31). As far as we ourselves are concerned, you may be sure we will exercise every effort in reforming, first of all, this Curia, from which perhaps the whole evil has proceeded. Just as she has occasioned the corruption of all her subjects, she will now bring about their healing and reform. We are committed to this all the more since we can see that the entire world eagerly desires such a reform.[2]

But Luther did not react. He missed his chance. According to Lutheran Church historian Martin Brecht, Luther, unlike his companion Melanchthon, generally brought into the disputes "a personal emotional quality that was not always appropriate or helpful".[3] Pope Adrian VI soon died. He was buried in the German national church of Santa Maria dell'Anima in Rome, and he was given the bitter epitaph, "Alas, how much even the best man's efforts depend upon the times in which he lives." His successor was another Medici. Under him, there was another dispute, with King Henry VIII of England. And even though the next pope, Paul III, was able energetically to advance the Catholic reform by convening the Council of Trent, by then the elderly Luther had already traveled too far down his path, away from the Church, and the hope for unity was crushed.

2. How Real Is Reality? The Black Legend and the Truth about the Spanish Inquisition (1484–1834)

When we speak about the atrocities perpetrated by the Inquisition, we are usually referring to the Spanish Inquisition. Supposedly, this cruel institution is answerable for hundreds of thousands, even millions, of victims throughout the vast Spanish global empire. Simply scandalous! Yet there is hardly a field of scholarship where recent research, analyzing ample source material, has cleared up historical myth so thoroughly as that of the Spanish Inquisition.

What are the reasons for the grotesque distortions of this Spanish institution? At this point, we need to address the famous *Legenda nera*, the "black legend". Not only was the venerable Spanish empire eventually defeated in their military feud with the rising Protestant powers of England and the Netherlands, but it also suffered a devastating and lasting defeat in the realm of publicity. Using outlandish distortions and—as we would say today—"fake news", Spain's journalistically superior opponents succeeded at diffusing a grotesque horror image of Spain in history, one that to this day remains largely unchallenged and continues to have an effect in the public sphere. And when the small, nimble boats of the English defeated the majestic Spanish galleasses in the battle against the Armada in 1588, the Spaniards, sad and indignant, looked on as many swift quills eagerly penned "alternative facts"—with great success. Few people know that the English Puritan leader Oliver Cromwell (1599–1658) had massacres carried out against Irish Catholics, or that the population of North America in that period was almost entirely composed of people who had fled from English religious repression. By contrast, it is common knowledge today that the Spanish Inquisition was a brutal criminal institution. Yet what does recent research have to say about that?

On April 18, 1482, Pope Sixtus IV founded the Spanish Inquisition with a solemn declaration: resistance to heresy should be governed by pure zeal for the faith, not greed for riches. Without legally valid evidence, no believing Christian could ever be thrown into prison, tortured, sentenced as a heretic, or extradited to the secular arm and deprived of property on the sheer testimony of slaves, enemies, or biased witnesses. Rather, the episcopal representatives were to work together with the inquisitors. The accused were to be told the names and statements of witnesses, defenders and witnesses for the defense were to be admitted, and before trial the prisoners could only be held in episcopal dungeons. Any violation of these regulations gave the accused a right to appeal to the pope, interrupting the proceedings. In general, whoever acknowledged himself to be guilty of heresy could be acquitted before the court, and his own conscience, by sacramentally confessing to an inquisitor or an episcopal official. There was no need for further renouncement—the acceptance of a simple penance was enough. The accused would receive an attestation about his absolution, which did not mention the kind of sin confessed and provided protection from any further harassment for past offenses. The only goal was, as British historian of the Inquisition Henry Kamen notes, to receive from the prisoners a confession of sin and a readiness to do penance.[4] In this way, Sixtus had wanted to acknowledge the lessons learned from the abuse of power.

But what happened afterward reveals the fundamental problem with the Spanish Inquisition: the powerful Spanish king soon thereafter forced the pope to suspend his declaration. And thus, over time, the Spanish Inquisition developed into a kind of Spanish intelligence service with no real religious motivation, an instrument of Spanish national interest entirely fixated on the idea that the unity of the state—which had at last been achieved, after many struggles—could only endure if religious unity was maintained.

The kingdoms of the Iberian Peninsula had been at war with the Muslim rulers of the Spanish south for centuries. In the last phase of the Peninsula's reconquest, a great number of Muslims came under Spanish rule. Some were baptized, but the Spanish harbored distrust toward the Muslims and suspected them of subversive activities that threatened the state. The same distrust was directed against Jews, too. Later on, those suspected of being Protestants were especially distrusted, because they were considered factionists of Spain's eternal adversaries, Protestant England and the equally Protestant Netherlands. The fear of being infiltrated became virtually obsessive. This is why the Spanish kings considered it their prime task to defend the unity and security of the state. To this end, they effectively brought the Inquisition under their control, and this would remain the case for the next three hundred years. The popes repeatedly made efforts to intervene and exert some mitigating influence, but they were powerless in Spain. The Spanish king even repeatedly forbade that papal decrees be published in his domain.

So the Spanish Inquisition was a hybrid institution: legitimized by the pope, but in reality run by state-appointed clerics and laymen. The trials themselves were considerably more restrictive than the pope had originally intended. The Inquisition used its own witnesses, and these remained hidden from the accused, supposedly for fear of possible abuse or even murder. Defense, too, was limited. Everything was geared toward obtaining a personal confession, as well as further accusations against others. Inquisitors even employed torture to obtain these goals, although this remained an exception. According to Kamen, torture was supposed to be avoided at all costs, used exclusively for confessions and never as punishment, and in practice it was relatively "gentle".[5] Edward Peters arrives at the same conclusion in his research on torture: the Spanish Inquisition used torture less than was the custom of the day.[6] American historian Stephen Haliczer confirms this.[7] Even Henry Charles Lea, who is very critical of the Inquisition, made some corrections to the popular imagination: the "impression that the inquisitorial torture-chamber was the scene of exceptional refinement in cruelty, of specially ingenious modes of inflicting agony, and of peculiar persistence in extorting confessions, is an error due to sensational writers who have exploited credulity."[8] In addition, American historian E. William Monter credits the Inquisition for not having treated defendants arbitrarily. There were precise distinctions, even, for example, in cases where a person was insane. During the fact-finding process, the inquisitors put their trust less in torture than in cross-examination, often with considerable psychological finesse: "Most of the time,... these inquisitors merely assigned penances of varying duration and intensity. Theirs was ultimately a culture of shame rather than a culture of violence."[9] Thus Stephen Haliczer is able to conclude that although the Spanish Inquisition was no modern tribunal, "it was willing to go further in the formal protection of accused than the French or English criminal courts."[10]

Sentencing ultimately took place in public. It was a beloved spectacle, drawing the presence of all the notable people along with huge crowds, often accompanied by fireworks, bullfighting, and amusements; for this reason, it was quite popular. The persons pronounced guilty had to appear in public wearing the capirote [a tall, pointed cap worn by penitents] and make a formal confession of faith, their *auto-da-fé*, or else, if they stood by their refusal, face extradition to the secular arm. Executions took place outside of the city, in most cases by strangulation before burning, in order to spare the convict the agony of incineration. If the convicts were absent, their images were burned. If instead the convict was sentenced to prison, this term—unlike the imprisonment before the sentencing—was served in "moderate comfort", as Henry Kamen reports, or at least was "more humane and enlightened" than secular imprisonment, often including the freedom to go out at certain times and an early parole.[11] Even the relentless Lea, who indeed spent his entire life critically examining the history of the Inquisition, describes the terror of the prisons as "less vile than that of other jurisdictions".[12]

Recent calculations have had a powerful impact on historical research in this field. Over the course of the Inquisition, one can note a "wild" phase lasting until 1530, followed by a "moderate" one. According to the source material, the comparatively short wild phase had about 5,000 victims. Danish social scientist Gustav Henningsen has thoroughly investigated the moderate phase and has tallied up for the entire Spanish empire 826 death sentences in the 160 years from 1540 to 1700—that is, 1.8 percent of all verdicts. And not all of these sentences were carried out.[13] This research allowed legal historian Edward Peters to conclude that the Inquisition exercised a lot more restraint when it came to the death penalty than secular courts did. Kamen speaks of a "proportionately small number", which contradicts the "legend of a bloodthirsty tribunal".[14] Outside of Spain, religious fanaticism "claimed more victims in a single night than the Spanish Inquisition did during its entire existence"[15]. The Saint Bartholomew's Day Massacre was initiated by the French queen with political motives, and recent studies estimate it claimed between 5,000 and 15,000 lives the night of August 23, 1572, and the days following. The French royal courts, moreover, had already ordered 500 Protestants to execution in the years leading up to 1560. That alone almost equals the number of heretics executed in the entire Spanish empire over 160 years.

A majority of the verdicts by the Spanish Inquisition did not even apply to deviant religious beliefs. In many cases, the Inquisition was a moral court for adultery and similar offenses, just like other European courts were, and of the 826 death penalties, probably only about 570 can be regarded as religious killings.

Over the course of the seventeenth century, the Spanish Inquisition lost its effectiveness, and executions were reduced to a minimum. By the time Pope Pius VII prohibited the Spanish Inquisition in 1816, torture had already long ceased to be practiced, which Kamen and others confirm. Thus, the torture and execution scenes that Francisco Goya illustrated at the beginning of the nineteenth century were not based on reality, but fantastical projections onto the past, part of a polemic that endured until new research provided clarification.

3. Giordano Bruno and Galileo Galilei: The Roman Inquisition (1542–1816) and Its Victims

The Roman Inquisition was founded by Pope Paul III in 1542. It was a response to Protestantism's spread into Italian cities and the situation's almost opaque complexity. Numerous reformed orders had been called into life by the Church for its spiritual renewal, not least the Jesuit order with papal approbation in 1540, which was to shape significantly the reform in the Catholic Church. But then in 1542, there took place a catastrophe in the Church's eyes. The general of the newly founded order of Capuchins, Bernardino Ochino, became Protestant, and indeed, for many people the difference between Protestantism and the new Catholic reform efforts was no longer very clear. The Inquisition was supposed to be a source of help in this situation, according to the pope's wishes.

Paul III was a remarkable figure. Originally, as a cardinal, he had completely given himself over to the worldly life of Renaissance princes, but then he underwent an interior conversion and became a reforming pope. He appointed credible personalities to the cardinalate and convened the Council of Trent, where his original goal was to restore the unity of the faith. Trent was chosen as a venue because it would be easier to reach for German Protestants.

To this pope, the Roman Inquisition was to be more of a defensive tool for guarding against errors in the faith. Thus its punishments were relatively moderate compared to other inquisitions. The proceedings were strictly regulated: thorough records had to be kept, and defendants were to have irrevocable rights, such as the right to know the accusations against them and the right to consult a defense lawyer, free of charge for those without means. Torture was never the first recourse but a last resort, and it was supposed to last no longer than a half hour. The Inquisition could take this route only when obvious evidence was being denied or when a confession clearly remained incomplete, and even then torture was to be carried out under strict supervision, i.e., after the approval of multiple consultants and a doctor. Statements attained by means of torture were valid if they were voluntarily repeated later on. Finally, torturers were to be punished for breaking the regulations or acting with inadequate caution. On the whole, torture seems neither to have yielded confessions, nor to have amended previously made ones, which perhaps indicates that torture was practiced very mildly. In case of imprisonment, prisoners were to be supplied with bread, wine, meat, vegetables, and fruit—the same as the security guards, in fact—all free of cost for the poor but otherwise by payment, with even inmates' servants permitted to work in the jail. The cell was to be cleaned every three days, and clothes as well as bedsheets were to be changed regularly. The cardinal inquisitor inspected the prisons on a monthly basis. There were physicians on hand in case of illness or, if necessary, a torture session. Lastly, the security guards were ordered to treat prisoners well and were forbidden from insulting them, failing which they were punished at the gallows. The death penalty only occurred in case of persistent and unrepentant behavior against key dogma or in case of a relapse after a previous sentence. Today, it is possible to determine exactly the total number of persons executed for religious offenses in the 220 years between 1542 and 1761: there were 97.

That means that the Roman Inquisition executed fewer heretics than many cities in the Netherlands, William Monter notes. Within a single year alone, in 1569, there were 78 executions of heretics in the denominationally split regions of the Dutch, almost as many as the Roman Inquisition carried out over 260 years. This is why American historian John Tedeschi confesses that during his research, he developed a new perspective that "differed from the traditional view I had always naturally accepted." In truth, the Roman Inquisition was "a pioneer in judicial reform", and also "a pioneer in the field of penology, at a time when secular judges, in pronouncing sentence, had as alternatives only the stake, mutilation, the galleys, and banishment."[16] And the respected historian Peter Godman, who refers to himself as an "unbeliever", has come to react with annoyance to common myths in his book on the Inquisition: one should not "pronounce yet another round of condemnations founded on the unstable ground of pseudo-facts. The Holy Office acted in its immediate sphere of influence far more gently than secular powers did."[17]

The Roman Inquisition's two "most prominent" cases were Giordano Bruno (1548–1600) and Galileo Galilei (1564–1642). Anti-Church propaganda spun both cases into the supposed departure point of the scandalous fight between modern science and the Christian faith. But in reality, things were completely different.

Giordano Bruno had joined the Dominican order at the age of seventeen and even then began to stand out for his remarkable behavior. When he was suspected of heresy, he left the order, eleven years after having entered it, and began a tenuous existence as a wanderer across Europe. In Geneva, he became a Protestant, but got embroiled in a theological conflict with the Calvinists, was thrown into a dungeon, and was excommunicated. Seeking release, he recanted. Then he continued on to Toulouse, where he briefly held an academic chair, then to Oxford, where he sought another professorship but failed thanks to accusations of plagiarism, along with his own rather bizarre ideas. With ruthless polemics, he then revenged himself on the scholars of Oxford and on London intellectual life in general, after which he returned to Paris. There, too, his provocations unleashed a great commotion among the Aristotelians, and he wrote a diatribe against a mathematician. Following this, he attempted to obtain an academic chair in Marburg, without success, and moved on to Wittenberg, teaching there for a brief time and then moving to Prague and eventually to Helmstedt, where he was excommunicated by the Lutherans, too—having already been excommunicated by the Calvinists in Geneva. In Frankfurt am Main, he started an argument with the city council and was banished from the city. After a short stay in Zurich, he returned to Italy, where he found himself a patron, who then turned him over to the Inquisition in 1592, so that he eventually ended up at the Castel Sant'Angelo in Rome. First, he offered to recant partially, then repeatedly wavered, and finally became set on denying Jesus' divine sonship and the Last Judgment and instead affirming his basic thesis about the eternity of the world and the existence of an infinite number of worlds. His concept of the temporal and spatial infinity of the cosmos rendered the Christian event of salvation "placeless". Eventually, in 1600, the Roman Inquisition decided after a long period of hesitation to exclude him from the Church for heresy, and they delivered him to the governor of the city of Rome with the usual request to exercise clemency and not to impose a physical punishment or a death sentence. The secular court of governors then sentenced Bruno to death at the stake, which took place on the Campo dei Fiori.

It was only much later that Bruno became a symbol. Basically, he was not a real scientist; rather, he indulged in shaky and fantastical speculations, and picked an argument with everyone—not only with literally every Christian denomination, but also with scientists and urban authorities. At the same time, he could also be a rather dedicated man, which disposed patrons favorably toward him. The atheist Georges Minois, in his classic work *L'histoire de l'athéisme* [*The History of Atheism*], writes of Bruno: "And thus, in 1600, he is a lonely man. No one wants to be associated with him, lest they compromise themselves. Neither Galilei nor Descartes mentions him." But neither do the atheists "want to have anything to do with a man they see as an enlightened mystic."[18] Thus, in the end, one has to assume that Giordano Bruno was certainly a man full of ideas, highly intelligent, but at the same time a psychically unusual man, antagonistic because of his extreme emotional volatility, a man whose chaotic life ended in tragedy.

But none of that troubled those who later on used him for their own purposes: the Freemasons, who, in order to annoy the pope, built a solemn monument to Bruno on the Campo dei Fiori, which the anti-papal Roman city government dedicated in 1889 with great joy. Nor did it bother the Giordano Bruno Fund; misunderstanding the thinker's character, which Minois says "retained a deep sense of the divine", the organization uses his name to promote atheism.[19]

Nevertheless, in 2000, at the Church's examination of conscience, Pope John Paul II declared the execution of Giordano Bruno an injustice.

And then there is the unavoidable case of Galileo, the Inquisition scandal par excellence. This, too, was more a psychological dilemma. For Galileo's case had precious little to do with the natural sciences, with the Copernican worldview, or with scholarship in general. At the time, the Copernican system was indeed contested, like so many other things in science, but the Church had long recognized it, both implicitly and even explicitly. It is said that when Pope Clement VII (1478–1534) heard about the new insights of the Frombork canon, Nicolaus Copernicus, he showed himself enthusiastic, and his successor, Paul III (1468–1549), accepted the dedication of Copernicus' revolutionary writings without delay. In 1582, Jesuit astronomers explained to Pope Gregory XIII the problems with the Julian calendar on the basis of Copernican astronomy, and this led to the Gregorian calendar, which we still use today. In Catholic Spain, the Copernican system had long become part of the syllabus, even while Calvin was still rejecting it. And Luther considered Copernicus a fool.

But then Galileo Galilei came along—a little late, but with much more of a spectacle. The first Inquisition trial in 1616 revolved around a question regarding the nature of science. Cardinal Bellarmine, a member of the Roman Inquisition, represented the standpoint that we still hold today: that scientific insights are always falsifiable and that Galilei was welcome to hold the Copernican system as a scientific hypothesis. In fact, the Inquisition only demanded of Galilei that he not say more than he was able to prove. The Copernican system wasn't scientifically proven until 1729. But Galilei turned it into a question of faith, a question of truth, and his approach was not scientific and empirical, but rather, as philosopher of science Hans Blumenberg observed in his work *Die Genesis der kopernikanischen Welt* [*The Genesis of the Copernican World*], speculative—and unfortunately also a spectacle.[20] Galilei had said about himself that he had "by his wondrous observations and clear demonstration" enlarged the world "a hundred, indeed, a thousand times more than any sage of the world had ever done before." "What can you do about it, Mr. Sarsi, if it has been given to me alone to discover everything new in the heavens, and no one else anything at all?" He approached the whole issue in this style. During his stay in Rome, he led such an extravagant lifestyle that the Florentine envoy whose house he lived in feared for his own good reputation. In the end, he was generously granted a papal audience and was received into the papal academy of science. The Inquisition's ruling of 1616 stated that he had only to promise to voice his opinion about the theory in a scientific capacity, and no longer in a quasi-missionary way in popular publications. Galilei accepted this. When gossip began to circulate that he had had to recant, Cardinal Bellarmine issued a formal statement for Galilei in the name of the Inquisition denying those rumors. As far as the scientific debate was concerned, that could have been the end of the matter. Werner Heisenberg, Nobel laureate for physics, called this verdict of the Inquisition a "justifiable decision".

But then Galilei broke the promise he had given. When his friend Maffeo Cardinal Barberini, who had helped him a lot in the past, became Pope Urban VIII, Galilei thought he could bring the question of the Copernican system once more into the public light. He did so with a particular barb in a pamphlet entitled *Dialogo sopra i due massimi sistemi del mondo* [*Dialogue Concerning the Two Chief World Systems*]— which he didn't publish in Latin, the language of science, but rather in popular Italian—by creating a figure called *Simplicio*, "fool", who effectively represented the position of his friend Pope Urban (still a mathematician after all), and having him counter Galilei's own brilliant Copernican position. The pope presumably did not think this was very funny, but most of all, the Inquisition saw in this pamphlet the very obvious break of Galilei's written promise. Consequently, in 1633, it ordered Galilei to recant and imposed subsequent house arrest, as well as what amounted to a ban from publishing. The court came to this decision by a tight majority, and this remained without the pope's signature. But we shouldn't get the wrong idea about this sentence, either. The house arrest confined Galilei to his splendid villa in Acetri, with a wonderful view of Florence and plenty of servants. Here, Galilei wrote his important scientific work. And he circumvented the ban from publishing by sending along manuscripts with friends who came to visit him, which were then published abroad. No one made the effort to prevent that from happening.

The case of Galilei is perhaps the greatest media hoax of all times. The myth remains unbusted to this day. But Jewish writer Arthur Koestler—who is above suspicion of harboring any sympathy for the Catholic Church, with a prize named after him by the German Society for Humane Death—tells the truth about Galilei:

In contrast to what most narratives say about the development of the natural sciences, Galilei invented neither the telescope, nor the microscope, nor the thermometer, nor the pendulum clock. He discovered neither the law of inertia, nor the parallelogram of forces, nor the parallelogram of movement, nor sunspots. He made no contribution to theoretical astronomy; he did not throw weights off the leaning tower of Pisa and did not prove the accuracy of the Copernican system. He was not tortured by the Inquisition, did not waste away in its dungeons, did not say "And yet it moves", and was not a martyr of science.[21]

In his *Crisis of the European Sciences and Transcendental Phenomenology*, the philosopher Edmund Husserl (1859–1938) even accused Galilei of "taking away from the knowledge of nature the status and claims of science and allowing it to degenerate into technique", [as Blumenberg puts it].[22] In our own days, Galilei's provocative thesis about the absolute priority of the insights of the natural sciences earned him the criticism of physician and philosopher Carl Friedrich von Weizsäcker (1912–2007), who saw a "direct path from Galilei to the nuclear bomb", as he wrote in his autobiography, *Im Garten des Menschlichen* [*In the Garden of Humanity*].[23] This recalls something Bertolt Brecht wrote in his notes for *Life of Galileo*: "Galilei's crime can be called the 'original sin' of the modern natural sciences. As both a technical phenomenon and a social one, the atomic bomb is the classic end product of his scientific achievement and of his social failure."[24] In any event, Pope John Paul II explicitly rehabilitated Galileo Galilei in 1992.

Even if scholarship has long cleared up the myths surrounding Giordano Bruno and Galileo Galilei, violence and threats of violence obviously remain un-Christian according to ancient Christian convictions.

Finally, we need to make another comparison with the secular world. In the free imperial city of Nuremberg, which had about 30,000 inhabitants at the time, there were altogether 939 executions between 1503 and 1743, 113 more killings than the Spanish Inquisition was responsible for across the entire Spanish empire during roughly the same period. Of the Nuremberg executions, 613 were carried out by sword, 295 by rope, 50 were wheeled, 27 drowned, 8 burned, and 6 buried alive. As reprehensible as the Inquisition may have been, it presented a contrast to justice by torture, the standard practice in the realm of secular law. The Inquisition did not, for example, practice mutilation.

Still, the early Christians would certainly have been stunned to learn about the Crusades and the Inquisition—as stunned as we are today. But these people lived under different circumstances, without any kind of state power or public responsibility—which, over time, has once again become the norm for Christians, after centuries of Christian public dominance. It is only fair, then, to investigate carefully the entirely different circumstances of the Middle Ages and early Modernity, in order to avoid making hasty judgments.

4. Catholics and Protestants in Competition: In Good Times and in Bad

But how were heretics treated outside of the jurisdiction of the Spanish and Roman Inquisition, especially after 1517, the beginning of the Reformation? What Christendom had already painfully experienced for a short time in the so-called Western Schism with its two popes—namely, that each pontiff excommunicated the other, leaving all Christians in the lurch—was now happening again. The Catholic Church had hurled her excommunication at Luther, and Luther fought back, calling the Roman Church the "whore of Babylon".

Now everyone was something of a heretic, at least from the other side's perspective. What was to be done? The Church was paralyzed; she basically did nothing, letting it all run its course. American historian William Monter says: "Everywhere one looks, from Scotland to Portugal, episcopal courts and papal inquisitors ... had the primary means of controlling heresy, but lacked the means to do so effectively," and in Germany, the Reformation's country of origin, the Inquisition was weaker than ever.[25] Luther had proclaimed "the freedom of a Christian". Was this the dawn of religious freedom?

Everything was supposed to turn out quite differently. Because it was also Luther who, in historian Gerd Schwerhoff's assessment, "labelled things as 'blasphemy' to the point of inflation."[26] But of course, with this, the state appeared on the scene, and there emerged a phenomenon that had already announced itself in times past, one that is impossible for us today to understand. It was not the Church, but the secular state—which was modernizing itself and acting with increasing self-confidence—that saw itself duty bound to persecute heretics and punish them severely, often even by death, in the interest of the general public. In pre-Christian times, every authority had considered this to be its task, in order to avoid incurring divine fury upon all of society. This is why the respected American historian Edward Peters has criticized how readily state executions linked to religious issues are overlooked, suggesting that the supposed alternative between a "tolerant" state and an "inquisitorial" Church is really false.[27]

The cities and reigning powers undertook the punishment of religious delinquency on their own authority and without previous ecclesial inquisition. That is why such executions were usually carried out by sword, just as in cases of high treason. This happened in Germany as well as other countries. In France, ecclesial jurisdiction was practically shut down for blasphemy trials. The royal courts claimed exclusive responsibility, and besides, there was no town or village community that would not have punished blasphemy, as French historian Alain Cabnatous found in a study.[28] In England, the monarchs had people decapitated: for example, 250 Catholics under Henry VIII, 300 Protestants under his Catholic daughter Mary later on, 180 Catholics under her half-sister Elizabeth I, and then parliament passed a "Blasphemy Act" as late as 1697. The burning of heretics was popular. For instance, a London goldsmith left money in his will for the collecting of wood for burnings. This is why the often-praised reform and liberation of the political sphere had a rather alarming side, giving rise to something that is downright bizarre to our eyes: an inquisition into religious issues carried out by secular authorities.

It was therefore not the Catholic Church, but Holy Roman Emperor Charles V who initiated a persecution of Protestants in the Netherlands after the 1521 Edict of Worms, resulting in the first burning of Lutherans in Brussels in 1523. But four years later, it was this same Charles V whose troops ravaged Rome and besieged the pope at the Castel Sant'Angelo. The Reformers, in turn, did not forgo the persecution and killing of heretics either, as became evident in their treatment of the Anabaptists, who later established a regime of terror in Münster and were generally considered a force of societal disintegration, since they rejected all authority and all duties. Catholic and Protestant lords took violent action against them immediately.

Luther and Melanchthon explicitly advocated the killing of Anabaptists. Though the first execution of an Anabaptist took place in the Catholic Schwyz [a canton in Switzerland], the next one took place in Zwinglian Zurich. In 1525, the city of Zurich adopted *sola scriptura* by community decision and with that basically became the "prototype for urban Reformation", as Dutch historian Heiko A. Oberman notes.[29] It was Zurich, of all cities, that drowned the Anabaptist Felix Mantz in 1527. In 1528, the later Holy Roman Emperor Ferdinand I sent Anabaptist Balthasar Hubmaier to the stake, a man who had called for a persecution of the Jews in 1519 in Regensburg, became an Anabaptist, and survived torture in Zurich in 1526. The 1529 Diet at Speyer established the death penalty for Anabaptists across the empire, and these punishments were to be carried out with full state and public power, without any ecclesiastical sentence of heresy.

But the death penalty did not apply only to Anabaptists. The jurors of Lutheran Leipzig had eight blasphemers decapitated in the first quarter of the seventeenth century. The reformed cities, too, particularly the Zwinglian ones, which could rightly be called "God's republics", intensified their persecution of blasphemers. Among the 471 people executed between 1526 and 1600 in Zurich, 56 were blasphemers, and there were another 22 by 1745; according to more recent research, it is thought there were 84 altogether. Thus a single Protestant city of only 10,000 inhabitants executed almost as many blasphemers as did the whole Roman Inquisition around the same time period: 97. In the theocracy of Geneva, Calvin pursued the burning of the Spaniard Michael Servet, who denied the divine Trinity. It took place in 1553, with the consent of Zwinglian and Lutheran authorities. It is true that in Catholic cities like Cologne, too, the members of the city council persecuted blasphemers. But we only have proof of a single execution there. Over the course of the 39 years alone between 1525 and 1564, the secular courts in Germany, Switzerland, the Netherlands, France, England, and Scotland sentenced 2,887 heretics to death, 3 times as many as the Spanish Inquisition did for *all* crimes over 160 years in the entire Spanish empire altogether. During this period, the role of the popes and the Roman Inquisition in all this remained "infinitesimal", with 25 death sentences, less than 1 percent. In general, there was a certain degree of moderation in the Catholic sphere, because the correction of faith and morality was ordinarily addressed first during confession, which offered "more opportunities to elude public discipline"[30]. In the left wing of the Reformation, some Anabaptists, who had meanwhile become pacifists, quietly reminded each other of the parable of the weeds among the wheat and spoke out—though not always consistently—against religious killing.

Secular authorities—Catholic ones to some degree, but Protestant one to a greater extent—not only concerned themselves with heresy, but saw themselves as responsible for the morality of their citizens. Legal historian Dietmar Willoweit notes that every duke, Protestant as well as Catholic, faced the concern "that the sins of his subjects would incite God's wrath and bring down his punishments." [31] Zurich, after converting to the new faith, was the first city to establish a marriage court, with the intention "that the council would ensure for its subjects a life pleasing to God, in order to divert God's punishments, such as epidemics, famines, and other catastrophes", explains modern historian Francisca Loetz.[32] From Zurich, moral discipline spread to other cities. Nowhere was it pursued more consistently in the beginning than in the equally Protestant city of Konstanz, where of its 5,000 inhabitants, at least 1,200 people were involved in some form of it between 1532 and 1534. In the Catholic Münster region, too, there was a so-called "synodal court" held annually in every parish in the name of the bishop, who was also the secular ruler; it served as a morality court, though it never imposed the death penalty.

Now a word on the censorship of books: book burnings have taken place as long as there have been books. Ancient Greeks burned blasphemous books, and Rome especially and unyieldingly persecuted invectives against the emperor. Judaism's reaction to heretical writings was the same. At first, Christians were the victims of such book burnings, forced to hand over their sacred texts during the Diocletian persecution. They reacted, at first, with surprising liberality, considering that in those days "even lascivious literature was only censured or destroyed in some isolated cases", in the words of religious historian Wolfgang Speyer.[33] When heretics were burned during the Middle Ages, their writings were always burned alongside them. But book censorship, which started to emerge in the thirteenth century, had a particularly life-saving effect, so to speak: the author was not sentenced, but rather specific publications of his were declared erroneous and then had to be withdrawn.

After the invention of the printing press, especially once the Reformation broke out, an entirely new situation presented itself, which Lutheran Church historian Berndt Hamm describes as a virtual "media event"[34]. Just as we see today with the challenges of new media, there arose the question of how to deal with the flood of writings, which were sometimes exceedingly polemical and seditious. Censorship was generally one of "the natural, largely unquestioned tools of state and ecclesial political procedure", so that "intellectuals, too, mostly saw it as a positive instrument", says historian Hubert Wolf.[35] The universities, both Protestant and Catholic, compiled lists of prohibited works, which especially included writings by members of the other denomination. However, Thomas More (1478–1535), who has been canonized by the Catholic Church, already trusted "the truth would sooner or later emerge and prevail by its own force".[36] Only the Enlightenment later on made the case for the freedom to publish. That being said, even today, we still impose some commonly accepted limitations. In the European Union, it is punishable to deny the Holocaust.

Some have shaken their heads at the book censorship that persisted at least formally in the Catholic Church up until the Second Vatican Council. But at the same time, Hubert Wolf reminds us that something can be said to the Church's credit: "By consistently taking action against astrology, naturalism, and occultism, the Inquisition and the Congregation of the Index helped—whether intentionally or not—to excise these elements from the emerging natural sciences and thus helped to modernize science".[37]

VI

The Biggest Judicial Error of All Time

Astonishing Facts about the Witch Hunts

Imagine it: someone dares to say that witch hunts were not in line with Church teaching, had not been conducted by the Inquisition at all, and had appalled the popes. Yet this is just what is written in the catalogue of an exhibition called "Hexenwahn" ["Witch Craze"], held at the Deutsches Museum in Berlin in the summer of 2002, organized by a research group from Trier. The curators emphasized: "The presumption that witch trials took place on a massive scale at the hands of clerical inquisitions persists with a special stubbornness. In those countries where the persecution of witches was handled by the Inquisition, there is evidence of a moderate, cautious treatment of the crime of witchcraft, especially by modern-period Inquisitions."[1] Historian Wolfgang Behringer, a leading expert on the topic of witches, had previously put it even more explicitly: "In Spain, it was the institutionalized Inquisition that first brought witch hunts under control and effectively ended them in 1526." And as completely unbelievable as it may sound, "popes and inquisitors of the seventeenth century did not conduct the sort of witch trials that spread fear and terror in central Europe during the same period."[2]

1. Outlandish Myths: Theological, National Socialist, and Feminist Versions of the Witch Hunt

To illustrate just how fresh is this perspective of Behringer's, let us compare a lecture series in religious studies and theology at the University of Tübingen from 1978–1979:

Not even the pope in Rome allowed for any clemency, so the danger must have been tremendous! There is no exact estimate for the number of women who were murdered in this way. In some places, after the "work" of the Inquisitors, only a handful of frightened women remained. This epidemic obsession with killing claimed more lives relative to the population density at the time than Hitler's unfathomable project of exterminating Jews. What the latter did, the inquisitors also did on an even greater scale—in the name of the Church, to exorcise and fight the devil, but with the same order and diligence, driven by an incomparable hatred, an irrational fear, and convinced of the righteousness of their actions. And this mass killing no doubt can be traced back to the Christian interpretation of the devil. Paganism knew good witches (fairies), too. The conditions that gave rise to the witch craze can be found in the theological interpretation of the inferiority of women, which must have had a far more devastating effect than did females' lesser status before the Church or outside it.[3]

If all this were true, it would indeed be an unbelievable scandal. But in the light of current research, almost everything about these statements is false. One gets the impression that current prejudices, in their own way, rage no less intensely than the witch fires of old.

The history of the witch hunts has long been used to absorb blame, and in fact, the topic of witches "like perhaps just a few other subjects in German history, has been heavily overlaid with political and ideological interests and instrumentalizations up to the most recent past", as the Berlin "Hexenwahn" catalogue puts it.[4] Nineteenth-century anti-Church polemics mostly considered the Catholic Church guilty, but it soon became clear that Luther, too, endorsed the elimination of witches. But since then, historian and Inquisition scholar Rainer Decker has noted that the Papal States are among the areas with the least persecution. Indeed, after the turn of the seventeenth century, when witch burnings really flared up north of the Alps, the Holy Office and its judges effectively no longer sentenced witches to death at all.[5] The Swiss historian Kim Siebenhüner reports that the Roman Inquisition fought witchcraft "not with severe sanctions, but with penance and pastoral enlightenment."[6] And Arno Borst summarizes: "Almost all early witch trials were arranged not by clerics or intellectuals, but by politicians and laypeople."[7] Historian Gerhard Schormann states unequivocally that witch trials had "nothing to do with Church jurisdiction."[8]

During the Nazi period, Heinrich Himmler had a "witch file" compiled, featuring as many trials and executions as possible to gain material for anti-Church propaganda. Supposedly the Roman Church, in particular the Jesuit order, had sacrificed nine million people of Germanic blood and had thus attacked the biological roots of a sound race. However, when Himmler's researchers looked at the actual data, they found not nine million, but a few thousand. Then, in the 1960s, comparisons with the Holocaust became popular. But the great Behringer has commented that likening of witch persecution to "the systematic extermination program of the Nazi period is untenable."[9]

Around the same time, feminist variations started to appear. Mathilde Ludendorff (1877–1966)—wife of the formidable German World War I general and co-founder of the "Bund für Deutsche Gotterkenntnis" [Society for the German Knowledge of God], which was active in the interwar period—discovered a "Christian cruelty to German women".[10] According to her, witch hysteria took on the status of Church doctrine, and the persecution of witches was proclaimed a religious duty. This movement of Ludendorff's resisted the spiritual laws of Christian priests, laws that were foreign to the Teutonic race. The allegation was that the Church had tried systematically to exterminate blond women and mothers, carriers of the Nordic genome. Feminists of the 1980s once again invoked the Holocaust as a comparison. According to the founder of feminist theology, Mary Daly, women suffered more than all the victims of racism and genocide; the persecution of witches escalated into femicide on a larger scale even than the genocide of the Holocaust.[11] The scenarios vary, but the judgments remain the same. Behringer says: "On this point, the new feminism, the ethno-nationalist [völkisch] women's movement, and national socialist neo-paganism all agree."[12] The bestselling book Die Vernichtung der weisen Frauen [The Eradication of Wise Women] by professors Heinsohn and Steiger—one a social pedagogue, the other a professor of economics—prompted great joy among reviewers in the 1980s. The work posited that the persecution of witches had been set in motion by the Church and the state with political-demographic motives, in an effort to eliminate wise women's knowledge about contraception.[13]

Research today invalidates these claims. Social historian Franz Irsigler speaks of "abstruse theses".[14] As early as 1986, the newly founded Feministische Forschung [Feminist Research] magazine diagnosed a use of "cheap polemics" based on primitive, materialist points of departure.[15] One dissertation on the history of pharmacy arrived at the conclusion that there simply had been no systematic elimination of birth control in the sixteenth and seventeenth centuries, and gender research has added that the persecution of witches had more perhaps to do with a standard conflict between the upper class, the Church, and male doctors on the one hand and peasants, magical folk medicine, and female healers on the other; in this sense, the conglomerate of "*Witches, Midwives, and Nurses*" [the title of a book by Barbara Ehrenreich and Deirdre English] was bound up rather with everyday politics.

Serious research about witches has long since risen to a remarkable level of quality. Since the 1980s, there has been an effort to work in a way that is free of any ideology, obtaining clear definitions, precise descriptions, and substantiated numbers. There are conferences on the study of witches, whose proceedings are published at regular intervals. The process of research is interdisciplinary, and obviously includes women's and gender studies.

2. Belief in Witches in the Middle Ages:
Regino von Prüm—"Delusions"

Belief in witches is as old as mankind itself. Black magic was already a punishable offense in the Code of Hammurabi (1792–1750 B.C.).[16] Magic was considered an infraction in the Roman Empire, too, and could be punished by death in late Antiquity. Even in the modern age, people generally assumed that it was possible to harm people with evil magic. But Christianity, true to its nonviolent attitude, rejected persecution or execution, and from the beginning relied on enlightenment and re-education. Research has always supported this view. Even the fiercely anti-Catholic *Geschichte der Hexenprozesse* [*History of the Witch Trials*] by Soldan and Heppes in the nineteenth century reads: "The idea of prosecuting superstitious practices through criminal law was completely foreign to the Church."[17] Instead, the Church always prescribed penance, a way of dealing with witchcraft that did not use coercion, as the American historian Richard Kieckhefer writes in his book *Magic in the Middle Ages*.[18] Like other religions, Christianity believed in the Devil, in personalized evil, and in the tempter, who was, however, in no way equal to God and, most significantly, has actually long been overcome by Jesus Christ. The New Testament is full of stories where demons have to flee the power of the Son of God. Still, according to Christian understanding, man—Christians included—remains corruptible. He can sell his soul to evil, out of his own free will. As early as the fifth century, Augustine, wanting to explain the origins of black magic, warned of such an alliance with the Devil. According to new, comprehensive research on this topic, Augustine considered contact with demons, which many in his time held possible, to be a subversion of the order willed by God and therefore a pagan and sinful act that contradicted the covenant of baptism.[19] These reflections had nothing whatsoever to do with witches or the persecution of witches, either explicitly nor implicitly. After all, the Church thought of belief in witches as pagan humbug, the delusion of excitable minds. The Council of Paderborn in 785 declared: "Whoever, seduced by the devil and following pagan beliefs, claims the existence of witches ... and burns them at the stake ... shall be punished by death." Regino von Prüm (ca. 840–915) puts it very clearly in his famous *Canon episcopi*: "It must not be overlooked that some unfortunate women, seduced by demonic pretenses and hallucinations, now believe and proclaim to ride on some animal in the deep, silent, uncanny night, traversing many of the earth's lands in the company of the pagan goddess Diana and an innumerable host of other women."[20] This is the first testimony to the flight of witches, presented as a hallucination, not a reality. Under the influence of Regino, canon law henceforth spoke of delusion and relegated night-traveling women to the realm of fantasy. Basically, the Church did not really take the belief in witches seriously. Even a man like Thomas Aquinas, whose expansive intellect perceived everything that moved the people of his time, speaks about pacts with demons, even reflecting on the possibility of sexual contact between human beings and demons, but draws no conclusions from all this. It was only several hundred years later that his statements were misused to completely different ends. At any rate, in the Middle Ages, the whole issue remained marginal. Wolfgang Behringer says, "Early Christian doubt about the efficacy of any kind of magic was very effective in curbing the desire for persecutions." But precisely because the persecution of witches was held illegal by the Church, grassroots-led persecutions, unapproved by the Church, forged ahead in a disordered and tumultuous way. Behringer provides a psychological explanation: "We can generally say that the Church- and state-imposed suppression of the urge to persecute witches, combined simultaneously with a strong belief in witches across many parts of Europe, led to acts of justice by lynching."[21]

For instance, in the Bavarian town of Freising in 1090, according to a report of the Benedictine Abbey Weihenstephan from the same time:

> the inhabitants of Vötting were stirred up by envy and kindled to a devilish rage against three poor women, who were allegedly poisoners and corrupters of men and crops. They seized these women early in the day, when they were still lying in bed, subjected them to ordeal by water, but found no guilt in them. Then they cruelly whipped these same women and sought to extort confessions for things they falsely accused them of, but they did not succeed. And they took the women, seized them, and led them to Freising. Again they whipped these same, but could not draw out a confession for poisoning. Then they led all three to the banks of the river Isar and burned all three of them together; one of them was pregnant with a living child. And thus they suffered martyrdom on June 18 and were buried by their kin on the riverbank. Later, a priest and two monks carried them away and buried them in the court of Weihenstephan, in the hope that they were truly worthy of Christian community.[22]

Popes and bishops opposed such campaigns by the populace. Gregory VII (ca. 1025–1085), for example, wrote in a letter to the Danish king Harald Bluetooth: "Do not think that you may sin against women, who according to a barbarian custom are cruelly condemned for the same reason (i.e., for having allegedly caused severe weather, storms, and illnesses). Rather, learn to divert through penance the divine judgment you have merited, instead of further provoking the wrath of God by bringing ruin upon those innocent women."[23]

Secular justice, however, reacted to black magic with violence. The *Sachsenspiegel* by Eike von Repgow prescribed around 1230: "A Christian man or woman who is without faith and practices magic or mixes potions and is convicted must be burned on the pyre."[24] Of course, magic in the Middle Ages, as legal scholar Günter Jerouschek says, was "a completely marginal offense."[25]

3. The Belief in Witches in Modernity: "Death Is a German-Born Master"

The catastrophe started to unfold only at the beginning of the modern age, in the fifteenth century, and it is difficult to say how things came to this point. Many have assumed that it was due to the age's characteristic need for a new beginning, which led to the decision to "cleanse" everything with zeal. And "cleansing"—not only at the beginning of the modern period, but also at the end—was to become another word for modern mass murder. Entire villages rose to hunt down magicians. In this period, there developed an outright doctrine of witchery, which no longer merely indulged itself with fantastical speculation, but now pressed for real practical consequences. Discussion about black magic and pacts with the Devil was nothing new. But what led to terrible consequences was the emerging conviction that witches' flights and the "witches' sabbath" were not delusions, but reality. If these were true, then logically, witches could denounce other witches who accompanied them in flight or at the sabbath—if they were only tortured long enough. And that is exactly what people did. In human history, there are likely few invented ideas that prompted as many cruel human sacrifices as this one. None of these ideas were fabricated at universities; they fermented among the population and called on the Church and the state to come along. The attitude of theologians as well as ecclesial courts was reserved and dismissive, while secular law showed itself to be accessible. Historian Arno Borst observes that the local clergy were not at the forefront of persecutions and that some actually "energetically defended the orthodoxy of women who were allegedly witches".[26] In Spain, the Inquisition practically ended witch hunts in 1526. British historian of the Inquisition Henry Kamen says, "The inquisition is completely justified in priding itself on having energetically extinguished a superstition in Spain which in other countries claimed more victims than any other wave of religious fanaticism."[27]

Germany, by contrast, was to be the center of witch hunts. The code of criminal law issued by the Holy Roman Emperor in 1532, the so-called "Carolina", immediately claimed to be the authority on witch trials, although it authorized such trials only for verifiable black magic and permitted only a limited use of torture. As legal historian Winfried Trusen explains, these provisions "were intended to inform uneducated jurors and to obligate them to consult with learned jurists in difficult cases."[28] Thus, it was clear from the beginning: witchcraft had become a matter of secular justice.

As early as 1487, a dubious German Dominican, Heinrich Kramer, who had adopted the fine-sounding name of "Institoris" and had been reported on several occasions for the embezzlement of indulgence money along with other shady dealings, fanned the flames with a ruthless piece of work, the famous *Hammer of Witches*. Most recent research has by now exposed all the falsifications Institoris needed in order to spark a furor with this text. He had skillfully obtained a routine decree from papal bureaucracy, which he combined with a forged report by the University of Cologne and an imperial charter to launch a polemic against witches, with dire consequences. The pamphlet contrasted sharply with ecclesial tradition, and he himself readily admits to having written it because "some curates of souls and preachers of the Word of God feel no shame at claiming and affirming in their sermons to the congregation that sorceresses do not exist or that they are unable by any working to bring about an effect resulting in harm to creatures."[29] But among the people, Institoris' work really struck the "nerve" of his time. Secular courts especially referenced it. Even the arch-Protestant constitutions of the Electorate of Saxony adopted parts of it; the Spanish Inquisition, however, rejected the *Hammer of Witches*.

That is how disaster took its course. The images of flying witches and the witches' sabbath were now taking their brutal toll through extremely cruel torture. Even though there were differing notions about the necessity of witch trials, in the great persecution waves, the supporters included "the contemporary bureaucratic ruling elite", as Behringer notes.[30] Even the atheist Enlightenment philosopher Thomas Hobbes (1588–1679) held the opinion that witches "are justly punished".[31] Modernizers of the legal system, such as Jean Bodin (ca. 1529–1596), the inventor of state sovereignty, and Benedict Carpzov

(1595–1666), a father of modern trial law, especially advocated for the persecution and death of witches. Around the end of the sixteenth century, most jurists subscribed to the idea that witches and sorcerers made a deal with Satan, and this had the extreme consequence "that even without black magic, the mere pact with the devil was equally punishable by death", writes historian Sönke Lorenz.[32] A single praiseworthy exception was Bavaria, where elite jurists fundamentally opposed the enduring persecution of witches and who in their resistance relied on the publications of the Jesuit Adam Tanner (1572–1632), whose student, Friedrich Spee, was to achieve fame later on.

The witch trials were almost always initiated from the bottom up, that is, by reports from neighbors and village communities. Along the river Saar, for example, every village had so-called "witch committees", and their well-prepared trials, with up to a fifth of the adult population participating as witnesses, ended in death sentences 96 to 98 percent of the time. Litigation was the responsibility of local secular courts and often of the courts of local nobility, who occasionally retained their pre-juridical practices, which often meant being sentenced to archaic ordeals by water that were long prohibited by the Church. However, in an effort to follow the "Carolina", landlords attempted to ensure greater legal certainty, specially appointing a graduate jurist for witch trials or sending the trial documents to a faculty of law. In sum, these trials had nothing to do with ecclesial jurisdiction. The Dresden historian Gerd Schwerhoff found that the people who had a final say in witch trials came "from the ranks of that circle which was afforded a significant role in the process of state formation and of rational administrative practice from the second half of the sixteenth century onwards: the jurists in the service of cities and territorial lords."[33] American historian Brian Levack confirms this idea: "Without the mobilization of this secular power, the great witch-hunt would have been a mere shadow of itself."[34] Finally, we have to note with dismay what the above-cited Berlin exhibition catalogue says: "In the period between 1560 and 1700, during the peak of the western and central European persecution of witches, the mass trials with their high rate of executions were the work of secular judges."

And what do the numbers say? The figure of nine million, absurdly "calculated" in the eighteenth century, is still haunting newspapers. In 2000, according to *Der Spiegel*, "one million devil women" fell victim to the "misogyny of the Church", and the estimates of its rival magazine *Focus* were also up in the millions in 2002. But clear, scholarly data has long been available on this issue. Danish social scientist Gustav Henningsen arrives at a total of 50,000 victims in all of Europe, most of which were in Germany (25,000) and the surrounding lands, in both Protestant and in Catholic areas equally.[35] However, the clerical prince-electors who ruled along the river Rhine evidently distinguished themselves with such ugliness because, wanting to be especially modern and "exemplary" as secular rulers, they left the legal proceedings to their leading secular jurists. In contrast, all of Europe's Catholic regions were affected to a vanishingly low degree. While in Germany a frightening 1.6 of every thousand in the population are calculated to have been affected, in Ireland it was 0.0002, in Portugal 0.0007, in Spain 0.037, and in Italy 0.076. So the persecution of witches constitutes an imposing piece of German guilt. "Behold Germany, mother to so many witches", Friedrich Spee, the great opponent of belief in witches, would lament in the end.[36]

None of this should obscure the fact that even 50,000 is a disturbing number of victims, when we bear in mind the terrible agonies these people had to suffer. It is no coincidence that the term "judicial murder" was coined during the course of a witch trial. The high percentage of women among those killed has always particularly triggered outrage. Scholars today assume that women made up 75 to 80 percent of the total. On this point, women's studies scholarship sees a particular challenge; after all, the implication of these figures seems so simple and consistent: misogyny, as it is so strongly evident in the *Hammer of Witches*. But these are only simplistic explanations for bygone days, says historian Ingrid Ahrendt-Schulte in a recent volume entitled *Geschlecht, Magie und Hexenverfolgung* [*Gender, Magic, and the Persecution of Witches*], which she edited. The misogyny of Scholastic theology, she explains, falls short of providing a complete explanation; the idea that women were supposedly easier to seduce had the effect not only of making them more suspect, but of mitigating their punishment. It could be more fruitful, adds Ahrendt-Schulte, to look for gender stereotypes in magical folk culture, where women were not only victims, but also agents: "New regional studies prove that suspicions and reports of witchcraft within communities often came from women."[37] A more recent examination conducts a cross-check with men and takes into account the creedal aspects of the phenomenon: because of Eve's corruptibility, Luther understood magic more as a women's act, whereas Catholic regions were more likely to recognize a broader understanding of magic, one that accounted for male sorcerers.

4. The End: A Horrified Inquisitor, a Courageous Jesuit, and the President of the Federal Constitutional Court

The end of the persecution of witches came about especially through convinced, convincing Christians, and specifically through Christian reasoning. From the beginning, as we saw with Regino von Prüm's *Canon episcopi*, the Church had considered the ideas about flying witches and the witches' sabbaths pure make-believe, which meant that denunciations extorted by means of torture, whether spoken or not, were unfounded anyway. Levack notes with surprise that it was the papal inquisitors, of all people, who "were among the first to recognize that [torture] had led to numerous miscarriages of justice."[38] In 1623, a papal announcement still declared, "His Holiness has instructed me to write to you not to give credence to the testimonies of possessed persons and of witches who attest to having seen other persons at the witches' sabbath, because of the deceptive nature of such actions."[39] For black magic, one received, at most, a Church penance. Ecclesial courts consistently rejected physical punishment.

The city of Münster is a striking example. As long as it still enjoyed its secular autonomy, witch trials took place, leading to the death penalty in only 5 percent of all cases, although there were a number of defendants lynched by mobs after acquittal. When Prince-Bishop Bernhard of Galen (1606–1678) took away the city's autonomy and exercised jurisdiction himself, he immediately barred further witch trials and severely punished judges of noble birth in his territory who were still utilizing the ordeal by water. In Rome, women had still been burned as witches as late as 1572, but since then, the Inquisition and the papacy prevented any further persecutions of witches; while north of the Alps, the witch burnings were only just really beginning. Traveling through Germany in 1635 in the company of a Roman inquisitor, the Roman Cardinal Francesco Albizzi (1593–1684) was appalled at the persecution, which contradicted all Christian principles. He also spoke of a praiseworthy book by an anonymous author, entitled *Cautio criminalis*.

This author was Friedrich Spee (1591–1635). The deeply pious and highly intelligent Jesuit, whose famous church hymns have been passed down and are still being sung with fervor today, wrote the text *Legal Objections, or the Book about the Witch Trials* (short Latin form, *Cautio criminalis*). It would become an epochal work, eventually adding a crucial contribution to the abolition of witch trials. Spee writes:

> After a long time of dealing with these prisoners in the confessional as well as outside of it, after I had examined their nature from all sides, consulted God and man for aid and advice, searched evidence and documentation, spoken with the judges themselves as far as possible without breaking the seal of confession, carefully thought through everything and weighed the arguments of my considerations against each other—there was no other verdict I could arrive at than this: innocent people are being declared guilty.

With these words, he vehemently opposed the German practice of torture, calling for it to be "completely abolished and never used again".[40] Spee's great achievement consisted in criticizing witch trials from a legal perspective. The secular courts that had conducted these trials were not in a position to express such self-criticism. And so, too, it should be up to the president of the federal constitutional court to apologize for the scandalous, murderous persecution of witches by his legal ancestors and, at the same time, to thank the Church for putting an end to this horrific specter. The *Handwörterbuch zur Deutschen Rechtsgeschichte* [*Dictionary of German Legal History*] says of Spee:

> Although he was not a jurist, he recognized the crucial flaws of the witch trials and had a knack for formulating a list of trial maxims for witch trials with irresistible logic and imagination, which only found general acknowledgment in Germany after the French Revolution, in liberal criminal trials. Spee's masterful legal achievement consists in having recast the principle of presumed innocence and having emphatically demanded its application in witch trials.[41]

Of course, his motivation was emphatically Christian. He, too, was impelled by the ancient, life-saving Christian parable of the wheat among the weeds: "If there is a danger of uprooting the wheat at the same time, then the weeds must not be destroyed." His conscience would not let him rest: "How often have I pondered this over sleep-less nights, with deep sighs..."[42]

So in actual fact, it was Christianity that ended the persecution of witches that had developed out of pagan folk superstition. The theological first commandment of love helped the Jesuit Friedrich Spee bring about a legal turn against witch trials:

> Love of neighbor consumes me and burns like a fire in my heart; it drives me to step in with all fervor to prevent my fear from coming true: that an unhappy breath of wind could spread the flames of these stakes to innocent people. Indeed, it must be shown that our God is not like the idols of the pagans, who cannot leave off their wrath; he is filled once and for all with an incomprehensible love for mankind, a love too deep for him to revoke now the promise of his affection.[43]

Christianity, which in a period of weakness was unable to over-come the persecution of witches, prevailed in the end after all. However, in places where Christianization has taken place only very superficially, the belief in witches is once again making head-way. On July 24, 2002, the *Frankfurter Allgemeine Zeitung* newspaper reported on a conference held in Kenya by the British Institute in Eastern Africa:

> More and more putative witches, often elderly women, are brutally dispatched. In a province in northeastern Tanzania, there were 185 people between 1997 and 1999 alone. Often, it is hired killers who undertake this bloody business; the clearance rate is low. The gov-ernment, the police, and local elites have to put up with vehement accusations. It is not uncommon for them to be accused of complic-ity. The press in Uganda, Kenya, and Tanzania fuels the craving for sensation. Stories about bestial killings and the mixing of witchcraft and politics make for popular reading material and ensure wide circu-lation. Courts often base their sentences on the "expert knowledge" of "witch doctors", so that putative witches are often punished dra-conically without further evidence. Politicians everywhere in Eastern Africa are convinced that occult powers are trying to weaken poli-tics and that this realm needs to be governmentally controlled. But members of the modern elite, too, are calling on the state to take legal action against the danger posed by witches; according to them, current legislation contains great gaps and even protects witchcraft.[44]

VII

Legends of the Indian Missions

What We Know and What We Ought to Know

1. Mission and Violence: The Question of Human Sacrifice

Isn't missionary work scandalous all by itself? Shouldn't people be allowed to go on believing in their ancestral belief systems? Many people think that way nowadays. But what if these systems of belief are violent, if they contradict human rights, if they are inhumane? Do they have a claim to religious tolerance even in this case? And can we remain indifferent about this matter?

Christians definitely did not remain indifferent, above all because they knew that God had tasked them with proclaiming belief in Jesus Christ to all nations. Christians from the beginning had no doubt that such a mission had to work with respect for the other's free will—by preaching, by example, and by reason. But with these good intentions, they nonetheless encountered irritating phenomena, especially that of tribal religions, which, according to Jan Assmann, are "ethnocentric powers" and hardly react to reason alone.[1] For religion of this sort creates an intoxicating feeling that one's own people, and religion, is incomparably superior to all others—a belief that finds expression in ruthless violence toward other nations. The modern substitute religion of nationalism, which operates on a very similar worldview, has brought forth extermination programs on an utterly monstrous scale, adding the proclamation that "God is with us."

The great Enlightenment philosopher Immanuel Kant (1724–1804) explained in his famous essay on perpetual peace, "No other

138

beginning of a law-governed society can be counted upon than one that is brought about by force: upon this force, too, public law afterwards rests."[2] Even in our days—at the behest of the United Nations and with the consent of even the otherwise pacifist German Green party—an international coalition used force to prevent Serbians from killing Kosovans simply for being Kosovans. "Ethnic cleansings" have always taken place and have continued right up to the present. Experts do not believe that they will cease in the twenty-first century. After all, Gaius Julius Caesar also had to use violence to ban human sacrifice from the Gauls' tribal religion. Was that religious intolerance? Force is not bad in itself; it takes state authority to guarantee human rights, and it takes the power of international institutions to stay the hand of unjust violence.

Was it intolerant and xenophobic for Christians to denounce the immensely popular gladiatorial games? In the year 107, over a period of just 123 days, 10,000 gladiators took part in these spectacles and, in many cases, died. Should human sacrifice, as practiced by the Celts, the Germanic peoples, and the Slavs, have been tolerated? At times, Christian missionaries made compromises: in the year 1000, Icelanders about to be baptized posed the condition that they be allowed at least to continue abandoning children.

The same problem occurred with Native Americans. Their religion also exhibited all the characteristics of tribal religion. One Native Mexican man called the Aztecs, to whom his tribe was subjected, "the most cruel and evil people imaginable, treating their subjects much worse than the Spaniards ever did".[3] The Aztecs burned books, too, but even worse, they were proud of their human sacrifices. One local account relates how they dealt with the Spaniards: "All would be sacrificed, eaten, or thrown before wild beasts, and when they took prisoners, they arranged for them to be killed and eaten in the eyes of Cortés' soldiers. Indeed, they sacrificed everyone else in this manner, eating their arms and their heart and offering the blood to the gods."[4] How could one confront such evil without violence? How was one supposed to do missionary work there?

Before modern times, no religious missionary from India or China had ever come to Christian Europe to preach there. But according to ancient Christian accounts, the apostles had already gone out into the world—as Thomas did to India, for example. Indeed, there were already Christian communities in India by the third century at the very latest. In China, the Nestorians founded the first Christian community in 635. From the beginning, the Christian mission was directed at the whole world and hoped to overcome all borders. In his classic *History of the Expansion of Christianity*, the American historian Kenneth Scott Latourette emphasizes the following fact about the modern transatlantic mission: "Never before had any religion been propagated over so large a proportion of the earth's surface."[5] In the sixteenth century, the religious map of the world changed: Christianity became a global religion. This outreach was mainly Catholic. No real missionary effort in the New World developed among Protestants, while Catholic religious orders, which had been geared toward missionary work since the High Middle Ages and now included the newly founded Jesuits, followed the explorers and made inroads on the new continents. As a result, Christianity became the largest world religion and Catholicism the largest Christian denomination.

Urgent questions posed themselves to the missionaries of those days: How should one deal with the people of these distant worlds? Were they men at all, and if so, did they have the same status as Europeans?

2. Effective Ideas: Natural Law, Human Rights, and the Law of Nations

Antiquity generated the notion of natural law, which concerned the rights that derive from the nature of man himself and thus apply to every person. But natural rights only held in theory. To the Greeks, Greek men alone had full rights—not Barbarians, not women, and certainly not slaves. The philosopher Plato only knew a sliding scale of rights, and his student and opponent Aristotle considered equality not only unattainable but, when it came to slaves, inherently impossible. Only later Stoic philosophy envisioned a common nature for all human beings, based on humans' intellectual endowment. Yet not even this notion produced any practical consequences.

In early Christianity, natural law was set on more solid ground. Christians held that everyone was created by God and therefore had good origins and should be treated accordingly. Two passages from the apostle Paul's Letter to the Romans were especially foundational for this view.

For one, there is his appreciation of reason in all men: "Ever since the creation of the world his invisible nature, namely, his eternal power and deity, has been clearly perceived [through reason] in the things that have been made" (Rom 1:20f.).

Then there was Paul's conviction that every man has a conscience: "What the law requires is written on their [the pagans'] hearts, while their conscience also bears witness" (Rom 2:15).

The *Decretum Gratiani*, an authoritative compilation of canon law drafted in 1140, defined natural law right at its outset: "that which is common to all peoples because it is valid everywhere, impelled by nature and not by some decree."[6] On the basis of this formula, the Middle Ages' greatest thinker, Thomas Aquinas, drew conclusions that would prove decisive for centuries to come. For him, every man had the natural disposition to know, express, and carry out the most general principles of moral and just conduct. The principle that "good is to be done" constitutes for Thomas "the first precept of law".[7] This law deserves absolute obedience. If, for example, a usurper imposes a system of law that contradicts the norms of natural law, active resistance to it is justified, as long as no greater harm is created by it for the common good.[8] And Aquinas very clearly says, "If the written law contains anything contrary to the natural right, it is unjust and has no binding force."[9] This axiom would eventually prove fundamental in Christian resistance to unjust rule.

But most of all, Aquinas' vision had consequences for missionary work. In contrast to Islam, which only recognizes God's law, Christian natural law leads to a broader sense of tolerance. Belief in the good nature of all men profoundly affects Christians' attitude toward unbelievers: since pagans too are created by God, they are to be respected in all their individuality. Indeed, if through no fault of their own they have never heard about Christ and have simply followed their consciences and lived a God-fearing life, they can be considered saved, even without baptism. Later on, this concept even made it into *Lumen gentium*, the pivotal document of the Second Vatican Council.

3. Protestant Mission and Catholic Mission: A Small Distinction with Big Consequences

Although Protestantism made a decisive contribution to the modern legal tradition, it did not recognize any natural law; indeed, for Luther, man's nature was completely corrupted and entirely dependent on God's grace. Rarely in history have theological convictions had such far-reaching consequences. As late as 1652, a report on missionary work by the Lutheran faculty of the University of Wittenberg still stated that the rejection of the gospel by Jews, Muslims, and pagans was due to devil-born stubbornness and divinely ordained predestination. Only much later did a Lutheran revival give rise to the first Protestant missionaries; the first in Germany were members of the Moravian Church.

By contrast, Catholic missionary theology maintained from the beginning a distinctively positive attitude toward the nature of pagans. For the famous Dominican Bartolomé de Las Casas (1481–1566), the Native Americans were neither "unpardonable" nor "depraved", since they had followed the light of reason to the best of their abilities, even without the knowledge of Christianity. The consequences remain visible to this day. The tradition of natural law led to "the survival of most civilized Native American peoples, who were better protected by the Spanish colonial system," whereas in Puritan areas, Westerners used what they considered "formally, juridically clean contracts" to buy "more and more land from the Indian peoples", and "the damned masses were hunted like wild animals or deported to reservations", as historian Mariano Delgado recounts. Catholic missionary and settlement politics "aimed to mix the evangelized peoples and to create mixed societies of old and new Christians", while "the Protestant missionary and settlement policy amounted to apartheid, letting the European elect remain amongst themselves".[10]

In the Christian perspective, the common descent of all men from Adam and Eve was decisive in extending human rights to all people. Only Enlightenment thinkers such as Voltaire (1694–1778), increasingly distanced from Christianity, would later on doubt whether the minds of black and white people could be considered as belonging to the same species, and he viewed African sexuality as primitive and pathological. Immanuel Kant believed the white race to be the original phyletic type of mankind—a type that manifested itself in Europeans, who had at all times subdued and instructed other peoples. Political scientist Gudrun Hentges critiques the Enlightenment philosopher: "With this statement, Kant implicitly justified all territorial conquests and subjugation of native peoples to the arbitrary rule of European colonial powers."[11] The philosopher Johann Gottlieb Fichte (1762–1814) warned about a global rule of "Jews, Negroes, Tatars, and Indians".[12] Georg Wilhelm Friedrich Hegel (1770–1831) called Africa a "land of children" and attributed the extinction of the American native population to its own stupidity.[13]

Meanwhile, the Christian missionaries preached the unity of mankind as though it were an utterly obvious truth. Most importantly, they considered people of all colors and cultures capable—without distinction—of converting and becoming cultivated. Through missionary schools and their idea of personal freedom, they set into motion a process of individualization and modernization that eventually had a decisive influence on decolonization. The missionaries had always made themselves advocates for the natives. Thus it is no wonder that colonized peoples' opposition to conquest and desire for independence was mainly articulated among Christians and resulted from the Christian message, as historian Horst Gründer observes.

But what about the claim that Europeans brutally exterminated the native population on a massive scale? It is true that in the course of European world conquest, there occurred in some places a considerable population decline. Yet that decline was not caused exclusively by malice, but above all by tragic circumstances. Europeans spread illnesses that in many places decimated the native populations to a shocking degree. In South America, the population declined from an estimated 70 million to 10 million, and in New Zealand, it dropped from over 100,000 to just 40,000 between 1769 and 1890; in seventeenth-century New England, more than 90 percent of natives disappeared. This was especially due to European germs, but it was certainly also due to European firearms, which wrought violent havoc among the natives. But a more nuanced picture of this scenario has begun to emerge. As Gründer emphasizes, in Spanish and Portuguese South America, there was "not a single regulation or even announcement on the part of the Crown or the central administration that decreed or even approved the extermination of Indians";

the Spaniards generally granted "Native Americans a place in their colonial empire".[14] In the so-called "Jesuit state" of Paraguay, under the protection of the Jesuits and with reluctant approval of the Spanish kingdom, natives were safeguarded from exploitation and extermination up until the eighteenth century. English Protestant settlers were different. Their colonial expansionism took "an especially aggressive form", and they "enslaved, supplanted, or annihilated the original inhabitants", says Gründer, "according to whether or not they were needed". Alcohol was regarded among the settlers as "an effective and God-given means for the elimination of Native Americans".[15]

4. The Great Silence: The Forgotten Defenders of the Native Americans

Thomas More (1478–1535)—the great humanist, lord chancellor to the English king, and holy martyr of the Catholic Church—was full of admiration for the newly discovered strangers, who, though they were not Christian, lived in an exemplary community. Evangelization of these people, said More, should only take place with great tolerance. His famous work *Utopia* posits an ideal, imaginary civilization that does not accept intolerant jealousy:

> There was one member of our congregation who got into trouble. Immediately after his baptism, in spite of all our advice to the contrary, this man started giving public lectures on the Christian faith, in which he showed rather more zeal than discretion. Eventually he got so worked up that, not content with asserting the superiority of our religion, he went so far as to condemn all others. He kept shouting at the top of his voice that they were all vile superstitions, and that all who believed in them were monsters of impiety, destined to be punished in hell-fire for ever. When he'd been going on like this for some time, he was arrested.[16]

There is evidence that missionaries in South America carried this book in their suitcases.

Immediately, there was a conflict between the Church and the greedy Spanish conquerors. To the latter, the enterprise was mostly about gold; for this reason alone they kept from exterminating the natives, since they needed them as forced laborers. As early as 1500, the Franciscan missionaries were the first to protest, directly against Columbus and his men. In 1511, the Dominican Antonio de Montesinos gave an Advent sermon that immediately became famous:

> Tell me, by what right or justice do you hold these Indians in such a cruel and horrible servitude? On what authority have you waged such detestable wars against these peoples, who dwelt quietly and peacefully on their own land? ... Why do you keep them so oppressed and exhausted, without giving them enough to eat or curing them of the sicknesses they incur from the excessive labor you give them, and they die, or rather you kill them, in order to extract and acquire gold every day? And what care do you take that they should be instructed in religion? ... Are these not men? ... Do they not have rational souls? Are you not bound to love them as yourselves?[17]

The Dominicans were so outraged by the behavior of the conquistadores that they used unheard-of measures: they refused the sacrament of confession to people who kept slaves and would not promise to set them free. Bartolomé de Las Casas, another Dominican, was so shaken by the outrageous circumstances that he converted from a conquistador into a fearless, tireless defender of the Native Americans. He even spoke before Holy Roman Emperor Charles V and convinced him to enact laws for the protection of natives, though these took a long time to come into force, since they met with resistance.

In a major highlight of Spanish history, the foundations of modern international law emerged from discussions about the rights of the Native Americans. Relying on Thomas Aquinas, Francisco de Vitoria (1483–1546) developed some fundamental legal convictions: "Unbelief does not prevent one from being a true lord."[18] Here, de Vitoria expressed, among other things, the conviction that from the perspective of divine law, a man cannot be deprived of his goods. Not even the pope possessed temporal authority over Barbarians and other unbelievers. In the colonies, colonists had to behave in a way proper to guests. It is not permitted to force anyone to convert; the only right that one can insist on is the right to preach the gospel—in modern terms, freedom of speech. Unlike Las Casas, however, de Vitoria held the opinion that human sacrifice must be prevented by force.

To be sure, it is impossible to ignore the tendency toward exploitation and impoverishment of the native lower classes in the Spanish domain. Yet as historian Wolfgang Reinhard remarks, "No other colonial power practiced self-criticism as thoroughly and as early as did the Spanish courts in 1542 to 1573 and the Spanish theologians in the second half of the sixteenth century."[19] And Swiss scholar Urs Bitterli confirms this: "No other colonial power, neither Portugal nor the Netherlands, England, or France made such an effort in the beginning phase of its transatlantic activity to penetrate intellectually the fact of cultural contact and to regulate it legally."[20] Roberto Fernandez Retamar, a former follower of Fidel Castro, arrives at the following conclusion:

> If anything distinguishes the Spanish conquest from the depredations of Holland, France, England, Germany, Belgium, and the United States, to mention a few illustrious Western nations, it is not the magnitude of the crimes, in which they are all worthy rivals, but rather the magnitude of the scruples. The conquests carried out by these countries were not lacking in death and destruction; what they did lack were men like Bartolomé de las Casa and internal debates on the legitimacy of conquest such as the ones inspired by the Dominicans, which shook the Spanish Empire in the sixteenth century.[21]

This corresponds to the latest research. Nevertheless, surprisingly, all this remains unknown to the general public. Even after 450 years, the "Black Legend" of Spain—the most lasting historical hoax of all time, painting all things Spanish in the darkest colors and tacitly ignoring the much more radical extermination of natives in North America—continues to work its effects undiminished. A new French *History of Christianity* confirms that the Black Legend "falsifies the debate about Spanish colonial policy to this day."[22]

Meanwhile, one decisive move against the unbearable situation of the Native Americans was Pope Paul III's decree in 1537, *Sublimis Deus*, which has been celebrated as the "Magna Carta of Indian Rights":

> We define and declare [that] the said Indians and all other people who may later be discovered by Christians, are by no means to be deprived of their liberty or the possession of their property, even

though they be outside the faith of Jesus Christ; and that they may and should, freely and legitimately, enjoy their liberty and the possession of their property; nor should they be in any way enslaved; should the contrary happen, it shall be null and have no effect; [and] that the said Indians and other peoples should be converted to the faith of Jesus Christ by preaching the word of God and by the example of good and holy living.[23]

The Church has always rejected forced conversion. Though the Spanish Crown long forbid the publication of this encyclical, *Sublimis Deus* would be of inestimable value to all future missionaries across the world.

A deeply religious, deeply Christian motivation drove Bartolomé de Las Casas in his tireless defense of the Native Americans: "Indeed, Sir, I have but acted in that very manner. For I leave, in the Indies, Jesus Christ, our God, scourged and afflicted and buffeted and crucified, not once but millions of times, on the part of all the Spaniards who ruin and destroy these people and deprive them of the space they require for their conversion and repentance, depriving them of life before their time, so that they die without faith and without the sacraments. Many times have I besought the King's Council to provide them with a remedy . . . ."[24] The liberation theologian Gustavo Gutiérrez sees in this confession the heart of Las Casas' theological thought, whose spiritual, gospel-fed roots are plain.

VIII

The Enlightenment

Where Do Human Rights Really Come from?
And Who Freed the Slaves?

1. The Rise of Europe: The Enlightenment and the Battles among Christians

Right in the midst of these debates on Native American rights, there came the Reformation—a conflict not between Christians and pagans, but between Christians and other Christians. For the first time in almost a thousand years in the West, large swaths of Christians—even whole countries—no longer shared the fullness of the Catholic Christian faith. How was this to be handled? Here, in the intrareligious conflicts of the sixteenth and seventeenth centuries, the concept of "permitted religion" helped curb the strife. In times past, this model had given the Church a tool for managing her relationships with other religions, and now it served to overcome the conflict between Christian groups. The Peace of Augsburg in 1555 announced a state-established "tolerance of permission", which, while withholding full equal rights, granted tolerance to the various confessional minorities. Often, the Church's own representatives made a particular push for tolerance, such as Münster bishops Bernhard von Raesfeld (in office 1557–1566) and Johann von Hoya (1566–1574). In lands that remained intolerant, secret denominations emerged: crypto-Catholics in England and the Netherlands, crypto-Calvinists in Lutheran countries, and crypto-Lutherans in Austria. Before Holy Roman Emperor Joseph II's 1782 Edict of Tolerance,

tens of thousands of crypto-Lutherans managed to preserve their religious practice by outwardly going to Sunday Mass, confession, and
Communion, while holding their Bible services beforehand and, as
far as possible, avoiding the chrism of confirmation as the "mark of
the antichrist". Many who did not want to integrate into their state's
denomination emigrated to North America, where those "moved by
the spirit" could gather together once more.

During the Thirty Years' War, especially at its outset, propaganda expanded enormously against both Catholics and Protestants,
although in the last analysis the motives were decisively political. Still,
the respected historian Anton Schindling sees this period in a positive
light: "The *Pax Christiana* was often linked, in very subtle discussions
of conscience, to an ethically moderate view of national interest that
rejected a morally unrestrained Machiavellianism."[1] Without wish-
ing to deny the deep fault lines present, modern research considers
inter-denominational conflict with more nuance. Historian Heinz
Schilling describes religion and churches under confessionalization[2]
as "an agenda of modern change". The widespread disciplining
[*Disziplinierung*] of Europe through the various denominations made
possible an advancement in education and eventually even catalyzed
industrialization: "Compared to the Middle Ages, the European
man had become, in the broadest sense, something 'other'."[3] In this
respect, confessionalization had a positive lasting effect. So says historical research. From the standpoint of Christian theology, of course,
the Church schism continues to be an outrage, contradicting Christ's
task in the Gospel of John—that "they may become perfectly one, so
that the world may know that you have sent me and have loved them
even as you have loved me" (Jn 17:23).

To be sure, the armed conflicts between Catholic and Protestant
states were not really confessional wars, since for the most part, they
were politically and economically motivated. In the Thirty Years'
War, Catholic France was generally in league with the Protestant
princes, and even the pope was at times sympathetic to these coalitions. Still, after this endless struggle, people grew tired of religious
controversies and sought a common ground for social and political life, both of which could function without explicitly Christian
references. And thus natural law once again started to appear more
frequently on the scene, since its approach to the question of Good

and Evil is based on the general nature of man and requires no biblical foundation. In fact, the 1789 French Revolution's Declaration of the Rights of Man forgoes any religious terms whatsoever: "Men are born and remain free and equal in rights." This declaration breathes with the spirit of the Enlightenment, one of the intellectual impulses behind the Revolution.

Today, even in some ecclesial circles, there is broad agreement that it was a scandal for the Enlightenment—to which we owe so much—and especially for the cause of human rights to have met with so much resistance and even outright opposition from the Church. But is this narrative really true? What does modern, enlightened scholarship have to say about this theory?

Above all else, the Enlightenment was occasioned by an immense increase in knowledge. The discovery of the Americas and of many other lands and peoples had, in a flash, enormously widened the horizon of Europeans. Other religions had come into view, and their mere existence called into question the obvious nature of the Christian faith. Astronomically speaking, too, it was no longer possible to consider oneself the center of the world. Goethe himself would ruminate on this in later years:

> Yet among all discoveries and convictions none may have produced a greater effect on the human spirit than the doctrine of Copernicus. Hardly had the world been acknowledged as spherical and closed in itself when it should abandon the enormous prerogative to be the centre of the universe. Perhaps never a greater challenge has been imposed on mankind; for what did not dissolve by this acknowledgement into vapour and smoke, a second paradise, a world of innocence, poetry and piety, the testimony of the senses, the conviction of a poetic religious belief; no wonder that they did not want to let go of all this. . . .[4]

But Enlightenment philosophers continued to move forward. New scientific insights inspired human thinking and led to remarkable technical achievements. The consequences reached even into everyday life. Just imagine the effect of the lightning rod, invented in 1750. Until then, lightning and thunder had been visible proofs of God's wrath, his thundering voice, his punishments; people sought to protect themselves from it by prayer and good conduct of life. But then, in 1750, even an absolute villain could put a rod on his roof and be saved. More than this, an ever more optimistic brand of progressivist thinking spread among the people. Nothing seemed impossible.

When it came to natural law, which was the Enlightenment's point of reference, Catholics had far fewer problems than did Protestants, who ever since Luther had considered human nature completely corrupt and incompetent. Christendom had broadened ancient natural law to make it universal and had effectively implemented it, to the point that the Enlightenment was in turn able to declare it a secular right, with effects lasting to this day. Thus the definitive secularization of the state is doubtless one of the great achievements of the Enlightenment. With this, they overcame the forced confessional identification that had long prevailed in European lands.

In North America, modern liberties emerged from the separation of Church and state, which was taken for granted from the beginning of the United States, and thus these freedoms were never considered anti-Christian. This explains why religion is much more naturally present in the American public sphere than in the European. On the Continent, these liberties often had to be asserted against compulsory denominational adherence, which was the norm in many countries. Religious freedom stood at the heart of the new liberties. The Lutheran theologian Friedrich Wilhelm Graf notes that for Americans, it was clear from the beginning that the state "does not ascribe to itself any competency to interpret religious beliefs and does not pretend to know better than the believers themselves what they should believe."[5]

In the Enlightenment, one's own free conscience came to the fore, a conscience that refused to let itself be appropriated by the authorities. Jean-Jacques Rousseau (1712–1778) cried:

> Conscience, conscience! Divine instinct, immortal and celestial voice, certain guide of a being that is ignorant and limited indeed but intelligent and free; infallible judge of good and bad which makes man like unto God; it is you who make the excellence of his nature and the morality of his actions. Without you I sense nothing in me that raises me above the beasts, other than the sad privilege of leading myself astray from error to error....[6]

This is exactly what the apostle Paul wrote in the Letter to the Romans, albeit without the Enlightenment twist: the pagans "show that what the law requires is written on their hearts, while their conscience also bears witness" (Rom 2:15).

Thus, the Enlightenment was also a result of a process that Christianity itself had set into motion and then had further advanced. Monasteries made formidable contributions to civilization, culture, and art. Without them, the Enlightenment would have been cut off from its intellectual roots, because the monastic scribes and librarians passed down the intellectual life of the Middle Ages. For the founder of sociology, Max Weber, who declared himself "tone-deaf" in religious matters, the medieval monk was, in his time, "the first human being who lives rationally".[7] And this same Weber arrived at the conclusion that Western Christianity had achieved unique cultural feats, such as the rational experiment, which was missing, for example, even from the highly developed Indian natural sciences. Outside of the West, there developed neither rational chemistry nor rational harmonic music with all its accessories—scores, instruments, and orchestras. The Western political and social field are equally unique, said Weber: just consider specialized bureaucracy, the state as a political institution, even capitalism.

If the Enlightenment had simply developed as a reaction against unenlightened religion, there would presumably have been comparable movements in other lands that had been shaped by religion. Instead, the Enlightenment arose on Christian soil alone, which suggests that the movement drew intellectual nourishment from this soil that it could not find elsewhere.

And indeed, what the dean of Islamic theology at Istanbul University said about Islam in 2005 holds true: "We have to declare frankly that the Muslim states are not yet sufficiently developed for the requirements of the twenty-first century."[8] According to the 1999 *Arab Human Development Report*, compiled by Arab experts and commissioned by the United Nations, the gross domestic product of all Arab countries taken together was lower than that of the comparatively small Sweden.[9] Patent registration and book production are marginal. Hardly anyone works in the sciences. And most of all, there is little freedom or democracy. This of course does not stem from a lack of financial resources. Without a doubt, the European

Enlightenment yielded a harvest of knowledge and emancipation, enriching and humanizing society; but it did not bring all of this about on its own.

2. Being Made in the Image of God: On the "Genealogy of Human Rights"

"Then God said, 'Let us make man in our image, after our likeness'" (Gen 1:26). The history of human rights begins with this sentence from the first chapter of the Bible. Being made in the image of God called for divine respect toward every person and, consequently, a corresponding ethics and politics. Christians very quickly drew conclusions from this. The earliest theologians of the Church, the Church Fathers, condemned slavery on this basis. Pope Gregory the Great (ca. 540–604) declared in his doctrinal teaching that nature brought forth all men equally in the beginning and that only human law had introduced slavery. Through the Savior, man's original freedom was restored, and therefore the act of setting someone free constituted a salutary act. Though the Greeks spoke about the equality of all people, that equality was valid only in theory; in practice, they made considerable distinctions and, in the end, excluded slaves. In ancient Rome, there was no concept of legal or political equality whatsoever. Stoic philosophy was the first to argue more resolutely for equal human rights, but even Seneca (ca. A.D. 1–65), who wanted to see in slaves their humanity above all else, still did not call the practice of slavery into question. Lacking in all these reflections is a decisive impulse to bring about social change. This arrives only with Christianity, whose core conviction is that everyone is made in the image of God.

Thus medievalist Hartmut Hoffmann describes the circumstances in the Carolingian era, which were completely different from those of Antiquity. The unfree now had "subjective rights"—no longer mere objects, but "recognized as persons".[10] In the High Middle Ages, for example, Eike von Repgow (ca. 1185–after 1233), writing the *Sachsenspiegel*, deduced the impossibility of slavery from man's likeness to God: "We thereby know from God's words that man has God's image and shall belong to God, and anyone other than God who promises him something [such as a slave] acts against God."[11] When one attempts, as Antiquity did, to derive the dignity of man from general human nature rather than from man's nature as an image of God, then those who do not correspond to one's preconceived natural image get quickly dismissed as "inferior by nature", just as in Antiquity, certain peoples were considered to have been intended for slavery by nature.

The first significant expert of canon law on German soil, Burchard of Worms (ca. 965–1025), considered the argument of man's divine likeness to be universal, equally applicable to Christians as to non-Christians such as Jews and pagans: if any such person is "killed, an image of God is erased, and along with it the hope for a future conversion".[12] Meister Eckhart (ca. 1260–1328) put it poetically: he saw in the "noble man" God's image "impressed and sown"; this image can never be buried, and man must always be drawing it out, as an artist carves a sculpture from a block of marble.[13] Albrecht Dürer (1471–1528) created his self-portrait in 1500 with the features of the Savior reflected in his face—in other words, made in the image of God.

In the Spanish discussion about the problems of the New World, Francisco de Vitoria defended the Native Americans by saying that their independence was rooted in their likeness to God, that paganism and sin did not compromise this dignity, "for is the image of God by his inborn nature, that is by his rational powers. Hence he cannot lose his dominion by mortal sin".[14] He also recognized that Native Americans used their reason, and because reason is what distinguishes human beings, de Vitoria generated a body of reasonable international law, guaranteeing peaceful coexistence among peoples. Erasmus of Rotterdam (ca. 1467–1536) used particularly Christian reasoning when he spoke out against the killing of human beings: whoever "meditates war against christians ... is preparing to destroy those whom Christ died to save, to spill the blood of those for whom Christ shed his own".[15] And the English poet and Nonconformist John Milton (1608–1674) penned the often-quoted medieval phrase: "Who kills a man kills a reasonable creature, God's image."[16] The philosopher Jürgen Habermas says that such considerations belong "to the genealogy of human rights".[17] Tilman Nagel, a scholar of Islam, goes even further when he notes, "Christianity was a *conditio sine qua non* for the development of the secular state and of human rights."

3. The Drama of Human Rights:
The Abolition of Slavery

The history of slavery is instructive. It survived longest in Islam. In Saudi Arabia, the last slave market was closed only in 1963, under pressure from the West. As one study on slavery in the Arab world reports, "In no part of the Muslim world was an ideological challenge ever mounted against slavery."[18] Over the course of centuries, millions of people were enslaved there.

Unenlightened Enlightenment Philosophers:
Flat Noses and Human Rights

Enlightenment thinkers certainly had their share of trouble with slavery, too. Montesquieu (1689–1755), the great pioneer of the separation of powers in government, condemned slavery with noble words and yet, at the same time, described "Negro slaves" as soulless blacks whose work made it possible to produce sugar. In his most famous work, *The Spirit of Laws*, this leading Enlightenment thinker literally declared—in line with the best of Enlightenment thought—"But, as all men are born equal, slavery must be accounted unnatural."[19] But it almost takes one's breath away when one reads in the same work:

> Were I to vindicate our right to make slaves of the Negroes, these should be my arguments.... Sugar would be too [expensive], if the plants which produce it were cultivated by any other than slaves. These creatures are all over black, and with such a flat nose, that they can scarcely be pitied. It is hardly to be believed that God, who is a wise being, should place a soul, especially a good soul, in such a black ugly body. It is so natural to look upon colour as the criterion of human nature, that the Asiatics, among whom eunuchs are employed, always deprive the blacks of their resemblance to us by a more opprobrious distinction.[20]

People have wanted to see a distancing irony in this, but it is telling that in Reclam Verlag's edition of *The Spirit of Laws*, this paragraph is left out. Obviously, the text does not fit the prevailing radiant image of the Enlightenment as the age of light. Montesquieu is by no means an isolated case. There are other statements by Enlightenment thinkers on the question of slaves that must be hidden from the public eye today. American sociologist of religion Rodney Stark chastises Thomas Hobbes (1588–1679), John Locke (1632–1704), David Hume (1711–1776), Count Mirabeau (1749–1791), and Voltaire (1694–1778), among others, for supporting slavery or at least accepting it with a shrug.[21] Even the founders of North American liberty, such as George Washington and Thomas Jefferson, owned slaves. At least the publisher of the Enlightenment *Encyclopédie*, Diderot, resolutely advocated for the abolition of slavery, and during the French Revolution, the two Catholic clergymen Abbé Sieyès and Abbé Gregoire did the same. But overall the picture is rather murky. Most Enlightenment thinkers' statements on slavery were, in the words of historian Peter Gay, "well-meaning, often vague",[22] and when it comes to slavery, Christian Delacampagne speaks of the "indifference of humanists" and the "silence of the philosophers".[23] Just as the idea of equality in ancient Stoic philosophy remained ineffective, the Enlightenment produced no effective social movement for the definitive abolition of slavery. Only the English and North American Christian dissenters would accomplish this in the nineteenth century. In fact, the Enlightenment led to a grave step backward. Robin Blackburn, author of a large monograph on slavery, summarizes it thus:

> The Enlightenment was not so antagonistic to slavery as was once thought.... As religious justifications of slavery came to seem hollow and absurd the pseudo-science of racial anthropology was encouraged by the speculations of Linnaeus and such enlightened dabblers as the Scottish lords Kames and Monboddo. Even such distinguished intellects as David Hume, Immanuel Kant, and Georg Hegel casually employed racial stereotypes derogatory to Africans.[24]

At the same time, we must remember that slavery had been common practice in essentially all cultures from time immemorial, and our perspective today was not available to the people of the past. Slaves were property—objects, not persons. Rodney Stark observes, "Slavery was once nearly universal to all societies able to afford it"; it is "far older than the pyramids", and "there is no record that any philosopher in Sumer, Babylon, or Assyria ever protested against

[it]".[25] Hammurabi's laws primarily concerned slaves, and ancient China had "slave cattle", just like the native tribes did in North and South America. Not even the great Greek philosophers condemned slavery. Israel was the only exception, says Harvard religious historian Ephraim ben Isaak, since it "affirm[ed] the common humanity of the slave" and indeed had "strong anti-slavery sentiments".[26]

The Christians and the Slave: The Litmus Test for a Religion of Salvation

Only against this background can the downright revolutionary attitude of Christianity be adequately understood. If Christians believed that the Son of God, Jesus Christ, took upon himself the form of a slave, as the apostle Paul says in the Letter to the Philippians, and that he had come to free mankind, then this conviction was bound to lead to a conflict with slavery, which had existed since ancient times. Often misunderstood today is the apostle Paul's sentence, "In whatever state each was called, there let him remain with God" (1 Cor 7:24). Yet this passage was merely an expression of the imminent expectations of early Christians, who were still counting on Christ's immediate return. From that perspective, everyone should be concerned with the essentials, namely, with an interior conversion to Christ, with leading a life pleasing to God, and with not allowing oneself to be distracted by the exterior realities of worldly existence. In the same letter to the Corinthians, we have further evidence that the passage mentioned above was in no way intended as a reinforcement of slavery. "Do not become slaves of men" (1 Cor 7:23), Paul writes, prefacing this with a phrase that would later have intense explosive force: "For he who was called in the Lord as a slave is a freedman of the Lord. Likewise he who was free when called is a slave of Christ. You were bought with a price" (1 Cor 7:22f.). This means that Christianity understands itself as a salvific and liberating religion for slaves and free people. According to a Christian understanding, the Son of God, Jesus Christ, has bought all these people by his suffering and death on the Cross, saving them, and those who have been redeemed should also redeem others in this way. This bloody, sacrificial death of Christ—an event that might ring strange in our ears today—truly became the beacon of hope for the liberation of slaves. In the first Letter to Timothy, Paul even calls the slave traders "kidnapers" (1 Tim 1:10)! There is also Jesus' word in the Gospel of Luke, "For the laborer deserves his wages" (Lk 10:7).

The texts from the New Testament had their consequences. The Christian rhetorician Lactantius (ca. 250–ca. 320) declared: "For God, who produces and gives breath to men, willed that all should be equal.... In His sight no one is a slave, no one a master; for if all have the same Father, by an equal right we are all children."[27] In the third century, several freed slaves served as pope. The historian Egon Flaig makes the following observation about the first Christian centuries in general: "Almost all of patristics assumed that human beings were by nature free: slavery, therefore, is a sin."[28] This motivated Christians to stick by one other. Those who knew themselves to have been saved and bought by Christ's blood, saw themselves bound together by "blood brotherhood".

The freeing of slaves and of prisoners—which often amounted to the same thing—has been a key concern of the Church from her earliest days. Bishop Cyprian of Carthage (ca. 200–258) reports that his community raised one hundred thousand sesterces to buy the freedom of prisoners, because it was essential to pay for the liberty of Jesus Christ, who was present in every brother since Christ had "saved us by his blood on the Cross".[29] There is evidence of Christians giving themselves personally into slavery as ransom to set others free. Ambrose of Milan (339–397) supported the ransoming of prisoners with liturgical vessels made of precious metals, citing our own redemption through Christ: "So I once brought odium on myself because I broke up the sacred vessels to redeem captives."[30] His rationale was later included in the standard canon law code of the Middle Ages, the *Decretum Gratiani*: "The Church has gold, not to store up, but to lay out, and to spend on those who need.... Truly they are precious vessels, for they redeem men from death."[31] Bishop Caesarius of Arles (ca. 470–542) went even further and bought the freedom of prisoners who had previously besieged his city as enemies, for each was a "rational man who had been redeemed by the blood of Christ".[32]

Church treasuries belonged to the poor. The endless and lamentable loss of medieval art can be explained not least of all by artwork's role as a means for ransoming prisoners. In the thirteenth century, there arose the Mercedarian and Trinitarian orders, who especially dedicated themselves to freeing slaves and prisoners and bought the freedom of thousands of people from terrible conditions over the centuries. By the end of the 1700s, they are said to have ransomed almost a million slaves. Jews and Muslims, too, felt themselves bound to ransom members of their own religion, but they did so on a much smaller scale and not systematically.

The Christian approach to the freeing of slaves came from the core of the Christian faith and had far-reaching social consequences. It allowed the Carolingian preacher Heiric of Auxerre to cry out: "Every Christian is our brother, ransomed for the price of Christ's blood, born again through baptism, raised at the breast of Mother Church, and called to the same inheritance of the heavenly fatherland."[33] In an estate-based society, this sounded almost dangerously revolutionary. One study on the situation of female slaves credits the Christian insistence on partnership-based marriage as an essential factor in overcoming the old system of enslavement. The status of both unfree men and unfree women "enjoyed the same rise during the Carolingian period.... Both were regarded as wholly free in the eyes of the law".[34] Pope Hadrian IV (ca. 1110–1159) decreed that the unfree could enter matrimony without the consent of their lords. Since canon lawyers and theologians always emphasized the right of the unfree to marry freely even against the will of their masters, the Christian understanding of marriage as rooted in a free consent had an extraordinary emancipatory effect. Still, over the centuries, young men and women had to fight for this right—using Christian arguments—against the great opposition of their masters. Rodney Stark attributes the end of slavery in medieval Europe to the fact that "the Church extended the sacraments to all slaves".

Even secular law in the *Sachsenspiegel* uses Christian reasoning: "God created man in his own likeness and saved man, each and every one, with his martyrdom. The poor man as well as the rich one was dear to him.... [W]hen laws were first established, there was no unfree person."[35] Even Marxist medieval historian František Graus sees primarily religious grounds—namely, Christ's death on the Cross for all mankind—for the Middle Ages' emphasis on "the equality of all human beings before God" and the declaration that "all differences are secondary and finally insignificant".[36]

When texts by the Greek philosopher Aristotle resurfaced in Europe in the thirteenth century, they initially hindered the freeing of slaves. For Aristotle, slavery was natural. Nevertheless, the greatest medieval thinker, the Dominican Thomas Aquinas, did not follow Aristotle on this point, but rather accepted the medieval concept of serfdom, which unlike slavery does not involve ownership of human beings. A lord could not forbid matrimony for the unfree any more than he could prohibit eating and sleeping. The Franciscan philosopher Duns Scotus (ca. 1266–1308) spoke out against slavery even more resolutely. In 1435, Pope Eugene IV (ca. 1383–1447) commanded masters—"through the sprinkling of the Blood of Jesus Christ"—immediately to free the enslaved inhabitants of the island of Lanzarote, under pain of excommunication.[37] Later, Erasmus of Rotterdam used exclusively religious arguments to warn the young Holy Roman Emperor Charles V: "What a mockery it is to regard as slaves those whom Christ redeemed with the same blood as redeemed you, whom he set free into the same freedom as you, and whom he has called to inherit immortality along with you".[38] The explosive liberating force of the Christian message has been clear in every age, including the sixteenth-century Peasants' War, wherein peasants accused their masters of "counting us their serfs, which is pitiful when you consider that Christ saved and ransomed everyone by his precious blood".[39]

The Christian argument had resounding success as early as the early Middle Ages. Late Antiquity and the subsequent Germanic Barbarian empires all remained slaveholding societies. But the Carolingian period—the eighth and ninth centuries—presents "a fundamentally different picture", as French medieval historian Stéphane Lebecq notes.[40] The former slaves became bondsmen, who were now able to have families and own and bequeath property. Rodney Stark therefore arrives at the conclusion that medieval peasants were "not slaves, and this brutal institution had essentially disappeared from Europe by the end of the tenth century".[41] Not even prisoners of war were typically enslaved in the Middle Ages. The Third Council of the Lateran in 1179 excommunicated all "who dare to rob [or plunder] Romans or other Christians".[42] However, this image is marred by the slavery that took place among crusaders, influenced by the Muslim slaveholders they encountered. The crusaders' keeping of Muslim slaves, too, strained the intermittently peaceful relations with Islamic neighbors.

Even though slave markets definitively disappeared from Europe in the Middle Ages, the practice of slavery was still maintained through contact with the Muslim world. As a result—and an end—of military conflict, Muslim slaves played a role in the early Modern period, especially along the coasts of the Mediterranean. This form of slavery continued to persist until the late eighteenth century. But still, the Oxford *Historical Guide to World Slavery* points out that Europe became "the probable locus of a moral revolution against slavery".[43]

A Low Point: Transatlantic Trade

The lowest point, however, was the trading of African slaves across the Atlantic Ocean. Bartolomé de Las Casas, who had passionately spoken out against the enslavement of Indians, had indeed mentioned the possibility of importing a workforce from Africa in order to relieve the Indians—an idea he eventually came to regret bitterly. What followed, however, exploded all expectations. Between 1500 and 1800, more than ten million Africans were shipped across the Atlantic under inhumane conditions by European forces. Fed by the insatiable greed of European economic powers, this trade marked a terrible relapse into times that many assumed to be long outmoded. Naturally, these excesses had a fatal impact on Christian missionary work. The popes stood by their strict condemnation of slavery, but at first they did not explicitly mention the Africans. Pope Urban VIII (1568–1644) strictly forbade all clerics, religious, and laypeople— under threat of excommunication—from "enslaving, buying, selling the Indians, separating them from their wives, robbing them of their goods and property, and relocating them to different places".[44] In 1680, the Roman Inquisition delivered a renewed condemnation of the slave trade. But ecclesiastical interventions hardly had any effect. It was an altogether hideous business, which people justified using the line of reasoning that Montesquieu would eventually put to paper: without "negro slaves", there would be no sugar from overseas.

This time, it was not the major churches, but dissenting North American and English Christian communities such as the Quakers and the Adventists who wanted to abolish slavery once and for all.

These communities drew their arguments not from natural law, but rather from the specifically Christian teaching on redemption—the ransom attained through the shedding of Christ's blood—according to which one's own salvation demanded that others be freed as well. Rodney Stark emphasizes: "It was primarily the churches (often local congregations), not secular clubs and organizations, that issued formal statements on behalf of ending slavery."[45] This Christian movement resulted in a ban on the slave trade in England in 1807. In the United States, this prohibition came in 1808, and by the end of the century, the possession of slaves was outlawed, too, though of course, not without the devastating American Civil War, fueled by differing opinions on slavery. By contrast, revolutionary France proved itself completely ineffective when it came to slaveholding. And once again, the popes spoke out. Pope Gregory XVI denounced the slave trade in 1839, this time explicitly including the trade of Africans; in 1888, Pope Leo XIII expressed his joy at the end of slavery in Brazil.

In the end, slavery was subverted through religious thinking: the idea of man's likeness to God and, more crucially, of one's own personal redemption. The New Testament idea that the Son of God, Jesus Christ, took the form of a slave to buy the freedom of mankind is the very paradigm of a religion of salvation, and it had a liberating effect on slaves as well, even serving as a decisive motivation for granting them total freedom. For this reason, Rodney Stark explains that "Christianity was unique in evolving moral opposition to slavery."[46]

Harvard sociologist Orlando Patterson comments, "Thus Christianity became the first and only world religion to declare its highest religious goal to be freedom—the redemption, the ransom from spiritual servitude and from the curse of original sin through the sacrificial death of the savior", since it believes in a God "who sent his Son to liberate mankind".[47] Neither Judaism nor Islam are religions of salvation in this sense. Stark accordingly emphasizes "that of all world religions, including the three great monotheisms, only in Christianity did the idea develop that slavery was sinful and must be abolished".[48] Ultimately, as the sociologist Hans Joas soberly observes, "Religious enthusiasm was the driving force not only behind the establishment of religious freedom, but also behind the eighteenth-century pronouncements on human rights and the struggle for the abolition of slavery; in no way can any of these be traced back to Enlightenment ideas"[49]—even less than one might have imagined.

4. The Shadows of the Enlightenment: The Victims of the Revolution

One would think that the Enlightenment took great care to promote tolerance. But indeed Voltaire's battle cry, "Écrasez l'infâme!" (Crush the villain [that is, the Church]!), calls for anything but serene nonviolence. Habermas' student Rainer Forst points out that Voltaire himself wanted to exclude from state-protected tolerance not only atheists, but also potentially any who obstruct the path of the Enlightenment. Thus, the Enlightenment state, which had just freed itself from compulsory confessional loyalty and no longer had to justify itself to anyone or anything, was threatening to slide into compulsory tolerance. Forst speaks of the "fanaticism of tolerance".[50] The *Encyclopédie*—the "Bible" of Enlightenment thinkers—elaborates the concept of "tolerance" with the following: "How could we fault an Asian or New World prince if he had hanged the first Christian missionary we sent to convert him?"[51] Some Enlightenment thinkers turned the state into a religion no less rigorous than the sort that had earlier prevailed under established denominations. Jean-Jacques Rousseau said: "There is thus a profession of faith which is purely civil. . . . If anyone, after having publicly acknowledged these same dogmas, behaves as if he did not believe in them, then let him be put to death."[52] But to him, the Catholic religion was the worst of all, precisely because it split the sovereignty of the state and placed people under two different bodies of law: state and church. For this reason, some "enlightened" states raged against Christians. Frederick the Great had a chaplain hanged simply because he had been accused of giving absolution to a deserter. Historian Hartmut Lehmann describes the secularization of his homeland Württemberg: "After 1803, there was no religious freedom in the kingdom of Württemberg. Instead, the government determined the forms— that is, the ways—in which the Catholic faith could be practiced. The situation was no better for Protestantism. Many deeply pious Protestants who did not want to comply with the regulations of the new, enlightened church policy were persecuted and sometimes even sentenced to prison."[53]

Enlightenment thinkers' statements about Jews and Muslims do not speak for tolerance, either. Voltaire is accused by recent scholars of having "cleared the ground for a rhetoric of secular antisemitism", as well as treating Islam with nothing better than "admiring contempt".[54] Acclaimed historian Reinhart Koselleck considers the claim that the Enlightenment created modern tolerance to be a "touchingly optimistic statement".[55] And as philosopher Hermann Lübbe explains, the later Reign of Terror ultimately intended to implement "a social purification through death", for cleansing "is that specifically modern principle of legitimation for modern mass killings, owed to the spirit of the Enlightenment".[56] The Enlightenment's original goals of tolerance and humaneness got partly buried by its own intolerance and, indeed, fanaticism. Modern historians have arrived at the frightening conclusion that "the French Revolution's historic Reign of Terror" drew from the Enlightenment.[57]

More recent research, too, has yielded some grim results in this regard. French cultural historian Michel Vovelle explains that during the Reign of Terror alone (June 1793 to July 1794), "50,000 official and summary executions took place—that is, about 0.2 percent of the population was killed."[58] That makes as many victims within 13 months as were killed over 400 years across Europe because of witch hunts, and ten times as many as all the victims of the Spanish Inquisition over 350 years. There were many more victims beyond these 13 months and outside of Paris. In the counterrevolutionary Vendée, for example, revolutionary death squads (têtes de morts) ran wild; the region lost 15 percent of its population (117,257 of 815,029) and 20 percent of its homes (10,309 of 53,273).

IX

After the Bloodbath

The Church in the Nineteenth Century

1. The Opening Act: Popes Are Only Human

Human rights are madness, Pope Gregory XVI proclaimed, with an Italian flair, in 1832. Today, we would be more tempted to characterize a statement like this one as insanity or scandal. How can we account for such a change? Hardly a century before, the liberal Pope Benedict XIV, in a friendly correspondence with Voltaire, had expressed his admiration for him in flattering words. A statement like Pope Gregory's would never have crossed the lips of this enlightened pope. For centuries, Christian theologians had proclaimed freedom in matters of conscience and in matters of faith; the medieval papacy had even been credited with supporting democratic advances against Italian princes and noblemen.

Pope Gregory was not, of course, the first to reject the French Revolution's declaration of human rights. In 1791, in a resolute statement, Pope Pius VI had previously pronounced the revolutionary declarations on equality and liberty "nonsensical", indeed, a "veritable monstrosity". But one has to keep in mind that the sovereignty of the people, which was proclaimed by the French Revolution and which we take for granted today, was something completely new at the time. Authorities ruled by the grace of God all over the world except in the rebellious recently founded United States of America, which were, however, far away. And the brutal methods of the French Revolution evoked universal horror. When King Louis XVI and his family were forcibly led to Paris, the severed heads of two bodyguards were processed before the royal state coach. Moreover, even the Enlightenment philosopher Immanuel Kant had qualms about establishing human rights exclusively on the foundation of the individual, since according to him, human dignity was something "which we first and foremost have to prove by our own moral achievements, and not a claim, the acceptance of which others owe to us", as philosopher Otfried Höffe notes.[1] Pius VI's argument is very similar: "Who does not know that men were created to live not simply as individuals, but also for the benefit of others? Weak as human nature is, each needs the assistance of others to survive; and to this end, God equipped men with reason and language, so that they would know how to ask for help and to help those who ask it."[2] This is the origin of the debates that continue to this day about the dangers of unrestrained individualism and also of the insistence that certain social duties are attached to the owning of property. In the end, the pope mitigated his remarks by declaring that it had not been his intention "to contest the new civil code, which even the king saw himself able to approve, because it was part of the realm of secular governmental power," and that he had not meant to plead for the re-introduction of the Ancien Régime, either.[3]

The violent actions of the revolutionaries certainly accounted for the vehemence of the pope's reaction, and Pius VI was soon to experience this violence first hand. Five years after the declaration, revolutionary troops occupied Rome, and two years after that he was taken prisoner. The eighty-one-year-old died in 1799 in custody in the citadel of Valence in southern France. His successor, Pope Pius VII, elected in Venice, was taken prisoner by Napoleon, and it was not until the Congress of Vienna that secular rule was re-established for the popes, who now considered it to be all the more necessary for their freedom. Thus it was the inhumane blood-lust of the Revolution's year of terror that above all served to discredit the French Revolution's ideas about human rights across Europe in the first half of the nineteenth century, including among the successors of the imprisoned popes.

Still, the Church responded positively to the declaration of human rights in the beginning. The clergy involved in the National Assembly of 1789 did not display the least disapproval. Among the

291 clerical representatives, Marxist historian Albert Soboul counts "more than 200 were curés [parish priests] committed to the cause of reform".[4] The clergy voted in favor of the renunciation of privileges as well as the declaration of human rights:

> Art. 1: Men are born and remain free and equal in rights.... Art. 10: No one should be disturbed on account of his opinions, even religious, provided their manifestation does not derange the public order and established law. Art. 11: The free communication of ideas and of opinions is one of the most precious of the rights of man; every citizen then can freely speak, write, and print, subject to responsibility for the abuse of this freedom in the cases determined by law.[5]

However, it was surprisingly the most progressive member of the clergy, Abbé Gregoire, who critically remarked that there is no social bond without duties, which temper the primordial freedom, a statement along the same lines as Immanuel Kant's.

The French bishops, of all people, immediately turned against the harsh declaration of Pope Pius VI:

> We had wished to establish the true kingdom of public freedom in a hereditary monarchy, and had without any trouble recognized that natural equality, which does not exclude any citizen from the station where providence calls him by the voice of his talents and of his virtues. Political equality can be expanded or limited, depending on the different forms of government, and we had believed that our views on these more or less substantial questions, which God himself indicates have been entrusted to man's exchange of opinions, as well as the views of all citizens, would be free.[6]

The Catholic Church is no "papal Church."

2. Catholics Don't Do What the Pope Says: Catholic Revolutions

Catholics were also at odds with Pope Pius VI during the Belgian Revolution of 1830. They allied themselves with the liberals and together created the constitution that stands to this day and includes all modern liberties. Catholics in Germany also wanted "liberty as in Belgium", not only for themselves, but for all, and not even new liberties, but simply those delineated in the constitution. Belgium, Ireland, Poland—all these were Catholic countries where Catholicism had various liberating effects, especially with regard to modern liberties, such as a nation's right to self-determination. But the people were also pleading for religious freedom. It was precisely these liberal freedoms that Pope Gregory XVI had considered madness and that German Pius societies, named after the liberal new Pope Pius IX, were demanding immediately after Pope Gregory's death. On the occasion of the 1848 Revolution, the bishop of Mainz held a formal thanksgiving service at the cathedral of Mainz. A subsequent bishop of Mainz, Wilhelm Emmanuel von Ketteler (1811–1877), set forth the will of the people: "The people, the individuals among the people, are the legal subjects who derive their legal existence from themselves; but the state, the legislative and the executive power in the state, is only an authorized representative."[7] The famous article of the Frankfurt constitution on religious freedom was especially supported by the Catholic Club, the association of Catholic representatives. In contrast, Lutheran Church historian Kurt Nowak observes "that the Protestants, who could have seen the inheritance of the Reformation in the demands of liberalism, were altogether rather helpless, while Catholicism availed itself of the new instruments of politics as if that had been the most obvious thing to do."[8] The great expert on the nineteenth century, historian Thomas Nipperdey, comments regarding 1848, the year of the Revolution:

> the Catholic movement was in favour of liberty and emancipation; the struggle for freedom among the Catholic Belgians, Irish and Poles was followed with great interest in Germany. A pragmatic combination of liberalism and Catholicism evolved. Liberal demands for freedom of association, assembly and the press, limitation of state power, self-government, the rule of law and a constitution were also raised by the Catholics, not only because they offered potential assistance to church policies, but also because they were readily justifiable from the natural laws that formed an important element of Catholic thought. The citizens of the Rhineland with their Catholic and anti-Prussian outlook and constitutional aims, were natural liberals.[9]

According to Nipperdey, "anti-clericalism and crude atheism"[10] was especially opposed to these liberal positions. In 1862, Bishop Ketteler, supported by Catholic tradition, Thomas Aquinas, and late Scholasticism, was still advocating for full religious freedom.

But then Pope Pius IX published the *Syllabus of Errors* in 1864, a whole list of heresies that were to be denied, including a renewed, strict rejection of liberal democratic rights. How did this happen? Pius IX became pope in 1846 as a young cardinal and was considered a liberal beacon of hope. But then the Roman Revolution of 1848 degenerated into unbridled violence. The pope's prime minister was murdered, a republic was proclaimed, and the pope had to flee in disguise to the kingdom of Naples in the dead of night. These events obviously left Pius IX deeply unsettled and led him to change his mind radically. Thus, he reverted to the stance of his predecessors, especially that of Pius IX and of Gregory XVI; and because he reigned for thirty-two years, the position of the papacy did not change for a long time.

A new pope was not elected until 1878—Leo XIII, who brought a more pragmatic attitude to the times: actually, existing states founded on popular sovereignty, for example Belgium and the United States, should be recognized, and the pope explicitly called on French Catholics to accept the republic. "No one of the several forms of government" was to be "in itself condemned, inasmuch as none of them contains anything contrary to Catholic doctrine",[11] he said. In general, the papacy of Leo XIII at the end of the nineteenth century was now receiving many of the signals that committed Catholic laypeople had been sending to society, as well as to the Church, for a long time. Such preparatory work especially inspired Leo XIII's epochal encyclical, *Rerum novarum*, on the question of workers, which granted workers their own rights. These two new openings, i.e. regarding the mutability of the form of government and the plea for the individual rights of workers, strengthened the development of "social Catholicism" in Germany, which focused on the constitution, democracy, and social policy. In contrast, as the leading Lutheran encyclopedia of theology puts it, German Lutheranism was still oriented "toward authority, toward the doctrine of the divine right of kings, and toward the Christian, or at least moral, authoritarian state—in other words, anti-democratically."[12]

3. The Infallibility of the Pope: A Liberal Dogma?

After the fall of Communism in 1989, a cartoon made the rounds. The character it featured was unmistakably Karl Marx, his hands deep in his pockets, with a speech bubble that said: "I guess I was wrong. I didn't mean any harm." The joke was that Communism had always included the claim to infallibility, and that this mistake was not some little glitch.

Could the Church be wrong? Christians, too, have been asking themselves this question for two thousand years. If she was indeed a divine institution, it would of course be nonsensical for faithful Christians to assume that God was systematically and permanently leading his faithful astray through the Church, to whom he had explicitly sent the "Holy Spirit". Somehow, they thought, he will make sure that Christians are not led completely away from the truth by the Church. But how? Different Christian churches give different answers to this question. The Orthodox stick to the Bible, and especially to the early councils of the Church that defined which beliefs were correct, that is, what was orthodox. That is enough for Eastern Christians, and for this reason, they still mostly read the old Church Fathers. Orthodox thinking about the Church tends to be along lines that are more mystical than legal, and they experience their faith primarily in church services, in their formal liturgy, which means more to them than any theology. The Protestants, on the other hand, actually have it very easy. Of course they, too, have a church, which even formulates binding professions of faith, but the determining factor for them is the individual's relationship with God, which they primarily experience in their encounter with the biblical text and in their faith in the efficacious grace of God. Their church seems to be no more to them than a provider of services. Catholic Christianity, in contrast, has since Antiquity been more legally, rationally, and institutionally oriented. While Jesus remains silent in response to Pilate's question, "What is truth?", the Orthodox Christian excuses himself to go to his church service, and the Protestant consults his Bible in order to find a personal answer there—but the Catholic sits down and writes a document. But who decides whether the text he writes is true, Christian, Catholic—i.e., whether it corresponds to the faith of the whole Church?

In the early Church, the answer was simple. If there was a question that was difficult to answer, in many cases, the most venerable authority was consulted, which was Rome—i.e., its bishop, the pope—because the Christian community in Rome had been founded by Peter and Paul. Communities from the East did the same, and then the Romans would reply by explaining what they had believed since ancient times and what had resulted from it. "Roma locuta, causa finita" was a famous saying of Saint Augustine: if Rome has spoken, the case is closed. Of course, one can imagine that over the course of two thousand years, there have been conflicts again and again over the question of whether everything the bishop of Rome says is covered by Jesus' promise that God's Holy Spirit would always stay with his Church. Of course, popes have also spoken nonsense, especially whenever they have spoken a lot. But in particularly sensitive situations, when it was a question about the core of the faith, the popes have undoubtedly achieved great things for the unity of the Church and for the unity of all living Christians, but also for the Church's unity with all past Christians, which is called preserving one's identity.

Now, in the nineteenth century, the typically Western, typically Catholic question emerged of when exactly the pope could count on the reliable help of the Holy Spirit in making decisions—and when he could not. The so-called traditionalists went as far as to attribute to the pope direct access to "original revelation". He could, so to speak, voice his opinion on everything and everyone with a claim to infallibility. Remarkably, this notion had already been condemned as heresy by the popes themselves. At the First Vatican Council in 1869/70, certain "papists" had tried to widen the scope of papal infallibility as much as possible. That was also prevented. The result was that the pope is rarely considered infallible: his infallibility applies exclusively to questions relating to faith and morals, and only then by his formal and explicit declaration. No wonder this dogma has only been formally exercised once since then, namely in 1950, with the proclamation of the dogma that Mary was assumed into heaven body and soul. Pope Pius XII had previously consulted several thousand bishops from all over the world over whether that belief had been held in their dioceses since time immemorial, and only when almost all of them confirmed that that was the case, did the pope proceed to make it dogma.

So the pope cannot, according to Catholic doctrine, raise a teaching he just happens to like to the level of dogma; he can only express what the Church has already always believed.

In 1870, after the proclamation of the dogma of papal infallibility, a storm of outrage broke all over Europe. The so-called Old Catholics broke away from the Catholic Church. The content of this dogma was grotesquely distorted so that it became a scandal, and everyone pretended that Catholics had to bow from now on to the arbitrary whims of an old Italian man, something many people believe even to this day. The whole thing took on hysterical proportions, especially in Germany, where the arch-Protestant chancellor of the German Empire, Otto von Bismarck, instigated a virtual persecution of Catholics using the methods of a police state, when actually, what Catholics believed did not concern the state at all. Bishops were taken into custody, orders were suppressed, the freedom to preach was significantly limited. This ruthless "culture war" made a mockery of human rights and the right to freedom.

According to what it communicated, the dogma of infallibility of 1870 was actually not a conservative act. Since it is almost never applied, because of the significant hurdles in the way, in everyday practice it means that all Catholics are prohibited from claiming infallibility, and most of the time, the pope is, too. The dogma of infallibility therefore rather works as a prohibition of infallibility. It stops people from being opinionated; it prevents hubris and the emergence of sects. Basically, it could be called a liberal dogma, if we can say such a thing in this context without being too annoying.

At this time the situation of Catholicism was already being made considerably more difficult by denominational differences, especially in Germany. Germany, unlike all the other European countries, was a nation that was virtually split along denominational lines: even though Catholics made up a strong minority, there was a clear Protestant majority among the state authorities. Catholics were second-class citizens in the German Empire. The Bismarck empire emphatically understood itself as a nation state, with historians for priests and prophets and a close alliance between the Protestant throne and the Protestant altar. Catholics, on the other hand, because of the world-church, international alignment of their loyalties, were considered untrustworthy with regard to their country, "ultramontane", or "backward"—which at the time meant the same as "backwoods", because the seat of their authority was not in Berlin, but on the other side of the Alps. For this reason, the "pastoral nationalism" in the Lutheran Church had no Catholic equivalent. However, in the midst of all this discrimination, something happened no one had counted on: the Catholic sphere became stronger in resistance to obvious injustice. Since the old imperial legal regulations for the protection of denominations had been removed at the beginning of the nineteenth century, denominations had already had to assert themselves on their own. That led among other things to more inter-denominational polemics, but also to the heightened self-assurance of each denomination as it came to be supported by its own schools, societies, and publications.

4. Why Karl Marx Was Right: And Why Christians Followed Him

"The philosophers have only interpreted the world in different ways; the point, however, is to change it." This famous saying by Karl Marx was put into practice not by the Marxists, but by the Christian churches. The agitational and political efforts of Communists and Socialists were, at best, only moderately successful. They did not change the world. Even Bismarck's progressive social legislation at the end of the century was mostly derived from the Catholic Centre Party. And it was the newly formed Catholic orders who actually sought to help the suffering in a practical way, along with the intense efforts of Protestant Christians to face actively the misery of the masses. They did so very successfully. And that changed much, if not everything, for people in need.

For a long time, it was customary for Christians themselves to lament the supposed failure of the churches to address the labor question. People appeared to be contrite and promised improvement. But recent scholarly insights paint a different picture. Thomas Nipperdey described social Catholicism at the time as "a path between capitalism and socialism, a third path for the taming of capitalism in the welfare state."[13] And the political scientist Karl Rohe credits Catholicism in the Ruhr region with enormous achievements in integration, which is one of the "most remarkable phenomena in German social history of the twentieth century."[14] At the end of 1912, more than 300 Catholic workers' unions and miners' associations boasted more than 70,000 members. The reason for the astonishing appeal of such associations was "a presumably unique combination of religious meaning and social representation of interests. Catholicism in the Ruhr area was characterized by clergy who were open to the social interests and the concerns of the workforce."[15]

The nineteenth century was an exciting time for Christians. After the bloodthirstiness of the French Revolution, the ideals of the Enlightenment, which many people from the Church had subscribed to, had sustained damaged. The fact that those who were advocating for democracy were simultaneously fervent nationalists was a problem, especially for Catholics. The Germans' song "Deutschland, Deutschland über alles" (Germany, Germany above all) did not easily cross the lips of Catholics, since they belonged to a church that understood herself to be an international church, a church of all nations. Thus, the emerging, fatal nationalism drove Catholics in all European countries into a defensive position. But that did not weaken them. In fact, it made the Catholic Church in the nineteenth century attractive to many. There were numerous conversions and an unexpected revival that included the founding of many religious orders. New churches were being built everywhere, and Romanticism was downright intoxicated with the Middle Ages and especially with the ancient Church. However, the papacy occasionally tripped itself up, because after its traumatic experience of violence in the French Revolution, it was now too concerned for its own good with the maintenance of the Papal States; also, it did not yet recognize that the loss of secular rule, and even destructive secularization, could be liberating for the Church. Pope Benedict XVI candidly admitted this to be true in his speech in Freiburg in 2011.

At times, there have been complaints about a certain degree of intellectual narrowness in the Church. Opening herself up to the lofty ideas of the new philosophers might have suggested itself, because for Kant, Fichte, and Hegel, Christianity was at the forefront of religion, and some of their texts at first sight give the impression of being Christianity turned into philosophy. But that is also exactly where the danger lay. If we follow the conclusions that the various left- and right-wing Hegelians, thinkers like Feuerbach and Marx, drew from Hegel's Christian-sounding philosophical principles, we notice that they were straying miles away from the original intuitions of Christianity. In this respect, the abstention of the papacy and of the Catholic Church from some newer nineteenth-century intellectual developments, despite coming across as narrow-minded, has perhaps ensured that this Church, which had been written off at the beginning of the century, could enter the twentieth century remarkably strengthened. When we read the stories of the innumerable Catholic martyrs who gave their lives in resistance to National Socialism, we always encounter the great power they drew from the stable Catholic environment of the nineteenth century.

X

The Twentieth Century

*Christians and National Socialism, Original Sin
and Euthanasia, the Church and the Jews*

At the beginning of the calamitous twentieth century, in 1912, Joseph Mausbach, a moral theologian from Münster who was making appearances as a Catholic speaker, issued a warning:

> It is not only the exterior defense and armament of the nations that is becoming heavier and more oppressive; but an interior alienation and hardness fortifies their breast with triple steel, and robs the numerous assurances of peace by state leaders of a warm, penetrating tone of truth. The old idea of humaneness is mocked nowadays as a beautiful utopian ideal from the period of the Enlightenment; the new peace movement takes root only with difficulty in authoritative circles that influence the course of events. We as Christians are eminently right to call the nationalism that both spans and separates the nations, and an even more inhumane naturalist racial theory, a danger to humanity.[1]

Christians fought on both sides in World War I. But the top representative of Christendom, Pope Benedict XV, instead of war sermons, put forth a dramatic peace initiative in 1917, which was only to be met with contempt by warmongers on both sides. Even though historian Wolfgang Mommsen observes that probably no social group "supported the war efforts of the German Empire from August 1914 to the bitter end in 1918 with greater determination than the Protestant regional churches", it was the highly respected Protestant historian Adolf von Harnack who eventually advocated for a negotiated peace.[2] In the Catholic "soldiers' hymnal", which soldiers who were enthusiastic Catholic participants in the war carried to battle, there is a prayer that reads:

> Protect me from all unnecessary bloodshed, from all inhumane treat-
> ment of the wounded or imprisoned enemy. The memory of the
> cruel mistreatment or of the killing of a defenseless person would fill
> the hour of my death with bitterness and make dying difficult. Do
> not let me ever forget that only the fighters I encounter in the field
> are my enemies, and that the unarmed inhabitants of the country, the
> wounded, and the defenseless are my suffering brothers, to whom I
> owe mercy and compassion.

A petition on behalf of the rulers forms the end of the prayer: "Instill in them a peaceful disposition, shorten through them the misery of war, and grant us in the not-too distant future the great boon of a blessed peace again." [3] Besides, as Heinrich Missalla has noted, contrary to all other claims, "so far there is no proven case of a blessing of arms, either from the time of the First nor of the Second World War." [4]

1. Democracy: Christians on New Paths

In the twentieth century, the situation of the Catholic Church in Europe was highly varied. In Spain, there were villages at the beginning of the century where out of 18,000 parish members, only 200 women and 10 men attended Sunday Mass, and a quarter of the children remained unbaptized. In the Netherlands, in the industrial city of Tilburg, Catholic Mass attendance was at 97 percent. And in Germany, Mass attendance after World War I in the workers' city of Bochum was higher than in conservative Münster. According to Thomas Nipperdey, Catholicism was quite capable of assert-ing itself in the age of a faceless modern industrial society, and even entered the twentieth century and the Weimar Republic in 1918 with a latent potential for an awakening. [5] According to well-known liberal sociologist Ralf Dahrendorf, to the question of why so many intellectuals in the two decades after the World War I succumbed to the great temptations of either Communism or of National Social-ism, the answer is religion: "To many intellectuals, especially those who had lost the God of their Jewish or Christian parents, the hope of a socialist paradise appeared to be more than just a substitute, especially since it was a paradise on earth."[6] Given this situation, it was especially surprising that Catholicism, which had previously been generally berated for being "unenlightened", began to hold an attraction for some educated circles. Numerous intellectuals found the Catholic Church appealing, and they converted: famous essayist Theodor Haecker (1879–1945); Ludwig Dehio (1888–1963), a student of Ranke; and the art historian and German UNESCO representative Otto von Simson (1912–1993). The famous art historian Aby Warburg (1866–1929) also converted to Catholicism on his deathbed. The Benedictine abbeys of Beuron and Maria Laach exuded a special aura. The philosopher Max Scheler, who had become Catholic in 1899, found a confessor in Verkade, a painter monk at Beuron, who was a converted student of Gauguin. Edith Stein, a student of Husserl who was eventually murdered in Auschwitz, had become Catholic and later on joined the Carmelites; she spent days and weeks of spiritual and intellectual retreat there. Even the philosopher Martin Heidegger (1889–1976) experienced Beuron during the night offices of the Liturgy of the Hours: "In the Compline, the mythical and metaphysical primal force of the night is still there, which we must constantly break through in order to exist truly."[7] In Maria Laach, students and academics from Strasbourg, Metz, and Bonn gathered, such as the French Robert Schuman and the Rhinelander Konrad Adenauer, who would later become crafters of modern Europe. In France, at the same time, the so-called "Renouveau catholique", a Catholic renewal, was taking place.

In the period after the November Revolution of 1918, that is, after the end of the empire, all historical records show a clear distinction between Protestants and Catholics in Germany. For most Protestants, the collapse of Protestant authority was a catastrophe and the republic a national misfortune. The rejection of natural law, widespread in Protestantism, had an especially fatal impact on Protestants' attitude toward the idea and the practice of democracy. Arguments were often based solely on the Bible, and pious Protestants' interpretation of Chapter 13 of the Letter to the Romans sought to justify the divinely ordained monarchy of the royal Hohenzoller family: "Let every person be subject to the governing authorities. For there is no authority except from God" (Rom 13:1). Only later did many read into this passage the idea that democracy could also be pleasing to

God. So, while Catholicism became a supporter of Weimar democracy without further ado after the end of the empire in 1918, politically, Protestantism was largely at sea.

In the decades leading up to that, Catholics had already known how to utilize parliamentary debates to stir up opposition, even involving parts of the workforce. As Protestant church historian Gerhard Besier notes, they thus had "far better premises on which to address the social question constructively than Protestant Christians did."[8] As early as the Reichstag Peace Resolution of 1917, the Catholic Centre had allied itself with the social democrats and the progressives and had thus laid the foundation for the later Weimar coalition. Protestantism remained secluded for the most part. Catholic moral theologian Joseph Mausbach, cited above, who had an essential role in shaping the new relationship between state and Church in the Weimar National Assembly, legitimized the people's state as well as the sovereignty of the people. This Catholic priest also advocated for women's voting rights with the trenchant remark that the World War "hadn't exactly revealed the lords of the earth to be so overwhelmingly great that women should sink to their knees in amazement before their glory."[9] The Catholic Centre Party established the Weimar Republic, was represented in all government coalitions from 1919 to 1932, and had stable election results all the way to the last free elections. Even if some bishops in the beginning only hesitantly followed the Catholic laypeople who were leading the way in accepting the republic, historian Manfred Kittel notes: "Political Catholicism overwhelmingly sided with the republic, while Protestantism mainly allied itself with its opponents." The reason for that was, according to Kittel: "Protestantism proved not to be in a position to produce a 'theology of democracy', which would have corresponded to the needs of pluralist culture and parliamentary constitutional reality."[10] No wonder it could be said about Berlin that they were ecstatic about the end of the Weimar Republic.

2. Dictatorship: Christians and the Resistance

And how did the Catholic Church deal with National Socialism? Before 1933, the Catholic Church's opposition to it was radical and resolute. All members of the NSDAP [*Nationalsozialistische Deutsche*

Arbeiterpartei, the National Socialist German Workers' Party] were de facto excommunicated. They were denied not only the sacraments, but even church burials. The well-known historian Hans-Ulrich Wehler calls "the unambiguous criticism with which the Catholic institutional Church faced the Hitler movement until 1933, a glorious chapter in its political discernment."[11]

The behavior of the Protestant Church was, according to Wehler, "diametrically opposed" to that. There was "no fundamental distancing, to say nothing of official, outspoken criticism of National Socialism."[12] Seventy percent of Protestants at church elections declared themselves in favor of so-called "German Christians", who unreservedly used the Hitler salute in the spirit of National Socialism, while a minority had to improvise and organized into the "Confessing Church" movement. The Protestant church historian Kurt Nowak writes that Hitler's seizure of power became "a catalyst for unbridled hope" in Protestant circles. At the time, there was even "no one who surpassed the members of the Confessing Church" in enthusiasm for the national people's state.[13] In any case, the "Confessing Church" was vehemently opposed to National Socialist ideology and especially to the state's interference in the church, but not to the state itself, and in some cases their attitude toward National Socialist influence was even sympathetic, as Protestant historian Günther van Norden emphasizes.

Catholics, however, as always, were less susceptible to nationalist overtones, because they saw themselves as supranational. To them, Hitler's seizure of power in 1933 posed a problem. Through free elections, Adolf Hitler had risen to the position of the legitimate head of state government. Even though the Church kept her distance, at this point, she had to relinquish total opposition to the Nazi party and her general prohibition of membership in it. With a concordat between the Vatican and the German Reich, which the previous government had already prepared, the Vatican attempted to secure the position of institutional Catholicism under international law. At the very least, the Catholic Church managed, according to historian Rudolf Lill, "essentially to keep her independence in totalitarian Germany", especially since "Catholic clergy—in contrast to Protestant pastors— were protected from having to collaborate with the NSDAP."[14] That was certainly part of the reason why "Catholicism—unlike

Protestantism—was substantially spared the incursion of Nazi ideology into its cults and teaching", according to Protestant church historian Gerhard Besier's evaluation.[15] In Bamberg, contemporary historian Werner Blessing notes: "Active Catholic churchgoers, though they had become smaller in number, persisted in their religious habits, and withdrew themselves like no other large group from the Nazi regime's claim to control their worldview."[16] Russian civilian workers joined in the 1942 Corpus Christi procession in Bamberg.

How to evaluate the concordat between the empire and the Vatican remains controversial among historians, since it improved the image of the new Nazi government, and in the end was unable to prevent the totalitarian suppression of many ecclesial associations. Research has come largely to reject the claim that the concordat put massive pressure on the Catholic Centre Party (along with the small civil parties and thus such representatives as later president Theodor Heuss) to approve the 1933 Enabling Act that effectively disempowered parliament.

In any case, the party researcher Jürgen W. Falter, who has conducted new research on the Weimar Reichstag elections, notes: "Protestants were on average twice as susceptible to the Nazi party as Catholics were." And he arrives at the following conclusion: "If there had only been Catholics, a Nazi takeover would probably never have happened."[17] And regarding the subsequent struggle between the Church and the state, Günther van Norden arrives at the following conclusion: "While in the Protestant sphere there was broad—though decreasing—cooperation with the system, with a growing readiness to resist, there was in the Catholic milieu wide and increasing resistance to the system, with a decreasing readiness to cooperate." In his research project, historian Heinz Boberach notes that during World War II, Gestapo reports on Catholics repeatedly mention the topic of sermons "on the fact that the current war was a punishment by God for the godlessness and lack of morality in Nazi leadership."[18] The Protestant Church, by contrast, says Günther van Norden, "did not understand the unleashing of war by the German rulers as such; rather, in complete agreement within the official empire church all the way up to the 'Confessing Church', she called on her faithful to do their duty, perform their service, and make the sacrifice for their native country, true to tradition—in this area, she had no critical potential."[19] It is a credit to the "Confessing Church", of course, that even without a supporting structure, she then invoked Christian unity across all nations against the modern idols of state, race, and national character. And these Protestant preachers eventually saw the war as a punishment by God; indeed, they even feared—certainly not unjustifiably—a persecution of Christians in the event of a victorious outcome to the war.

The power of Christianity was evidenced most of all in the resistance of Christians to the violent dictatorships of the twentieth century. Martyrdom, which had shaped the image of the Church in the first centuries, returned on a massive scale. The Christian idea of sacrifice influenced many of those who gave their lives in the resistance. Innumerable Christians died for their faith in Russia, where churches were almost completely destroyed. The historian of modernity Hans-Ulrich Wehler from Bielefeld summarizes the situation in Germany in the following way:

> Overall, the Catholic Church demonstrates a record that is as nightmarish as it is proud of suffering and sacrifice. Half of all priests, 8,021 clergymen, were affected by coercive measures, and 418 priests were taken to concentration camps, where 110 of them died. Another 59 clergymen were executed or murdered. The number of victims and the extent of arbitrary acts [of cruelty] far outnumbers the burden placed on Protestant pastors and on the "Confessing Church".[20]

In 2017, leading expert Helmut Moll corrected the tally of German martyrs in the twentieth century to a total of 241 murdered priests.[21] Thus, Catholic priests were the most persecuted professional group in Nazi Germany. Worldwide, in the twentieth century, the Catholic Church has recorded more than 12,000 witnesses to the faith, i.e., those who died for their faith. However, to honor the many German Protestant martyrs, it must be noted that they often had to invent their resistance independently, so to speak, without a church, completely left to their own devices, and all the more heroically for that; consider, for example, the impressive Protestant pastors Paul Schneider and Dietrich Bonhoeffer, who both died for their faith with amazing courage. Catholics, however, had been familiar with state persecution since the culture wars under Bismarck, so that the

Catholic sphere and the Catholic Church itself proved to be considerably more resistant. We must acknowledge both churches, however, as historian Manfred Gailus does, for having been "probably the most difficult social and cultural barriers to a complete implementation of the totalitarian Nazi claim to rule and worldview."[22] A frontal attack against the churches "was an exceedingly risky venture even for the firmly established National Socialism, which was very clear to the more intelligent ones among its leaders."[23]

According to historian Thomas Nipperdey, "the intensity of Catholic subculture, and even the fortified ghetto, certainly made possible—and actually put into practice—the Catholic Church's self-identification as the people's church, her resistance in time of crisis to left- and right-wing totalitarianism after 1918 as well as after 1933, and—in the long run—her potential for self-renewal."[24]

3. Euthanasia: Why the Nazis Hated Original Sin

The idea of "inferior races" was forbidden to Christians by their conviction that they were made in the image of God. And their belief in original sin made the idea of a spotless "master race" unacceptable.

To many people, the idea of original sin actually seems completely absurd, even scandalous. If it exists at all, sin is something personal, and it cannot be inherited. Indeed, it is quite right to reject collective punishment, blood revenge, and collective guilt. Herbert Schnädelbach regarded the claim that all men are corrupted by original sin as an offense to his freedom and dignity, and he rebuked this idea as "inhumane".[25] However, he, too, drastically misunderstood this term.

In reality, original sin means a phenomenon that every person can experience on a daily basis: namely, the fact that, on the one hand, people always carry the notions of peace, joy, life, beauty, and perfection within themselves and are eager to realize them, but, on the other hand, they repeatedly fail to achieve them, or at least they never attain perfection. The Bible gives the following explanation for this failure: God created the world to be good, and he gave men the desire for perfection; however, a disruption occurred, which has since then been hindering men in their attainment of this perfection. Since the biblical image of God and man is personal, this disruption can only be explained by a malignant decision made all the way back by the first human beings, the original sin in paradise, which then had an effect on all their descendants. Regardless of one's stance on the biblical interpretation, the phenomenon it describes is indisputable: we are all born into a situation that is shaped by the guilt of other people. We cannot escape being formed by this guilt, either: man is "built from ... crooked wood", as the great Enlightenment philosopher Immanuel Kant (1724–1804) described him—that is, he is crippled by Evil.[26] Kant says, there is "innate guilt ... which is so called because it can be perceived just as early as the use of freedom in the human being may manifest itself."[27] And when Kant then states it more precisely, by saying that "we must indeed presuppose that a germ of the good in its entire purity has remained, that it could not be extirpated or corrupted", then he describes the Catholic understanding of original sin exactly, while for Luther, man is radically corrupted and therefore completely dependent on divine grace, without being able to do real good himself.[28]

Human weakness, which became a problem with original sin, was of course repulsive to all movements, left- as well as right-wing ones, that tended toward the worship of man: to some Enlightenment philosophers, to the bourgeoisie of the nineteenth century, who believed in progress, and most of all, to Friedrich Nietzsche, to whom original sin [because it requires the sacrifice of God himself for redemption] was the evil "stroke of genius on the part of *Christianity*".[29] In contrast, he made "strength" into the creed of an entire generation: "What is evil?—Whatever springs from weakness. What is happiness?—The feeling that power *increases*—that resistance is overcome. Not contentment, but more power; *not* peace at any price, but war; *not* virtue, but efficiency (virtue in the Renaissance sense, *virtù*, virtue free of moral acid)."[30] And Nietzsche drew ruthless conclusions. Inspired by the Darwinian idea of the battle for existence and the survival of the fittest, he wanted the higher breeding of a "European race": "The weak and the botched shall perish: first principle of *our* charity. And one should help them to it. What is more harmful than any vice?—Practical sympathy for the botched and the weak—Christianity."[31] This brilliant and passionate philosopher was clear-sighted in his recognition of Christianity as the resolute enemy of such misanthropic ideas. And we cannot really say that the euthanasia practiced by the Nazis, in the course of which tens of thousands of disabled people were murdered, was a misunderstanding of these ideas, even if Nietzsche also wished for some "well-bred" Jews for his "rule of noble races".

Friedrich Nietzsche was right: compassion is a Christian invention. Not that pagans were not compassionate at all, but the sick, the weak, the disabled were above all seen as those struck by the gods, with whom it was best not to be too concerned, so as not to lose divine favor the way these had. In contrast to that, even in the Old Testament, but most of all in the New, the poor, the sick, and the disabled are considered friends of God; Jesus calls them blessed. Moreover, he says that in these people, one encounters the Son of God himself. Of course, this entirely new attitude, this self-giving love for the weak, made Christianity incredibly attractive. Rich pagans had given buildings and entertainment to their fellow citizens, instead of giving alms to the poor. The Christians, however, sensitized an entire society to poverty. French ancient historian Paul Veyne notes: "Old people's homes, orphanages, hospitals and so on are institutions that appear only with the Christian epoch, the very names for them being neologisms in Latin and Greek."[32] When Roman emperor Julian the Apostate wanted to change course once more, twenty years after the death of Emperor Constantine, and re-introduce paganism, he invented pagan care facilities to this end, which were supposed to make the old gods look a little more warm-hearted. But in two years, this specter has already disappeared, and the religion whose two main commandments were "Love your God!" and "Love your neighbor!" continued on its path. For example, Gaul was covered with an entire network of xenodochia, i.e., hostels for pilgrims. When the cities dwindled, monasteries attended to the poor. Burgundian Cluny, which for a while was the largest abbey in the West, distributed seventeen thousand meals to the poor annually in the twelfth century. When the cities were re-founded after the turn of the millennium, soon each of them also had a Holy Spirit hospital. Saint Francis of Assisi is the towering example of merciful love in the Middle Ages. His conversion was set in motion when he kissed a leper for the first time, dismounting his horse and holding his nose because of the smell—a breakthrough that led to his new life. No order over the centuries has given rise to a social movement comparable to the one the Franciscans unleashed.

Passion piety, which is alien to us today, was of great importance to individual people, which made many capable of compassion in the first place; by compassionately contemplating the suffering of Jesus, one developed the fundamental attitude of actively sharing the suffering of other people, too.

Such compassion was alien to the new pagans, who wanted to form a "master race" in the twentieth century. It was Darwinism and genetics that paved the way: according to these, the law of the survival of the fittest is a natural law, according to which what is higher defeats what is weaker, and thus in the same way the stronger race defeats the weaker ones, which do not even have a right to exist. The idea was to demand a morality of high breeding instead of a Christian morality of weakness. The well-known literary historian John Carey provides evidence that many European intellectuals harbored such attitudes: self-aware mankind was supposed to rise to the status of the subject of selection, and would thereby arrive at hitherto undreamed-of utopian heights.[33] Josef Mengele was not alone intellectually when he was standing on the ramp at Auschwitz and selecting Jews, and neither were the doctors who carried out the euthanasia.

When we look at the pre-history of Hitler's euthanasia campaign, which was the killing of the terminally ill and disabled, in the course of which one hundred twenty thousand people were murdered, it becomes apparent that the discussion started around 1900 with the question of the "right to death". It was continued after World War I with "redeeming death for the terminally ill". Then the cost of the upkeep of "burdensome lives" was added to the issue. Finally, the killing of incurably ill newborns was approved, which then opened up the floodgates for the elimination of so-called "unworthy life". The Nazis simply ruthlessly implemented what had been previously thought.

Not only the functionary elite, but also the churches offered resistance, because euthanasia was diametrically opposed to basic Christian convictions. Pope Pius XI (1857–1939) declared categorically that state authorities may "never directly harm, or tamper with the integrity of the body, either for the reasons of eugenics or for any other reason."[34] It was Christians most of all who opposed this barbarism. The resistance came, as historian Michael Schwartz notes, "doubtless most strongly from the churches, and, much more inconsistently and conditionally, from the circles of physicians and jurists."[35] The

Protestant church historian Kurt Nowak further differentiates this by saying that, put simply, all the way to the end, the Protestant side did not find a way to resolve the practical ambiguities involved in the protective measures it took for the sick, while the Catholic side offered the most determined resistance, because it assumed "an uncompromising stance" and managed to achieve a breakthrough in at least one case: in the public outcry of indictment by "the lion of Münster", Bishop Clemens August Graf von Galen (1878–1946).[36]

4. In the Face of the Holocaust: Christians and Jews— Unmixed and Undivided for Two Thousand Years

However, as we know, the killing of the mentally ill and of the disabled in gas chambers during the euthanasia campaign was only the prelude, the rehearsal, for an even larger mass murder: the genocide on the Jews, the Shoa. The Nazis attacked two groups whom Christians actually cared about a great deal in different ways. But after the Shoa, Christians, too, had to question themselves critically about whether some things they had said and done in their two-thousand-year history may have been ill-fated, indeed, scandalous, when seen in the grim light of the horrors of Auschwitz. At this stage, though, every historical judgment is subjected to overwhelming scrutiny. For in view of the horror of the Shoa, even the smallest offense that at some point in the past might have represented a step toward this crime against humanity becomes absolutely unpardonable. At the same time, to avoid any historical evaluation would be dangerous, too, because it would make it impossible to speak in a nuanced way about what came before and what came after, and the Shoa would, so to speak, drop out of history; we would no longer be able to learn anything for the future from it. For this reason, we owe it to the victims to examine the often difficult relationship between Jews and Christians in a historically serious way, in light of current scholarship.

How It All Began: From Fraternal Strife to the Protection of Jews

The New Testament at times uses pretty strong words for "the Jews". Of course, it has to be taken into consideration that these are "negative judgments by Jews on Jews, by Jews who believe in the Messiah on other Jews", as the biblical exegete Gerd Theissen emphasizes.[37] They reflect the conflicts between early Christians and those Jews who rigorously rejected Christianity. At the same time, Paul's tone is very different in the Letter to the Romans, where the Jews are "brothers", children of the promise and of God's perduring predestination, whose lack of faith in the Messiah Jesus Christ would remain a "mystery". The Jewish religious scholar David Flusser can even understand the aggressive tone of certain other statements in the New Testament. For previous Jews, these statements were virtually a "historical necessity in order for Christianity to become a world religion." And, Flusser says, that is why these statements have to "be somewhat defended against the theology that came after Auschwitz."[38] Contradicting the notion represented by some theologians that the New Testament has strong anti-Jewish elements, scholarship has now arrived at a different conclusion. The prestigious Judaist Heinz Schreckenberg explains that "the assumption that the enmity toward the Jews is already inherent in the nature and the core of the New Testament is inaccurate."[39] As the ancient historian Alexander Demandt states so concisely, "According to Jewish law, Jesus' death was justified", since his claim of being the Messiah was considered blasphemy. For this reason, he says, it is certainly not an invention of the authors of the New Testament "that the high priests and their following were the driving force behind Jesus' trial, as the Gospels portray it." [40] These facts are not contradicted by the view of Haim Cohn, [who was] the supreme judge of the State of Israel, that "the crucifixion was ... carried out by Roman troops under the supreme command of the governor."[41] That was simply the legal situation at the time.

For this reason it was unjust for Christian polemics to raise the accusation of "deicide" soon afterward. Augustine had already rejected this accusation in the following classic way: "Had [the Jews] known Him, they would never have crucified the Lord of glory."[42] Pope Gregory the Great went even further by saying what is still convincing for many Christians to this day: all sinful men are guilty of Jesus' death, including sinful Christians. Gregory the Great also vehemently opposed forced conversions, just as popes would do repeatedly later on, and confirmed Judaism's status as a "permitted religion", which secured extensive rights for Jews. Origen (ca. 185–254), the great teacher of the early Christians, praised the Jews: "If anyone ... were to compare them with the present conduct of other nations, he would admire none more, since as far as it is humanly possible they removed everything not of advantage to mankind, and accepted only what is good."[43] And Gregory of Nazianzus (ca. 329–390) says: "Such noble figures, then, are not to be overlooked because they lived before the time of the cross, but should rather be acclaimed for having lived in accordance with the cross".[44] Nevertheless, there were also lapses, such as when John Chrysostom (ca. 390–407) allowed himself to be carried away and uttered vile invectives in the kind of tense situation in which many Christians tended to find themselves with regard to Judaism. He later regretted his words, speaking of the "nobility of the Jews" and even granting them a place of primacy in salvation history. Along with Michael Toch, who teaches at Hebrew University in Jerusalem, we have to note that the Christian understanding of the Jews as irrefutable witnesses to the Christian truth, which was already supported in their time, also led to "the categorical prohibition of violence"; indeed, it made "the protection of the Jews until the end of time a duty".[45]

But Jewish polemics weren't long in coming, either. The so-called Amidah, for example, the key prayer in Jewish prayer services, which pious Jews have prayed three times a day since the second century, reads threateningly: "For the apostates let there be no hope. And let the arrogant government be speedily uprooted in our days. Let the *noẓerim* and the *minim* be destroyed in a moment. And let them be blotted out of the Book of Life and not be inscribed together with the righteous."[46] This was meant to refer to the Roman authorities as well as heretical Jewish groups, among them Jewish Christians. According to Michael Toch, "Judaism in late Antiquity gave no sign of being ready to include Christianity in the blessing of divine revelation."[47]

In late Antiquity, Jews actively and vigorously participated in civic and urban life. Ancient historian Karl L. Noethlichs emphasizes that accounts of their miserable situation that are supposed to be general descriptions of Jewish life are "Christian ideology".[48] The medieval popes conscientiously practiced their duty to protect them, which they had been instructed to fulfill since Gregory the Great. Pope Alexander II (ca. 1010–1073) declared apodictically: the Jews shall be protected and their blood shall not be shed.[49] This statement was later included in the *Decretum Gratiani* of 1140. From then on, for four centuries, every pope issued a so-called *Sicut Judaeis* bull for the explicit protection of the Jews, with severe punishments for infringements. At times, special updates were included in these formal papal decrees: if trials against Jews were being held in order to extort money from them, false prosecutors were to receive the same punishment they had wanted to impose upon the Jews; insinuations of ritual murder and host desecrations were to be punished in the same way. Pope Gregory IX (1167–1241) insisted on the fair treatment of the Jews, because they "bear the image of the savior and are created by the Creator of the world", and regarding the murdering of Jews by crusaders, he gave the following warning: "They do not consider that Jesus Christ came in order to reconcile us in his blood, and to accept as children of God all human beings from every nation without difference in status and race." And for the German bishops, he arrived at the following formula: "Christians should share the same goodwill toward the Jews that we desire to be shown to Christians in pagan lands."[50] Nicholas IV (1227–1292) declared: "The Church has no patience for the subjection of Jews to injustice and accusations by those who confess to be Christians."[51] American historian Solomon Gayzel attests to the following about the popes: "When a Jewish community pressed its compliant ... the complaint was investigated, and if found justified, the guilty party was ordered to desist."[52] And as the prestigious Israeli historian Shlomo Simonsohn writes in the final volume of his edition of no less than 1,100 medieval papal proclamations regarding Jews, "It is probably fair to state that if the Apostolic See had had its way in the Middle Ages, the Jewish presence in most West European countries would have continued."[53]

The reason that the Jews lived such secluded lives in Christian surroundings had mostly to do with their strict food and purity requirements, which made eating with non-Jews downright impossible and forbade women to touch anyone. Provisions were put in place to prevent mixed marriages, which both parties rejected. One of these was self-identification through clothing. They tried to avoid conversions at all costs. According to the Babylonian Talmud, apostates from Judaism were even supposed to be killed, a requirement that was dropped, however, in the Middle Ages because of a lack of opportunities. Contact with non-Jews was generally avoided. Attempts were even made to prevent visual contact. Jews boarded up windows that looked out on a church or a crucifix.

While on the Christian side, there had long been a special genre of literature that was directed against the Jews, the general intellectual awakening in the twelfth century allowed for the emergence of vehemently anti-Christian literature. God's vengeance on the Christians became a key topic of Jewish Bible commentaries; Christians were enemies of God because of their worship of images alone, and were thus comparable to pagans. There was verbal abuse, admittedly mostly for use among the Jews themselves, of things held sacred by the Christians. But theological debates among Jews also became more heated, so that the Jews in France turned to the Inquisition, just then emerging, which as a result burned a work by the famous Jewish philosopher Moses Maimonides in 1233. But there were also efforts to bring about more tolerance. Thus, for example, the Talmud scholar Menachem Meiri (1249–1316) granted more legitimacy to Christianity than common practice at the time would suggest. On the Christian side, there were also very diverse statements made on the Jews, from Hildegard of Bingen's sympathetic attitude, to Bernard of Clairvaux's relatively friendly position, all the way to the invectives of Peter the Venerable, abbot of Cluny. Looking at this conflict between medieval Jews and Christians from a modern perspective, Viennese Judaist Kurt Schubert says that the following rule applies: "We need to distance ourselves from both."[54]

But there are also mutual positive influences. The great Christian Scholastics consulted the Jews to help them understand the Hebrew text of the Old Testament. Moses Maimonides exercised considerable influence on Thomas Aquinas, but also later on Meister Eckhart. Conversely, Israeli historian Avraham Grossmann describes the "distinct improvement ... in the status" of Jewish women in medieval Europe in comparison with the attitudes of the Talmud as well as of the Muslim world, which was due to the improvement of the status of women in the neighboring Christian societies.[55] Nevertheless, Jewish women remained disadvantaged. There is "no extant work created by a Jewish woman during the medieval period"[56] because "one of the major areas of discrimination against Jewish women in the Middle Ages was that of education and culture."[57]

There was no efficient administrative state in the Middle Ages, so that for Jews, there were only protection privileges that were personally granted by rulers, but that were nevertheless effective. But since these were not permanently valid "human rights", they had to be repeatedly renewed. At the same time, the absence of a strong state sometimes had its advantages, too. In the Middle Ages, every city was supposed to have only one synagogue, but in Rome, of all places, there were ten of them. And thus it was only the efficiency of the developing modern nation states that led to Jews being driven away on a massive scale from France, England, and most of all, Spain.

The Jewish Valley of Tears: The Medieval Persecution of the Jews

There were no Jewish pogroms in the first Christian millennium, except for the incidents in Visigothic Spain. Recent research has made astonishing discoveries about the causes of the terrible persecutions of the Jews in the High Middle Ages.

There were cock-and-bull stories that provided pretexts over and over for the tumultuous pogroms against the Jews that broke out in response to any old catastrophe. On the one hand, there was the absurd claim that Jews were committing ritual murder, that is that they were occasionally killing Christian children for their Paschal feast. On the other hand, there was the accusation of desecrating hosts, which to Christians were the "Body of Christ"; and finally, there was the charge of poisoning wells. Just as with the persecution of witches, in this case, too, southern European countries were hardly affected at all at first, and "this northern chimera could not even establish itself" in the south, as Michael Toch observes, while the lack of education and culture north of the Alps favored these mindless explosions of scattered popular rage.[58] According to Heinz Schreckenberg, they were mostly instigated by people "of low education and middling rank", "while it was often the prelates, of all people, who advocated for the persecuted."[59]

The Church vehemently opposed these outbursts of hatred and resentment. In a letter to the German bishops, Pope Innocent IV (ca. 1195–1254) makes the following complaint:

> Though the Bible lists among the commandments "thou shall not kill" and prohibits the Jews from touching any dead flesh on Passover, some falsely assert that the Jews share amongst themselves on that day the heart of a murdered child, believing this practice to stem from the

same Law, although it is clearly opposed to it, and thus they wickedly accuse them whenever a dead body happens to be found. These same people rage against the Jews because of this and many other figments of the imagination, depriving the Jews of all of their property, contrary to God and justice, despite the fact that they have been accused of nothing else, have confessed nothing, nor been convicted .... [And the Jews] are forced to wander in miserable exile from the places where they and their ancestors have lived since long before memory can recall.[60]

As far as the charge of host desecration goes, Pope Benedict XII ordered a thorough investigation of alleged incidents of this kind in Austria in 1338. If necessary, the Jews would be punished, he said, but if it turned out that they were innocent, the Christians involved would be charged, to ensure that such anti-Jewish riots, which often led to Jews being deprived of their goods, would no longer occur. Even an unfounded accusation of well poisoning incurred a penalty of excommunication, imposed by Pope Clement VI (around 1290–1352).

The popes repeatedly opposed the persecution of Jews. When in 1236, crusaders were raging against the Jews in Anjou, Poitou, and Bretagne, Pope Gregory IX wrote a sharply worded letter to the French bishops:

We have received a tearful and pitiful complaint from the Jews who live in the kingdom of France. The Crusaders of your districts and dioceses ... try to wipe the Jews almost completely off the face of the earth. In an unheard of and unprecedented outburst of cruelty, they have slaughtered in this mad hostility two thousand and five hundred of them—old and young, as well as pregnant women.... After foully and shamefully treating those who remained alive after this massacre, they carried off their goods and consumed them. And in order that they may be able to hide such an inhuman crime under the cover of virtue and in some way justify their unholy cause, they claim to have done the above and threaten to do worse, on the ground that the Jews refuse to be baptized. They do not sufficiently consider that ... those to whom God wants to be merciful are not to be compelled to the grace of baptism, rather they must want it voluntarily.... Therefore, lest such great temerity, if unpunished, continue to injure still others, we command that each of you force the inhabitants of your

dioceses who commit such excesses, to bring proper satisfaction for
the crimes perpetrated against the Jews and for the property stolen
from them. After giving due warning you may use ecclesiastical punishment without appeal.[61]

The wave of pogroms following the plague of 1348–50 affected
Germany especially. It was brutal, and in some towns even carefully organized by the authorities—for example, by Holy Roman
Emperor Charles IV and the city council in Nuremberg. Marxist
medieval historian František Graus emphasizes that there was a complete lack of this kind of agitation among the clergy. Pope Clement
VI even issued two bulls for the protection of Jews—without any
success. A coalition of patricians and guilds kept appearing on the
killing sprees. For the most part, it was all about money; they ruthlessly availed themselves of the opportunity to enrich themselves. In
Germany, there were thousands of victims. It is evident that even the
popes were powerless in the face of this superstitious popular turmoil.
In [the popes'] own sphere of control, in the Papal States, the Jews
were never seriously harassed. The well-known Protestant historian
Ferdinand Gregorovius (1821–1891) explains in his *History of the City
of Rome in the Middle Ages*: "Especially in Rome, Jews received a
more humane treatment than elsewhere in the Middle Ages."[62] In
1569, the creation of the ghettos took place, but there was no displacement, and the Jewish sermons prescribed by Pope Gregory XIII,
which the Jews had to attend, seemed to be merely a matter of duty,
and had no effect whatsoever.

Spain was a special case. In contrast to the prejudices that have been
voiced for a long time, research has found that the situation of the
Jews was no better in Muslim Spain. The first Jewish pogrom there
took place in 1066, in Muslim Granada, and previously, Jews had fled
from the Muslim regions to the Christian north. In fact, for a long
time Spain represented a great, positive exception; it was even spared
pogroms during the Great Plague in 1348. American Judaist Stephen
Haliczer notes: "In fact, during the High Middle Ages it seems that
Jews may have had more conflicts with each other than with their
Christian neighbors."[63] American historian David Nirenberg confirms this.[64] There was a relatively free atmosphere in Spain all the
way until the fifteenth century, according to Shlomo Simonsohn.[65]

But then Judaism itself fell into a deep crisis. In scholarly debates in Barcelona, in 1263, and also in Tortosa in 1413–1414, which were conducted in front of a large audience, an entirely new interpretation of Jewish Scripture, especially of the Talmud, emerged, spreading the impression that these Scriptures contained passages that confirmed that Jesus was the Messiah. They had a tremendous effect. Many Jews were profoundly unnerved, were voluntarily baptized along with their rabbis by the thousand, and became serious Catholics, according to Yosef Yerushalmi, professor of Judaism at Harvard.[66] Some even became priests and bishops. Today, it is estimated that the number of converts between 1381 and 1414 was in the tens of thousands and that because of this, the atmosphere among Jews was also troubled. In this situation, a pogrom developed in 1391 in Seville that spread all over Spain, whose perpetrators were immediately punished by the Aragonese king, who "took up a position of the clearest possible hostility to the murders and the forced conversions", as French historian Philippe Wolff says.[67]

But things were going to get even worse. The converted Jews were suspected of having only pretended to become Christians. Even though Pope Nicholas V (1397–1455) opposed such a disastrous development with all his might by ordering the punishment of anyone who did not acknowledge the converts as full Christians, he was not able to avert a catastrophe. People like Alfonso de Espina, the son of converts, enabled the Inquisition to track down and punish those converts who had not really become Christians. Many converts apparently had the notion, as Yerushalmi writes, "that, if the Judaizers could weeded out, their own Catholic orthodoxy would no longer be impugned."[68] That was a fatal error. It ended in the complete banishment of all Jews in 1492, although recent research has corrected the high numbers referenced earlier and assumes that there may "not have been much above 30,000 persons" (Henry Kamen).[69] But that was terrible enough. Tragically, during the phase of the "wild Inquisition", there was also a devastating persecution of the converted Jews who had originally set the whole development in motion, with four to five thousand victims. These measures, says the historian Horst Pietschmann, were not really taken for religious reasons, but were motivated by Spanish national interests, which demanded a unified religion for a unified country.[70] In the end, the notion of the "impure blood" of a person descended from Jews even emerged in Spain—an early form of racism, which completely contradicted Christian principles.

In addition, the so-called "Talmudic controversy" had been poisoning the atmosphere between Jews and Christians in Europe since the thirteenth century. The Talmud is a text that is deeply respected among Jews and that exists in two versions and includes doctrinal texts dating back to the second century. It was largely inaccessible to Christians because it was written in Hebrew. However, when the Jewish conflict about the "liberal" ideas of Moses Maimonides flared up and his followers were "excommunicated" by the Jewish communities, some of them had themselves baptized and then launched a counter-attack. One of these baptized Jews submitted to the Church passages from the Talmud that sounded anti-Christian. They were invectives about Jesus burning in hell, and about Mary as an impure adulteress and whore, etc. Jewish defenders of the Talmud attempted to interpret such passages as not being directed against Christians, but American historian David Berger is of the opinion that at the time, they could hardly have been understood in any other way.[71] Paris proceeded to burn the Talmud. But Pope Innocent IV made a different decision: he said that the Talmud belonged to Jewish orthodoxy, and it was only the blasphemies that had to be eliminated. This case was to be handled in exactly the same way as that of some Christian authors: by elimination of the offensive passages, but with no personal penalty. The Talmud conflict continued for a long time. Martin Luther's polemic against the Jews was kindled by the alleged blasphemies of the Talmud: [according to Peter von der Osten-Sacken, Luther believed that] "In the midst of Christendom—and with her tacit acquiescence—the Messiah, his Mother, even God himself are blasphemed. Wherever that occurs, it can only be the work of the devil."[72]

In any case, the Reformation did nothing to improve the situation of the Jews, but rather made it worse. Even though the Enlightenment was to contribute to the emancipation of the Jews, there were also opponents to this emancipation who are ranked among the greatest figures of their time: Voltaire called the Jews "the last of all nations", Kant called them a "nation of crooks" and unworthy of civil rights, Fichte saw a hatred of mankind in them, Herder made similar statements, and Hegel diagnosed them with a deficiency of personality and liberty.[73] Still, the progression could not be halted. In Germany, the emancipation of the Jews was first achieved by state bureaucracy, which instilled in the Jews a deep trust of the state. It began with Holy Roman Emperor Joseph II in Austria and was completed in the Revolution of 1848. Jews themselves had to adapt to the new circumstances—archaic religious rites were abolished, and it was the compulsory education of boys and girls that made the rise of the educated Jewish class possible. This was even more important than the increase in economic prosperity. In the nineteenth century, however, the pope's Papal States still had an anachronistic negative influence. More recent sources have revealed, however, that the Holy See still continued to intervene to prevent the forced conversion of Jewish children. Church historian Hubert Wolf, who has conducted research on this in the Vatican Archives, notes: "The fact that the Inquisition protected Jews from Catholics fits into our image [of the Church] as poorly as the [Church's] explicit renunciation of forced baptisms by fire and sword."[74]

Murderous Ideas: Racist Anti-Semitism and Its Consequences

In the nineteenth century, racist anti-Semitism began to appear, which, even though it had already been discernible in Spain, now developed into a pseudo-scientific system through the newly emerging field of genetics, among other ways. At the same time, the great success of Jewish emancipation led to social envy, and the liberalism of assimilated Jews who were distanced from religion led to resentment in conservative, including religiously conservative, circles. This mix was explosive. Karl Marx, himself the son of a Jewish convert, surmised: "What is the secular basis of Judaism? *Practical* need, self-interest. What is the secular cult of the Jew? *Haggling*. What is his secular God? *Money*."[75] And the Jerusalem historian Schulamit Volkov noted "that social democracy was not able to overcome anti-Jewish sentiments either at its roots or among some of its leading figures, where it existed 'subliminally'."[76]

To Christianity, which was sent "to all nations" and whose first followers had all been Jews, every form of racism was alien. However, František Graus, who himself survived Auschwitz, described with really moving psychological empathy the temptations that can occur in the ongoing coexistence of two religions: "The idea of possessing the 'right faith' makes it possible for the have-nots in town and country, as Christians, to feel superior even to the rich 'believing' Jews, just as it allows Jewish beggars to look down on Christian authorities with a certain degree of contempt."[77] The reciprocal negative stereotypes and standard reproaches that developed between these two religions in centuries-long conflicts have to be seen against this background, with the understanding, of course, that the anti-Jewish stereotypes held by the Christians had a much more devastating effect because the Jews were always a helpless minority. Pope Gregory the Great had already rejected the charge of deicide, and the Roman Catechism, which had been forming people for centuries, confirmed this rejection; and the popes (the last one was Pope Benedict XIV, 1740–1758) had repeatedly intervened against the malignant accusation of ritual murder and sacrileges involving hosts. In 1882, several Protestant faculties participated in an investigation, requested by the Hungarian chief rabbi, which came to the conclusion that the charges of ritual murder "had to be deemed a wicked untruth."[78] The popes had also regularly issued declarations of protection, but all that could not prevent a theologically coarse anti-Judaism that broke forth repeatedly, and also ensured that the increasingly rampant racist anti-Semitism did not meet with sufficiently resolute resistance.

However, the historian Olaf Blaschke notes that Catholics "rejected the hatred of Jewish people, which was nothing more than racial ideology, and distanced themselves from anti-Semitic parties."[79] In fact, as Thomas Nipperdey says, "all anti-Semitic propositions were rejected by the Centre; anti-Semites considered both the Centre and Catholics to be their opponents. There were anti-Semitic incursions in Protestant voting districts, but not in Catholic ones."[80] At the end of the Weimar Republic, about 25 to 30 percent of Jews voted for the Catholic Centre Party. In 1928, Cardinal Faulhaber of Munich explicitly instructed his priests to avoid all anti-Semitism, for the reason that the Church and the synagogue belonged together, and that the sins of the Christian people must share in the indictment for the Crucifixion. He was a member of the society of the "Friends of Israel"—which had been established in January 1926, and which eventually numbered 19 cardinals, 278 bishops, and about 3,000 priests worldwide—and he declared: "All kinds of anti-Semitism are to be avoided; moreover, they shall be fought explicitly and torn out by their roots."[81] Because of its political plans, which were more extensive, this society had to be disbanded later on, but Pope Pius XI declared on that occasion: the Holy See "condemns with all its might the hatred directed against a people which was chosen by God; that particular hatred, in fact, which today commonly goes by the name anti-Semitism."[82] In his encyclical *Mit brennender Sorge* ("With Burning Concern"), which was the first ever to be written in German and had to be smuggled into Germany in adventurous ways and reproduced in secret in order to be read on Palm Sunday 1937 from all the pulpits, the pope severely attacked Nazi racism. Eventually, his statement that Christians were "spiritual Semites", which he made in 1938 to Belgian pilgrims, became famous. In general, Pius XI acted in a demonstratively pro-Jewish way, housed Jews in the Vatican, employed them, and befriended them. Finally, he had an anti-racism encyclical prepared shortly before the outbreak of the war, which, however, was not published by his successor, Pius XII.

On the Protestant side, however, there were downright bizarre developments among some theologians. They claimed that Jesus had in truth not been Jewish, but Arian. On the whole, in Protestantism there was, according to Hans-Ulrich Wehler, a "stark ethnonationalist anti-Semitic coloring to the new political theology",[83] and the Protestant historian Gerhard Besier paints a gloomy picture of official German Protestantism, where Protestants of Jewish descent were asked no longer to attend "German" services, but to found their own parishes.[84] In contrast, in October 1943, the Synod of the Prussian Union of Churches issued a proclamation that denounced the mass murder of Jews and that was to be read out on the Day of Repentance and Prayer (*Buß- und Bettag*). And then there was also Dietrich Bonhoeffer, who found his way out of the entrenched thought patterns of anti-Judaism, and who spoke about the permanent revelation from God to the Jews and advocated for the church's support of Jews as Jews. The Protestant priest Helmut Gollwitzer preached at the Day of Repentance and Prayer in 1938 about solidarity with the persecuted, saying "we have to become red with shame and are all afflicted with guilt."[85] His parish rectory became a refuge for non-Arian Christians. On the Catholic side, the dean of

the cathedral of Berlin, Bernhard Lichtenberg, who was later beat-
ified by Pope John Paul II, had people praying "for the priests in
the concentration camps, for the Jews, and for the non-Arians", and
on the occasion of Kristallnacht in 1938, he declared: "Outside, the
synagogue is burning. It is also a house of God."[86] Lichtenberg was
arrested and died as a martyr. The chair of the German Bishops'
Conference, Cardinal Bertram, had resorted to submitting petitions
continually to the government of the German Empire. These protests fizzled out and were to a large degree ineffective, but he did not
leave it at that. In 1943, the German Bishops' Conference published
the "Pastoral Letter on the Ten Commandments", which was read in
all Catholic churches: "Killing is in itself evil, even if it is carried
out allegedly in the interest of the common good: the killing of the
mentally disabled or mentally ill who are innocent and defenseless, of
the incurably ill and the mortally wounded, of people with hereditary
illnesses and newborns unfit for life, of the innocent hostages and the
unarmed criminals and prisoners of war, of people of foreign races or
foreign descent."[87] It was most of all the courageous Berlin bishop
Konrad Graf von Preysing who urged such interventions and who
sought to move Pope Pius XII, who he personally knew well and
who held him in great esteem, to advocate publicly for the Jews in
that same year.

The Deputy: The Controversy over Pope Pius XII

But Pius XII hesitated. He was a diplomat, highly educated, subtle,
pious, but also courageous. When he was papal nuncio in Munich,
at the beginning of the post-war period, he intrepidly withstood the
pressure from the Spartacists. As early as 1924, he had called National
Socialism "perhaps the most dangerous heresy of our times".[88] Then
he had loyally and wisely served the temperamental Pope Pius XI
as cardinal secretary of state. On the eve of World War II, the cardinals had elected him pope perhaps also because they were hoping
to find in him the skill required in the terrible situation of a cruel
war, where Catholics were shooting at other Catholics. On the one
hand, he had to manage not to be perceived as taking sides in the
war, so that he could act as peacemaker; on the other hand, he had
to make sure especially that Catholics, who were in a permanent state

of mortal danger on both sides of the front, would not be misled by their chief shepherd. In the face of unbridled, naked violence, displayed especially by the Nazis and impervious to moral arguments, these tasks essentially amounted to squaring the circle. But there was no possibility of escape from this task, and Pius XII was not thinking of fleeing, either.

His appeals for peace were dramatic and characterized by real passionate concern, but they were all completely ineffective, just as Benedict XV's suggestions had been during World War I. The Vatican was also tirelessly committed to helping prisoners on both sides. When Rome was threatened by bombing, the pope publicly declared that he would immediately proceed to the site of the bombing. In doing so, he saved the Eternal City from destruction. On the day when the armistice was signed, Romans spontaneously flocked to St. Peter's Square to thank the pope. After the war, since he had lived in Germany for twelve years, he contributed to Germans' being able to take their place in the world again. At his death in 1958, there was shock all over the world. Leonard Bernstein, before lifting his conductor's baton, asked the auditorium in New York to observe a minute of silence. Practically all Jewish organizations as well as official representatives of the state of Israel thanked the pope for saving thousands of Jews from being murdered, especially in Italy, but also in other countries, through his tireless individual actions. According to today's research, some 100,000 to 200,000 people were spared. Pius XII was an unquestioned global authority when he passed away, almost excessively venerated by Catholics.

But then, on February 20, 1963, the play *The Deputy* by the hitherto unknown young author Rolf Hochhuth was performed in Berlin, which subjected the pope to scathing criticism. Pius XII's "silence" on the extermination of Jews had been a scandal, it said. Therefore, the pope was to be blamed for the Holocaust. The piece proved to have been poorly researched and was criticized for formal defects, but it was so geared to make an impact that it immediately cast the pope in an evil light not only in Germany but worldwide. Since then, the "pope's silence" has become the hallmark of Pope Pius XII. After the vociferous battles between outraged followers of the pope and admirers of the author died down, historical research led to more clarity:

On July 26, 1942, a declaration by all ten Christian churches in the Netherlands, issued by Cardinal de Jong from Utrecht, was read from all pulpits in Catholic and reformed churches in the Netherlands, which was occupied by the Germans; this declaration denounced in no uncertain terms the deportation of Jews. The Nazis' reaction was rapid and harsh: the immediate deportation, this time of all baptized Jews, too, among them the philosopher and Carmelite Edith Stein. Sister Pasqualina, Pius XII's German housekeeper describes how the pope, when he heard about it, threw a letter of protest on the persecution of Jews that he had already completed into the fireplace, with the following words as she remembers them: "If the letter by the Dutch bishops cost 40,000 lives, then my protest would perhaps cost 200,000. I cannot take the responsibility for that. It is better to remain silent in public for the sake of these poor people, just as I have done up to this day, and to do everything that is humanly possible in silence." Nevertheless, Cardinal de Jong, just as the bishop of Preysing would do later, asked Pius XII to make a public appeal. But after the experience in the Netherlands, Pius apparently feared that a similarly aggressive protest would unleash a global catastrophe, the victims of which would be many innocent people. Protestant martyr Dietrich Bonhoeffer took a similar view when he said that "today in the matter of the Jewish question" the Church could "not encroach on the state's sphere of responsibility." Resistance, he said, was an issue of "the individual Christian, who knows himself called to the task." Declarations by "the Church" would inadvertently involve all members of the church, including the weak.[89] Despite all this, the pope spoke out. In his Christmas message of 1942, broadcast on Radio Vatican, he spoke in an accusing tone about "hundreds of thousands, who through no fault of their own, at times because of their nationality or race, are abandoned to death or continuing extermination."[90] These words were understood not only by the international press, but also by the Nazis, as unambiguous protest against the persecution of the Jews, and the Nazis immediately reacted with repressive measures. That was still not enough for some. Instead, American president Roosevelt expected the pope explicitly to take sides against Germany. But Pius XII considered that irresponsible. Thus, he encouraged the bishops of Germany, in private letters that have since been made available, to raise their voices in public. In

Rome and all of Italy, he urged monasteries and other ecclesial institutions to hide Jews, so that there were hundreds of Jews in the Vatican alone. Because the Nazis in turn wanted to prevent a more dramatic protest, they did not interfere with this and deported only 1,000 of the 8,000 Jews they had been ordered to take from Rome. In France, Serge Klarsfeld, who for decades after the war tracked down Nazi leaders, confirmed that the high clergy, who answered to Pius XII, were effective in their protest against the Vichy regime, apparently saving many Jews.

But is that enough? In light of the Holocaust, from today's secure position, one can only answer, with the wisdom of one who has come later: no! This wise pope certainly knew that a great show of protest would certainly have benefitted his reputation. He would have been regarded as the resplendent confessor pope, as Pius VII had been as a prisoner of Napoleon. But Hitler was no Napoleon. He was capable of boundless vengeance and would have mercilessly struck down many simple Catholics while he was lashing out. For this reason, research agrees that no one knows if even worse things would have happened in the event of a more extensive public intervention by the pope. And it is also clear that pressure from the Roman pope would not have induced the Nazis to abandon the core of their ideology, their fanatical, murderous anti-Semitism. After all, they were still murdering Jews when the Russians were standing at their gates. The euthanasia program had been a different issue; it did not touch upon this ideological core, and to that extent, the protest by Bishop von Galen succeeded temporarily. Besides, the "moral capital" of the Vatican, which has been discussed, had already been exposed as worthless during World War I.

Pius XII was no anti-Semite, and he was a determined opponent of National Socialism. But he found himself facing a terrible dilemma. After the well-known terrors of the Stalin era and the hundreds of Catholic priests murdered by Communists worldwide on the one hand, and the mass murder by the Nazis on the other hand, the victory of either the Communists or of the Nazis would have been an equal nightmare for the Church. That explains the mode of desperation Pius XII was in during the entire war. It was certainly not a lack of courage, and it was also not a narrowing of this cosmopolitan man's perspective so that he was focused only on the Church; it was probably rather the fear of something worse—worse for others—that held him back. His contemporaries, who had themselves been subjected to circumstances of naked violence, were probably better able to understand this than his accusers were. Thus we may say with all due caution: Pope Pius XII was a sensitive intellectual who was overwhelmed by the tragic task that was set before him. He says so himself in his will: "The realization of the deficiencies, shortcomings and faults of so long a pontificate in an epoch so grave, brings my insufficiencies and unworthiness more clearly to my mind."[91] But no one has been able to show persuasively what man would not have been overwhelmed by such as task as this.

The radical shift among Germans from exuberant adoration to aggressive rejection of the pope continues to astonish everyone. It was here in Germany, of all places, that a person like Rolf Hochhuth was to arise, and here, later on, that Daniel Goldhagen, with his controversial theses, was to celebrate his greatest success. The well-known British biographer of Hitler, Ian Kershaw, who considers Daniel Goldhagen's sweeping accusations against the Germans and against the churches to be groundless, explains it in terms of "the continuing troubled relationship of Germans with their own past".[92]

It will be necessary to draw on social psychological explanations in this context. Authorities apparently hold a special attraction to Germans. No other Catholics are so fixated on the pope, either, whether as followers or aggressive opponents. For this reason the papacy is especially well suited to serve as a means of exoneration for their own burdensome past. When the author of this volume was in Vienna with a group of students in 1976, the state secretary in the Austrian ministry of foreign affairs said to the students, with hardly any irony, that the greatest achievement of Austrian foreign policy had been to make Beethoven Austrian, and Hitler German. Many Austrians to this day consider themselves victims of the German Nazis. For a long time, Germany did not want to hear anything about a common past, either. After a long delay, the Frankfurt trial of Auschwitz was finally held in 1963. The solicitor general, Fritz Bauer, was subjected to terrible invectives. Many people simply did not want to hear anything about it. In that same year, it was a welcome outlet to be able to accuse the Italian pope of culpability for the Holocaust, even though at the time he was held up as the highest moral authority imaginable. The title "the deputy" takes on a very different meaning against this background. This was also the time when many were hypocritically rebuking the army officer von Stauffenberg for not simply shooting Hitler.

Of course, the socio-psychological impulse to distance oneself from one's own history and to blame others for it does not lead to healthy self-confidence but to a distorted perception of reality. That is an essential reason for the particular aggressiveness and resistance to facts to be found in German criticism of the Church. A general attack on Church history helped make it easier to overlook the past guilt of one's own parents and grandparents, almost all of whom failed to protest—or worse. And such mechanisms of self-justification are still at work to this day. In 2000, when the old and ailing Pope John Paul II stood at Yad Vashem, the Holocaust memorial in Israel, and with a trembling voice lamented the horror of this crime against humanity, even Israeli and American critics fell silent. Only in Germany did a few people level the criticism that the pope should have apologized for the Holocaust more clearly and more vehemently. Consider this: the Polish pope, himself a victim of German forced labor, is accused by the Germans of not having apologized for German injustices unreservedly enough. *Difficile est satiram non scribere*—it is difficult not to write a satire about that!

The End of Fraternal Strife: Confessions of Guilt and Understanding

Despite the indisputable failure of many Christians, in the end we have to remember that the operators of Auschwitz and of the entire machinery of human extermination were enemies of Jews and in the same way enemies of Christians, and that Goebbels noted in his journals that after the Jews had been dealt with, after the "final victory", the Catholics would be "attended to" next.[93]

In August 1945, the Catholic bishops thanked those "who had shared their sparse daily bread with the innocently persecuted non-Arians", and they admitted: "Many Germans, even from within our ranks, allowed themselves to be beguiled by the false teachings of National Socialism and remained indifferent in the face of crimes against human liberty and human dignity; many aided and abetted the crimes through their attitude, many became criminals themselves."[94]

Cardinal von Preysing from Berlin, who of all the Catholic bishops had perhaps the most clear-eyed perspective on the crime of National Socialism, and who had repeatedly urged the chair of the German Bishops' Conference, the hesitant Cardinal Bertram, but also the pope, to stage resolute protests, spoke in 1949 of five million Jews having been killed. Pope Pius XII had made him cardinal, together with Bishop von Galen from Münster, even though their dioceses were actually too small for that. It was a recognition of what the two had done, and of what the pope himself believed he was not able, or not allowed, to do. The Lutheran Church in Germany declared with all clarity only in 1950: "We openly state that by omission and silence, we have become guilty of the crime which was committed by people of our nation against Jews."[95]

It is legendary how Pius XII's successor, Pope John XXIII, greeted a Jewish delegation on October 17, 1961 with the words: *Sono io, Giuseppe, il fratello vostro* ("It is I, Joseph, your brother"—he had originally been called Giuseppe Roncalli), reminding them of the biblical story of the brother of the sons of Jacob, who had been lost. For the Catholic Church, the encyclical *Nostra aetate* of the Second Vatican Council pointed the way, which after intense international public debates began a new chapter in the relationship between Christians and Jews. In very clear words, it rejected the charge of deicide and vigorously opposed anti-Semitism. It was also important that Pope John Paul II, during his visit to Germany in 1980, spoke in Mainz before the Jewish community of "the old covenant," which was "never revoked",[96] a conviction over which Catholic theologian Klaus Berger had been accused of heresy at the time of the Council.

Jews and Christians, said the Auschwitz survivor Jehuda Bacon, belong together so closely that they cannot live without each other.[97] That is what the New Testament says, too. The fact that Judaism survived is the "Jewish miracle", which the well-known cultural studies scholar George Steiner calls an "indispensable miracle" because of the incomparable Jewish contribution to world culture.[98] The history of persecutions had seemed to come to an end in the nineteenth century with the emancipation of Jews. Indeed, by their very perseverance, they were thought to have proven their mettle. Today, we have to make a correction: the Shoa has surpassed all previous horrors. The well-known Jewish Holocaust scholar Steven T. Katz notes that previously "the physical elimination of Judaism had at no time been the official political goal of any church or any Christian state."[99] And Yoseph Yerushalmi, professor of Judaism at Harvard and at Columbia University in New York, commented in 1993, in a talk on anti-Jewish violence in the Middle Ages: "There was no slaughter [of Jews in the Middle Ages]. No medieval king ever decreed it, no pope ever sanctioned it. Where it occurred it did not emanate from above." The Nazis' ordering of such murder from the top down was an "unprecedented phenomenon", i.e., not the continuation of medieval pogroms: "We have all lost whatever remained of our innocence, and by this I mean not only Jews but the entire world."[100]

From the very beginning, the apostle Paul had called the Jews "my brothers", because "they are Israelites, and to them belong the sonship, the glory, the covenants, the giving of the law, the worship, and the promises" (Rom 9:4). The relationship between Christians and their "elder brothers" (Pope John Paul II)[101] has seen highs and lows over the course of two thousand years—with the lows over and over at the cost of the Jews, who were oppressed and discriminated against as a minority. It was only the terrible crime of the Holocaust that brought about a true new beginning. However, a new beginning that is meant in earnest requires an honest confession of guilt.

For this reason, Pope John Paul II had formally proclaimed on March 12 of the Jubilee year in 2000, at St. Peter's Basilica: "Let us pray that, in recalling the sufferings endured by the people of Israel throughout history, Christians will acknowledge the sins committed by not a few of their number against the people of the Covenant and the blessings, and in this way will purify their hearts."[102] And after a silent prayer of all the faithful gathered at St. Peter's Basilica, the pope personally prayed: "God of our fathers, you chose Abraham and his descendants to bring your name to the nations: We are deeply saddened by the behavior of those who in the course of history have caused these children of yours to suffer, and asking your forgiveness we wish to commit ourselves to genuine brotherhood with the people of the Covenant. We ask this through Christ our Lord."[103]

5. After the Catastrophe: New Beginnings and the "Second Papal Revolution"

After 1945, both churches in Germany were held in high regard because of the many Christian opponents to National Socialism. They were also needed in order to create the foundation of the new state. Thus, for example, the judiciary could not manage without recourse to natural law, which had always been upheld by the Catholic Church. It was the only possible way to condemn people for following the unjust laws of an unjust state even though by nature, they should have known that they were unjust. For "a law that is not right has to yield to justice", said legal philosopher Gustav Radbruch (1879–1949).[104]

The experience of common persecution welded the two Christian churches together, so that the age of denominational parties like the Catholic Centre was over. The Christian union parties offered the opportunity to Catholics and Protestants to shape the new state on the basis of the spirit of Christian social teaching. And that is what they did. The harrowing experiences of totalitarian dictatorships induced the world community to declare the General Proclamation of Human Rights in 1948, which was prepared with the help of representatives of Christian churches. As early as in the interwar period, Protestant theologians in particular had advocated for an international peace organization. After World War II, the churches spoke out more and more radically against any war and supported the right to conscientious objection. When on the occasion of the second Iraq war in 2003 the politicians of the war coalition were consulting with Pope John Paul II, the old, ailing pope maintained his strict rejection of war.

In France, the Pax Christi movement was formed immediately after World War II, following a bishop's appeal for reconciliation with Germany. Its German branch was established in 1948 and was able to take up the work of the German Catholics' Peace Association from the interwar period. It was particularly the Catholic politicians Alcide de Gasperi, Robert Schuman, and Konrad Adenauer who advanced European unity. Charles de Gaulle and Konrad Adenauer attended Mass together at the cathedral of Reims on July 8, 1962, symbolizing the new German-French friendship. Observers agreed that the fact that both were practicing Catholics especially fostered the rapprochement between Germany and France.

On the subject of human rights, Pope John XXIII, drawing on ancient traditions, declared in his 1963 encyclical *Pacem in terris*:

> When, furthermore, we consider man's personal dignity from the standpoint of divine revelation, inevitably our estimate of it is incomparably increased. Men have been ransomed by the blood of Jesus Christ. Grace has made them sons and friends of God, and heirs to eternal glory. But first We must speak of man's rights. Man has the right to live. He has the right to bodily integrity and to the means necessary for the proper development of life ... He has a right to freedom in investigating the truth, and—within the limits of the moral order and the common good—to freedom of speech and publication, and to freedom to pursue whatever profession he may choose. He has the right, also, to be accurately informed about public events ... Also among man's rights is that of being able to worship God in accordance with the right dictates of his own conscience, and to profess his religion both in private and in public.[105]

And the Second Vatican Council (1962–1965) formally declared: "This right of the human person to religious freedom is to be recognized in the constitutional law whereby society is governed and thus it is to become a civil right."[106] And in a different passage, the council supports that "the choice of a political regime and the appointment of rulers are left to the free will of citizens."[107] That is an unambiguous recognition of the sovereignty of the people. The number of statements on human rights by succeeding popes, especially by John Paul II, is impossible to overlook. The *Frankfurter Allgemeine Zeitung* newspaper went as far as to note on the occasion of the death of John Paul II: "It is John Paul II's legacy that in the predominantly Christian areas of the world there are almost no dictatorships left (quite different from 1978), while dictatorships have been maintained or have been able newly to establish themselves in non-Christian countries."[108] The respected historian Heinrich August Winkler speaks of a "second papal revolution"—after the Gregorian Reform in the Middle Ages: "Within the Catholic Church itself, the second papal revolution in history was a conservative revolution. Politically, however, it was a force for liberalization, and it played a crucial role in undermining and eventually bringing down the communist system."[109]

On the Protestant side, the 1985 memorandum "Evangelische Kirche und freiheitliche Demokratie" (The Lutheran Church and Liberal Democracy) spoke out on democracy. Protestant social ethicist Trutz Rendtorff wrote in its foreword: "For the first time, liberal democracy as a form of government is receiving such a thoroughly positive valuation in a statement by the Protestant church."[110] In contrast to previous [Protestant] arguments, the dignity of man is connected with his being made in the image of God, and the passage from the Letter to the Romans—"There is no authority except from God, and those that exist have been instituted by God" (Rom 13:1)—is placed after the following biblical passage: "We must obey God rather than men" (Acts 5:29).

Thus, at last in the twentieth century the ecumenical movement was able to make progress, too, and its efforts to bring about understanding and communication between denominations in order to overcome the scandal of the schism are meeting with more and more success. Besides, the conflict between Christians has long been an annoyance to outsiders. At the beginning of the third Christian millennium, the question about God is high on the agenda of Western Christian societies. It is crucial for Christians to be able to respond to this question convincingly and live persuasively according to their answer, as different kinds of Christians, but still with a view to one day being unified.

XI

Ongoing Scandals

*Everything You Always Wanted to Know about
Christianity but Were Afraid to Ask*

1. The Emancipation of Women and the Priesthood of Women: How Christians Have Dealt with Fifty Percent of Humanity

The twentieth century is also the era of the modern emancipation of women. This began around 1900, and it is a unique, first-time phenomenon in the history of the world. Whatever part of the past one examines, no matter which culture or epoch, one encounters the supremacy of men everywhere. By contrast, the effects of the women's emancipation movement mark "one of the great revolutionary changes in world history", notes historian Thomas Nipperdey.[1] It had its beginnings in countries shaped by Christianity. But what does Christianity have to do with it?

In the Palazzo Barberini in Rome, there hangs a famous painting by Jacopo Tintoretto (1519–1594): *Christ and the Woman Taken in Adultery*. It depicts the ending of a highly dramatic scene that was a matter of life and death. Jesus looks intensely and with utmost compassion at a woman standing beautiful, free, and confident before him. In the background, some figures are leaving the scene. The disciples, standing in the front, seem irritated. What has happened? Jesus had already thrown the merchants out of the temple in Jerusalem and had then even healed a man on a Sabbath day, against the prescriptions of Jewish law. These had been provocations. And now, the scribes and Pharisees have set a cunning trap for him. They have dragged before him a woman just caught in the act of adultery, asking him what should be done with her. The Law of Moses indeed says that she must be stoned. In this moment, Jesus' fate might have already been sealed: if he opposed the stoning, he would have thereby made himself guilty of breaking the Law; if he supported it, his divine message of love and compassion would have been discredited, making him just another rabbi, one among others. Even today, the tension in this scene from the Gospel of John comes through to us. So what does Jesus do? "Jesus bent down and wrote with his finger on the ground." Imagine the situation: he does not answer, but neither does he shy away. "And as they continued to ask him, he stood up and said to them, 'Let him who is without sin among you be the first to throw a stone at her.' And once more he bent down and wrote with his finger on the ground." This is a completely unexpected response, and John the Evangelist reports: "But when they heard it, they went away, one by one, beginning with the eldest, and Jesus was left alone with the woman standing before him." This is exactly the moment Tintoretto has painted, the moment when Jesus sees only this woman, looks into her soul, and asks, "Has no one condemned you?" and she answers, "No one, Lord." Jesus says, "Neither do I condemn you; go, and do not sin again" (see Jn 8:2–11).

This story is above all about mercy, but it is also about equality. Unfaithful women were to be stoned according to Jewish Law, while men—as in this case—could avoid punishment. Jesus broke with this tradition of discrimination against women, which existed in Antiquity outside Judaism also, and he did so not merely in this single case, but systematically and radically. Men had hitherto been able to release their wives from marriage; Jesus forbids men from doing so on the grounds that man and woman are equal from the beginning of Creation and become "one flesh" in matrimony. In Luke 7:47, he praises an indecent woman, a prostitute, forgives her many sins, and then denounces the hard-hearted men with the provocative comment, "But he who is forgiven little, loves little" (Lk 7:47). Then there is the New Testament story of the "woman who had suffered a hemorrhage", who touches Jesus and is restored. This stands against the perpetual discrimination against women in all cultures on account of their monthly periods, during which they were not to be touched because they were considered impure. At the grave on Easter Sunday, it was women—women, who could not serve as witnesses in equal measure with men in any culture of the time—who became the first witnesses of Jesus' Resurrection. The apostle Paul's words in the Letter to the Galatians are decisive for the future: "There is neither Jew nor Greek, there is neither slave nor free, there is neither male nor female; for you are all one in Christ Jesus" (Gal 3:28). Paul wanted to see all discrimination—of race, social class, educational background, or sex—overcome, and there are few texts that have truly liberated as many people as these few phrases.

This applied especially to the role of women, although the potential for societal change contained in these words unfolded through history only little by little. Paul acknowledged the crucial guardianship provided by a husband and father. Yet he added another, more uncommon duty on the part of men: "Husbands, love your wives" (Eph 5:23–25). Or again, even more insistently: every man, along with his wife, should "know how to control his own body in holiness and honor" (1 Thess 4:4). The first Latin theologian, Tertullian (150–220), describes marital equality simply:

> They are truly "two in one flesh". Where the flesh is one, one also is the spirit. Together they pray, together prostrate themselves, together perform their fasts; mutually teaching, mutually exhorting, mutually sustaining. Equally are they both found in the Church of God; equally at the banquet of God; equally in straits, in persecutions, in refreshments. Neither hides anything from the other; neither shuns the other; neither is troublesome to the other.[2]

The well-known French ancient historian Paul Veyne notes that "nothing was more alien to the Romans" than such a concept.[3] The indissolubility of marriage, described in the Gospels, destroyed the old male privilege of dismissing wives at will. French legal historian Jean Gaudemet considers this "a revolutionary contribution to the further development of the family structure."[4]

No wonder, then, that Christianity was extraordinarily attractive to women from the beginning, especially women from society's educated classes. In Antiquity, there were twice as many Christian as pagan female doctors. Compared to ancient (and early Germanic) law, according to which women could not act in public in a legally binding way, Christianity offered a considerable improvement in the status of women. Even the mere fact that women, during Mass, publicly participated in the liturgy in the same room as the men, instead of remaining in a side room, the fact that they spoke for themselves in confession, and most of all, the fact that marriage required equal consent—all of this radically changed the situation of women. As historian Peter Blickle observes, medieval sources always talked about both men *and* women: "Men *and* women are permitted or prohibited from entering into matrimony, men *and* women are granted or denied freedom of choice, men *and* women can or cannot leave an inheritance."[5] For Paul, equality in marriage also explicitly means sexual equality: "For the wife does not rule over her own body, but the husband does; likewise the husband does not rule over his own body, but the wife does." Such a concept was unheard of outside the Christian sphere.

Christianity's entry into the world of the Germanic tribes was bound to bring on a particularly intense collision. In medieval Germanic and even in early German national law [that is, in the late nineteenth century], women had, as legal historian Reiner Schulze notes, "a considerably weaker legal status than men; in early times, they were almost excluded from legal relations and were generally subject to the individual legal power of male relatives or husbands."[6] The free consent to marriage required by Christianity had a decisive and revolutionary impact here as well. In the face of traditional parent-arranged marriages, the popes were a final authority in defending the free decision of bridal couples. They even defended this freedom against kings. When the daughter of King Charles the Bald fled to Pope Nicholas I (820–867) in Rome, seeking help in marrying the man she loved against her father's wishes, the pope resolutely supported her. Later on, too, women, even from the lower classes, including servants, turned to Rome time and again when forced to marry or to enter a convent, or when men did not accept their own responsibility toward women and children—and they won their cases. In the event of violence in marriage, Rome would decide to separate spouses. There is evidence from the sixteenth century of a man being sentenced on account of rape within marriage. The *Decretum Gratiani* from 1140 makes it clear that a woman "may only be married to someone by her own free decision."[7] In fact, early medieval canon law, according to medieval historian Wilfried Hartmann, gave women a decidedly better position in comparison to secular law, tending even toward equality. This also applied to adultery, where canon law chastised men and women alike with exclusively spiritual punishments, while secular law, for example in the *Sachsenspiegel*, demanded that both be decapitated.

Remarkably, even when it came to the so-called "marital duties", the Middle Ages were downright emancipated. Ivo of Chartres (1040–1115), a canonist, explains: "If a wife is overcome by a desire for sexual union, she should by no means keep it secret from her husband, and the husband shall in no case use force with the wife, believing that his subordinate owes him her consent to intercourse at all times."[8] The right of women to intercourse was so important to canon lawyers that they drew up absurd examples in its defense: should a married man be elected pope, he would first need the consent of his wife in order to make the obligatory renunciation of marriage required upon assuming office; if the wife denied her consent, the man had to renounce the papacy. Protocols of the ecclesiastical marriage courts of Canterbury and York report that if a woman lodged a complaint over her husband's impotence, honorable women were officially sent to the suspected husband to allure him until it became evident whether or not the defendant was indeed capable of intercourse. In the case of his inability, these honorable women submitted the impotent man to abuse and shame. The court was in the habit of annulling such marriages. Critics readily cite the *ius primae noctis*—the right of noble men to spend the wedding night with bondswomen, before their husband did—as a sign of the oppression of women at the time, but this, too, is more legend than reality. Legal history has no knowledge of a single case in which the *ius primae noctis* was in fact exercised; *The Marriage of Figaro* is merely entertaining fiction.

In Christianity, moreover, women were not commanded to marry and so to submit themselves to a man's protection. Rather, they could choose celibacy for the sake of the kingdom of heaven. This was a highly esteemed practice related to with the maxim of Paul—who had in view the imminent end of the world—that the unmarried are able to dedicate themselves to God with undivided hearts and for this reason it is better not to marry (1 Corinthians 7). However—as Paul continues—this is only a piece of advice, not a commandment, and ultimately everyone must see for himself what God has called him to do. Thus this counsel had nothing to do with a hostility toward the body, nor with a disregard for marriage. Yet it offered an attractive alternative, especially to women. Later on, the temperamental Saint Teresa of Avila would say that she had entered a religious order because she did not want to fall under the yoke of a stupid man. Increasingly in the Middle Ages—compared to Antiquity, where it was quantitatively rare—women became influential leaders. In the thirteenth century, a hundred years before the male mysticism of a Meister Eckhart, there was a spring of female mysticism, as represented by Gertrude the Great, Saint Mechtild, and Mechtild of Magdeburg at the monastery of Saint Mary's in Helfta, Germany. This phenomenon did not consist of just some crazy daydreams, but rather of expressions of deep spiritual experience—which, incidentally, these women described in German for the first time, prompting them to find a completely new vocabulary. One could therefore make the claim that the German language was invented by women. Education was key, and convents provided education to women. At that time, there were far more noblewomen able to read and write than men.

Ultimately, the Protestant Reformation resulted in a step backward for women in their social roles. Consecrated religious life was not available to Protestant women. If a woman remained unmarried, she was often mocked as an "old maid". The Enlightenment, too, brought no real progress, but rather propagated biological hypotheses on female inferiority. Jean-Jacques Rousseau (1712–1778) declared that woman was there to please man and had to subject herself to him, since her "tender muscles are without resistance."[9] With the daughter of a washerwoman, who according to Rousseau's description united intellectual simplicity and a good heart, this author of the novel *Émile* fathered five children, all of whom he delivered to an orphanage. Even though the Enlightenment finally abolished the legal disadvantage of women considered "dissolute", it did not fundamentally change anything about the terrible fates of many. Indeed, well into the later twentieth century, women still predominantly carried the blame for sexual mischief. They were socially discriminated against, falling into mortal danger if they became pregnant, and their children were stigmatized as well. Men dodged all that. Even the philosopher Georg Wilhelm Friedrich Hegel (1770–1831), writing of law, impassively declared that when a girl surrenders to the senses, she gives up her honor, though this is "not the case for a man."[10] Authorities issued laws on compulsory education for "fallen women", but not for "fallen men". This latter term did not even exist. Even in Karl Marx' case, the socialists tried to deny that he had fathered a child out of wedlock. The pagan sense of honor was quite fashionable, especially in the nineteenth century. Spectacular duels took place, which the Catholic Church prohibited. This disastrous concept of honor spread throughout society, and it particularly discriminated against women. Even in the period of the Weimar Republic, the Association of Female Postal and Telegraph Officers, which consisted mostly of unmarried women, called for the dismissal of one member on account of her illegitimate child, though the Reichspost minister rejected the motion.

While Catholic society was mainly characterized by agriculture, where husband and wife went to the fields and then worked together at home, Protestantism coupled with industrialization tended toward a social model that in the nineteenth century kept bourgeois women at home while the husbands pursued gainful employment outside the house. Historian Heinrich von Treitschke (1834–1896) praised the ambitious Protestant Prussia: "There is no state that has seen as little female rule as Prussia."[11] German novelist Thomas Mann, too, was leery of "the independence and liberation of the biking, driving, studying, strong-minded, somewhat masculinized woman" of 1925.[12] Even social democracy, whose program called for a kind of egalitarianism, was more concerned with "women in their role as homemakers and mothers than in their role as factory workers," as historian Thomas Nipperdey observes.[13] At the end of the nineteenth century, women were not really able to conduct business in the secular sphere, could not select or practice a profession of their own accord, and also lacked the right to vote. Such discrimination against women prevailed in other cultures as well, but in Christianity the concept of a partnership-based marriage relying on equal spousal consent—which Austrian social historian Michael Mitterauer calls an "essential, fundamental principle" in Christianity[14]—created a situation in which a distinctly Christian claim came into ever more fierce conflict with male dominance.

This explains why around 1900 the women's suffrage movement developed not in Asia or Africa, but in those countries of Europe and America that had been shaped by Christianity. One of this movement's important protagonists was the first German female social policist, Elisabeth Gauck-Kühne. She converted to Catholicism because she saw there, in the ideal of virginity, a respected role for women even apart from marriage. Criticisms came from the "anti-feminist alliance" attacking Catholic positions as "clerical feminism". Later, the founder of feminist theology, Mary Daly, praised the (Catholic) dogma of the Immaculate Conception of Mary, because it makes it clear that women were redeemed not by men, but by God alone.

Comparing the roles of women in the three chief monotheistic religions, the Jerusalem historian Avraham Grossmann notes that in Christian Europe, women had a distinctly larger space of freedom with regard to their public presence than in Islamic countries or in Jewish areas. This had positive effects for Jewish women in Europe, even under the persisting objections of the rabbis. Jewish men consistently lived in monogamy in Christian environments, but not in Muslim environments, where polygamy was common among Jews as well. One look at the Muslim position confirms just how special a development Christian marriage is, with its focus on the spouse. In Islam, the status of women did improve in comparison to the pre-Islamic way of life, but the significantly superior legal status of men remained untouched, including their right to initiate or dissolve a marriage and their right to have multiple wives. Professor of Islam Gudrun Krämer emphasizes that even in more recent Arabic literature, the question of women is "hardly ever systematically discussed".[15] To this day, parents in non-Islamic regions of North Africa, China, and India, and even in Japan, determine the lives of young women and arrange their marriages. But today, the Christian "invention" of partner-centered monogamy, determined by the two people involved in it and no one else, is spreading, albeit in a secular form.

But at the end of the day, isn't it a scandal that women cannot become priests in the Catholic Church? No, because in the "sacred theater", as the Mass has been called, the Catholic priest acts in the role of Christ. In this moment, he is—for the faithful—Christ. Because Christ was a man, nobody has ever in two thousand years thought that a woman might take on this role. In many Protestant denominations, women can become pastors, and it is telling that they still typically wear men's clerical clothing and vestments, probably because there remains a consciousness that they are filling a masculine role. The priesthood of women would probably never have been demanded at all in the Catholic Church if the role of priests had been confined to the liturgical sphere. In secular theater, no one demands that Prince Hamlet be played by a woman.

However, Feminists and others are right to raise the issue of power. The office of a priest plainly comes with the spiritual authority [*Vollmacht*] granted to it by Christ to forgive sins, to preach in his name, and to consecrate the Eucharist, but it can also be bound up with power [*Macht*] plain and simple. And women, on principle, no longer accept exclusion from power simply because they are women. In point of fact, the positions of [secular] power in the Catholic Church, even beyond spiritual authority, remain by and large in the hands of men. Pope John Paul II repeatedly called for an expanded role for women in the Church, and Pope Francis has done the same. In recent times, bishops have started to entrust real leading positions to women, but this is not enough, either. The Second Vatican Council points out an important path. It calls for conceiving of clerical offices no longer in terms of "office" but rather in terms of "service". If bishops and priests saw themselves as "servants" of women and men in the Church—not just in words, but in deeds—and more crucially if they were also perceived this way by others, then surely the question of power would no longer be posed with such intensity. Most importantly, this would enable us to recognize that state and ecclesial power had never been particularly desirable to Christians, but in fact were viewed as threats to the salvation of one's soul.

2. The Church, Celibacy, and Sex: On a Vast Misunderstanding

For Christians, Emperor Constantine's victory on the Ponte Milvio in 312 A.D. was not only an occasion for joy, but also a problem. And this problem, too, was related to the issue of power. Until then, being a Christian had meant having no power and accepting significant disadvantages on account of one's faith. Shortly before, the brutal persecution of Christians under Emperor Diocletian had demanded the lives of numerous martyrs—now it was suddenly an advantage to be Christian, since Emperor Constantine privileged Christians when assigning key positions. This was a big chance for some opportunists, who became Christians in order to rise in their career. How many of these there were, no one can say. But it is no coincidence that right at this time, there sprang up a movement whose impact has endured into our own age: the celibacy movement.

The term "celibacy" is used here as it is broadly understood, namely remaining unmarried for the sake of heaven, as Catholic priests and religious do today. To be very precise, the word "celibacy" today only applies to "secular", or "diocesan", priests. For consecrated religious—even men!—the technical term is "virginity", which today is liable to sound unintentionally odd.

In the early centuries of Christianity, many men who wanted to follow Jesus more closely left society for the desert of Egypt. There they lived austerely and unmarried, whether alone or in community with others wanting to share this way of life. News about them reached the cities, and soon people from across the Roman Empire were flocking to Egypt to behold the spectacle—only to realize that it was no spectacle at all, but rather, for many, a significant enrichment of the Christian life. Desert Father Saint Anthony became exceedingly famous and renowned, thanks to a much-read biography by Athanasius. It was expected that these men—and among them a few women—would teach something about the essentials of life. Soon, the people wanted them to abide not only in the Egyptian desert, but also in their own locales. They needed celibate priests and bishops who weren't under suspicion of pushing their way into Church leadership for the sake of a career, but instead had spiritual substance and were able to dedicate themselves completely to their task. The great freedom and unselfish integrity of these people kept the Church strong through the tempests of the ages, even later on in the oppressive dictatorships of the twentieth century.

By now, research has revealed that celibacy is in no way an invention of the Middle Ages. Rather, the renunciation of marriage for the sake of heaven was already highly valued in the Church at the time of the apostles, because it was the form of life of Jesus himself, as well as of the apostle Paul. The Council of Elvira in Spain around 300 A.D. had already legally prescribed celibacy for deacons, priests, and bishops. In times of weakness in the Church, there has come again and again a crisis of celibacy, with too few people ready to put everything on the table. However, in times of Church reform, even after the Middle Ages, it was most often people living a convincing celibate lifestyle who set spiritual revivals in motion. Time and again in the course of history there have been measures to strengthen celibacy, for example the legal regulation in 1059 that the marriages of priests were to be considered invalid a priori. There were also different lines of reasoning behind such measures, such as the un-Christian notion—especially prevalent in Antiquity—of "pollution", that is, the "corruption by intercourse" that made one unfit for liturgical acts; more recently, there has emerged the idea that unmarried life makes one more available to live in solidarity with the lonely and the abandoned. Voluntary celibacy is generally common in many religions for people of a particularly spiritual bent. Though married, Mahatma Gandhi took a vow of continence.

Anti-celibacy polemicists like to talk about forced celibacy. Forced celibacy is a scandal, they say. However, setting such polemics aside, one can see plainly and soberly that there is no compulsion at work here, because the decision of celibacy is a free decision made by adult human beings and weighed for many years before, making it in this respect even freer than some marriages. There is, however, a package deal. One can only become a Catholic priest if one renounces marriage. Of course, this is just an ecclesiastical regulation of the Latin Church, fundamentally subject to change. In the Eastern church, the rule exists only for bishops, not for priests. The Church could modify or abolish its regulation. Whether the dramatic lack of priests would be sustainably eliminated by such a change, however, is questionable, considering the lack of pastors even in Protestant churches; it remains doubtful, too, whether the compromise of leaving celibacy up to individual election would really help either. The Old Catholic Church, which separated from the Roman Catholic Church in the nineteenth century, adopted just such a compromise in 1878, but this marked the de facto end of celibacy in that denomination.

Moreover, the consistent negative public depiction of the celibate way of life has a regrettable side effect. It often unintentionally discriminates against single people who are not "celibate" by choice, quite numerous now, who live alone after a string of temporary relationships, each occupying one of the many single apartments of our cities. They do not like being told that this is "unnatural". The zeal of some critics of celibacy who are far removed from the Church calls to mind—in a certain sense—the story of the manic patient who breaks into a nightclub armed in order to set a dancer free, when she did not even want to leave in the first place. The point is simply that celibacy has nothing to do with an animosity toward sexuality. It was precisely celibate people who, across Church history, unreservedly defended marriage against sects that were hostile to the body.

For people in every age, sexuality has been a strange, and sometimes uncanny, phenomenon, which has been shown reverence in every culture by various rites of passage or initiation. Ancient philosophy and medicine saw in it the most powerful and most destructive of all drives, because it inhibited reason, the guiding light of man. Roman philosopher Musonius Rufus said, "People may only consider matrimonial love morally permissible when it aims at the begetting of children."[16] Seneca calls homosexuality "contrary to nature".[17] French ancient historian Paul Veyne, too, surprisingly states, "The rumor about pagan sensuality is due to a succession of traditional misinterpretations."[18]

Aurelius Augustinus, from Late Antiquity, often gets pointed to as evidence for Christianity's alleged animosity to the body. This major Doctor of the Western Church had a truly enormous influence, especially on the Middle Ages, and when it came to sexuality, Augustine had a rather turbulent past life. Before he became a Christian, much to the distress of his Christian mother Monica, he lived in concubinage and had an illegitimate son. He called the boy Adeodatus (gift of God), but this did not quite reassure his mother. On a passionate search for truth, Augustine then joined the Manichees, who disdained the body. Only at the end did he arrive at Christianity, for which his pious mother had been praying tirelessly. Owing to this past, it may be that Augustine's comments on sexuality as the "lust of the flesh", a product of original sin, do come off as a little too pessimistic. To be sure, the ancient historian Peter Brown, a Princeton professor who specializes in this period, does not believe that these ideas of Augustine generally met with a positive response in his time. However, it is in Augustine, of all people, where we surprisingly find this rather modern-sounding passage:

A further question often raised is when a man and a woman, neither of them married to anyone, have sex with each other not to have children, but merely to indulge in intercourse because they cannot control their lust. But they show fidelity to each other in that the man does not have sex with another woman, nor the woman with another man. The question is whether this should be called a marriage. Doubtless without absurdity it can indeed be labelled a marriage, provided that they agree to maintain the relationship until one of them dies; provided, too, that that they do not avoid having children.[19]

He recognized that marriage indeed has spousal love as its aim.

In fact, the celibate Paul is in no way opposed to sexuality, and he definitely recommends marriage: "If you marry, you do not sin" (1 Cor 7:28) and "It is better to marry than to be aflame with passion" (1 Cor 7:9b). Nor is Thomas Aquinas prudish at all when he writes: "The principal reason why a man loves his wife is her being united to him in the flesh."[20] Pope John XXI (1205–1277), a learned physician and theologian, goes into detail: kissing and erotic play are prerequisites for the noblest thing there is in marriage, that is, intercourse.[21] Denis the Carthusian (1402–1471), who after all belonged to the strictest religious order, offers an argument for his conviction that one can only enter such an order after having learned a thing or two about life: "Desire can be a kind of incentive toward greater friendship, and so, too, the marital friendship is, in a way, a sexual friendship."[22]

Martin Luther's declaration that marriage is "a secular thing" had significant consequences.[23] Thus it happened that in Protestant cities, secular powers introduced so-called "morality courts", which punished extramarital sexuality, especially adultery, with the strictest secular penalties. This is why Reformation historian Heinz Schilling has been able to say that "the basis of Protestant marriages was more stable in practice than Catholic sacramental marriage."[24] The intervention of the state, which sometimes even forbade sleeping naked, had fatal consequences. The secular prohibition of marriage for all those who lacked the necessary financial means to feed a family—resulting in more people without families and an increase in extramarital births—seriously interfered with the basic Christian right to marry. By contrast, ecclesiastical marriage trials ensured a significant decrease in male violence in marriages, since wives had the option

of suing their husbands. This does not change the fact that society
at large was still characterized by male domination. In the Catholic
Münster region, the punishment of public shaming for sexual delin-
quencies was almost exclusively carried out against women, and exile
was imposed more often upon women than upon men.

Ecclesiastical marriage trials led not only to a decline in male
domestic violence, which had prevailed since ancient times, but
also to increased intimacy in marriage, where affection and responsibility started to play greater roles. This development was catalyzed
at the beginning of the nineteenth century by Romanticism. After
the excessive violence of the French Revolution and the European
powers' harsh antiliberal reaction, the Romantic movement not only
harked back to an idealized Middle Ages, but also brought on a cult
of romantic love that would influence marriage from then on out.
This romantic love is considered a product of Christianity. In 1900,
Thomas Nipperdey noted that "love rooted in partnership" is "a basis
of marriage and of parent-child relationships". It is in this form that
marriage has "indisputably its highest validity" and indeed articulates
itself as a "family religion".[25] Only at the beginning of the twentieth
century did something new rear its head. Sexuality was declared to be
liberation and ecstasy, and people demanded a corresponding reform
of lifestyle and a culture of nudism—in other words, a loosening of
past restraints.

After the introduction of the "pill", the sexual revolution of the
1960s led to the definitive decoupling of sexuality from procreation,
with serious social consequences. Frank Schirrmacher, the late publisher of the *Frankfurter Allgemeine Zeitung* newspaper, described the
dilemma in his bestselling book *Das Methusalem-Komplott*: "While
the old live and don't die, the young, whom we need for the future,
are never born."[26]

In public debates, it has long since become standard practice to
link the topic of sex first and foremost with the Catholic Church and
what is commonly known as "Catholic sexual morality". There are
socio-psychological reasons for this, since all the old authorities for-
bidding sexuality have by now given up, leaving only the Catholic
Church to offer her own form of resistance—a resistance that some
in the new school actually think they need in order to prove their
own sexual liberation. But that is based on a fatal misunderstanding.

In truth, the Catholic Church, in her two thousand years of existence, has repeatedly—and successfully—defended herself against merely prudish opponents of sexuality, without exception excluding them from the Church or at least vehemently fighting them. In Antiquity, the Encratites, the Montanists, and the Manicheans were all excluded; in the Middle Ages, the Cathars; then in Modernity the Church fought against the Jansenists, a group of rigorists that even Blaise Pascal followed. In the nineteenth century, the respectable Protestant bourgeoisie, with its bizarre sexual preoccupations, considered Catholics to be sexually lax. This relative "liberality" of Catholicism, so to speak, in the realm of sexuality is confirmed by scholarship on the history of morality. However, at some point, even Catholics conformed to the anti-sexual spirit of the age, with heavy consequences, even though this did not at all correspond to their own centuries-old tradition. And because some Catholic Christians today are no longer aware of this history, two extreme camps have emerged: on the one hand, conservative Catholics who, out of ignorance, "boldly" defend cramped Puritan notions of sexuality, and on the other, progressive Catholics who, out of the same ignorance, make apologies for them. Because many journalists are generally unfamiliar with the Church, they follow this conflict and believe that sexual prohibitions are the heart of Church teaching, and so they harp on the topic time and time again. For this reason, we have to stand by and watch old unmarried men awkwardly try to answer any number of highly detailed questions on sexuality. Not a pretty sight and, unintentionally, a singular bit of disinformation. At the World Youth Day in Cologne, Germany, Pope Benedict XVI—probably on purpose—did not say a word on sexual morality, speaking instead about faith in God, about deepened spirituality, about the beauty of Christian life; nevertheless, many media sources reported mostly on condoms.

For nineteen hundred years, no successor of the apostle Peter had ever commissioned any systematic statement about sexual morality. On July 25, 1968, the moment came. Pope Paul VI published the encyclical *Humanae vitae*. To be sure, Pius XI had already commented on this topic on December 31, 1930, in his encyclical *Casti connubii*, but by no means as thoroughly and spectacularly as Paul VI in this new document. In his encyclical, Pius XI had for the first time referred in passing to the use of certain methods whereby Catholics didn't have to procreate "like rabbits" (Pope Francis, January 2015). Today in the Church, this is called "responsible parenthood". According to this view, a married couple should decide for themselves how many children they can take responsibility for and then use the woman's naturally fertile days for "the most noble thing there is in marriage" (Pope John XXI, ca. 1275).[27] That is how the Second Vatican Council saw things, too. Besides, the pill did not yet exist at the time of the Council, so this approach of natural family planning was Catholic pragmatism. But then the "anti-baby pill" entered the market, and the whole world put pressure on Pope Paul VI to comment on it. He did so in 1968. He forbade the pill. Then, as if by reflex, there came an outcry: a scandal! First off, people did not want to have anything forbidden to them, much less by an unmarried man and least of all by a pope. What's more, women brought with them into the debate their fully understandable anger over the uncontested rule of men in the Church. Lastly, three years after the end of the Second Vatican Council, moral theologians had just rediscovered Immanuel Kant, and they could not reconcile what this German philosopher had written in Königsberg in 1788 with what the Italian pope was now declaring in Rome. Soon, no one quite understood the debate anymore. Only one thing was clear: whoever was for the papal encyclical was considered conservative, whoever was against it, progressive. The misapplication of sexual morality for the purpose of strident, narrow-minded thinking reinforced the tendency of less-informed journalists to see the Catholic Church wrongfully as, in the main, an institution for the prevention of sexual joy.

The truth is that the Catholic Church has always had a holistic and, shall we say, ecological understanding of sexuality. One part of fulfilled sexuality is sexual desire, which is something good and beautiful (the popes confirm this: see John XXI, 1205–1277, John Paul II, 1920–2005), along with personal love and, ultimately, vitality—that is, "openness to children". Thus, if a man had one wife only for sex, another one only for love poetry, and then a third one only for having children, he would instrumentalize all three women and not truly love any of them. For the sake of this holism, a marriage that excludes children from the outset is not valid. Neither is it all right if

one purposely tries to prevent oneself by artificial means from having children, according to the encyclical *Humanae vitae*, because this
manipulates nature, which is not the case when spouses instead simply mind the natural periods of infertility in a woman's cycle. Sure,
one can see things differently, and many moral theologians nowadays
do. But recently, many women who are not Catholics have refused
to take the pill for these same reasons, because they do not want to
expose themselves to the manifold "unnatural" effects and side effects
of hormone preparations. These tend to be more ecologically minded
women or else feminists, who, as Adrienne Rich once put it, consider the pill "a mechanistic and patriarchal device".[28] Sociologist
Herrad Schenk puts it this way: "Feminists' weariness of the pill is
not prudishness, either, but a refusal to play by the rules of patriarchal
stage directions and is itself a new context in which to rethink these
rules, and perhaps to rewrite them according to the needs of both
sexes."[29] Alice Schwarzer had already lamented the "side effects" of
the pill: "In the past, if a woman had no desire to be with a man, she
could refuse him out of modesty or out of fear of an unwanted pregnancy; but today, thanks to enlightenment and to the pill, women
have to remain available."[30]

Still, Catholic women ultimately decide according to their own
conscience whether to follow the Church's teaching on the pill. And
whatever they decide, nobody is going to excommunicate them for
it. At any rate, the encyclical *Humane vitae* pertained above all to
Catholic marriages. In the Catholic holistic-ecological vision of reality, sex outside of marriage contradicts the order of creation, which
holds for all unmarried heterosexuals, all civilly remarried people, and
all homosexuals. But not even this is the worst transgression Catholics
can imagine. It is likewise important to the Church, for example—as
it says in the *Catechism* (CCC 2358)—that all discrimination against
homosexuals be avoided; and without a doubt, to reduce homosexual
individuals to their sex organs is a kind of discrimination. Nevertheless, public discussions on the theme of the Catholic Church and
homosexuality, as a rule, always focus on sexual intercourse.

Saint Alphonsus Liguori (1696–1786), the strict patron of confessors, advises that priests hearing confession should not inquire too
concretely into sexual matters, which changed altogether in the
nineteenth century, when Catholics began adapting to the prevailing

Victorian zeitgeist, to become just as "puritanical" as "everyone else". By and large, this spirit arose not so much from religious convictions as from what was then considered "science", which led to some absurd—and frightening—kinds of repression. On the basis of certain studies on human sperm, the secular jurist and co-founder of modern trial law Benedict Carpzov dealt out severe punishments for masturbation (exile), homosexual acts (beheading), and intercourse with animals (burning). Denmark, too, punished homosexuality by death in 1683. The Enlightenment was especially rigid, contributing new pseudo-scientific insights that would lead to further criminalization. Because masturbation, it was said, led to the drying up of the brain and the spinal cord, which later on was called "the softening of the spine", philosopher Immanuel Kant considered masturbation an "injury to humanity" and found it to be worse than suicide. Even the famous physician of the Berlin Charité, and militant atheist, Rudolf Virchow (1821–1902) called for state measures against masturbation.

Obviously, such radical punishments create a highly embarrassing impression, making it preferable to attribute them to religious obscurantism. But historical facts suggest something different. The churches only absorbed what so-called scholarship was furnishing them with—which had dismal effects on the Christians of the time.

As a matter of fact, in the past, Catholics were generally considered rather lax, even "piggish", when it came to sexual matters, appalling righteous Protestants for centuries. Many laypeople, priests, bishops, and even some popes saw things more according to the old Rhenish motto, "The good Lord is not that tough"—for better or for worse. Although sexual misdeeds have been extensively brought to the fore in social debate for two hundred years, this fact does not stem from the Catholic Church, but distinctly from the Enlightenment, which found that the individual person was most vulnerable when it came to sexual sins. By contrast, since the earliest Christian age, the gravest sin for monks has been, not some kind of sexual transgression, but acedia, indifference. For even murder gets committed, in the last analysis, out of indifference, indifference toward another person's right to life. Love is the opposite of indifference. That is why Jesus controversially encourages a prostitute who is despised by all: "Her sins, which are many, are forgiven, for she loved much" (Lk 7:47). That, if you will, is Catholic sexual morality.

3. Christianity and Pedophilia: "It's Easier to Get Pregnant from Kissing Than to Become a Pedophile from Celibacy"[31]

"Did not he who made me in the womb make him?" So it is written in the Old Testament's famous book of Job. For Christians, even in the earliest days of the Church, every child remains under God's protection starting in the mother's womb. While abortion and the killing of children were common practice in Antiquity, one of the most ancient Christian texts—the *Didache*, which may have been written as early as the first century—states: "Do not abort a fetus or kill a child that is born."[32] Likewise, the *Epistle to Diognetus*, which is dated only slightly later, says of Christians: "They marry like everyone else does and have children, but they do not expose them once they are born."[33] All this was revolutionary, and above all, it interfered significantly with the rights of men over women and children. Christians and doctors who took the Hippocratic Oath were among the few people in the Roman Empire who thought abortion was wrong. Medical historian Robert Jütte summarizes: "Nothing like an unborn child's right to life could exist in the occident until the appearance of Christianity."[34] Not even infanticide was punishable under Roman law. Children only obtained a right to life as a result of a legal "reversion" by the father, who in the event of a visible disability or for other reasons could just as well withhold this right or else freely decide to abandon the child in the mountains or some other place, leaving it to die an agonizing death. This held true for the Greeks, the Romans, and also the Germanic tribes; even today, among the tribes of New Guinea, 30 percent of all newborns are killed, according to anthropologist Wulf Schiefenhovel's estimations.[35]

But Christians especially cared about the growing child. Indeed, Jesus himself had treated children with exceptional kindness and respect. The extrinsic reason for this special attention on the part of Christians was, among other things, infant baptism. With the emergence of the doctrine of original sin, such baptisms became common practice, as a clear sign for the pure grace of God destined for the child without any prior merit on its part, by which it was saved from mankind's entanglement in original sin. Since children of course could not be expected to make a profession of faith, the consequence of infant baptism was that education—Christian education by Christian parents as well as by the Church—assumed crucial importance. Children had a right to this education, a right to a formation with all its cultivating effects on society. French historian Philippe Ariès, in his famous *History of Childhood*, has said that schools organized by bishops were "the original cell of our entire scholastic system in the West."[36] By contrast, the ancient Roman *paterfamilias* could not only "abandon newborns, but also sell or pawn children of any age, or place them at the disposal of others as servants", states the ancient historian Otto Hiltbrunner.[37] The father's right to kill his children was only abolished in the fourth century, after the Christianization of the Roman Empire.

The sexual exploitation of children, too, was a depressing fact of life in ancient times. As Bettina Stumpp explains in her dissertation, *Prostitution in Antiquity*, "Prostitutes were recruited from among abandoned children. They were raised by pimps or madams and 'trained' for prostitution from an early age." This was especially the case with slave children. They "were at times already sold by the age of three in order to serve as amusements, and some were certainly looked upon as sexual toys." Christians protested against this: "The abduction of abandoned children for a 'career' in brothels attracted harsh criticism from Christian authors as early as the first century of the imperial period."[38] Of course, children did not ordinarily grow up among such conditions in Antiquity, but neither was there any legal protection for them.

The early medieval penitential books, unlike secular law, already directly punished abortion, not to mention the killing of newborns and the sexual abuse of adolescents. Only around 1500 did secular law follow suit. The Church was already founding orphanages in Antiquity to protect children. To this day there stands a foundling hospital in Rome, built by Popes Innocent III and Sixtus IV in the vicinity of the Vatican, with exterior baby hatches where children could be dropped off—a system that has recently been revived all over the world. The extent of this kind of aid was astonishing: in 1844, the foundling hospital in Milan took in 2,700 children annually, a third of all newborns in the city. By 1900, that number had increased to 6,000 per year. In Paris, over the first third of the eighteenth century, there were 7,000 foundlings; in London, 15,000 within four years.

There were probably about a million in total in the nineteenth century alone.

As the influence of Christianity has diminished in recent times, concern for the treatment of born and unborn children has begun to slacken again. In Germany, the political compromise over abortion rights in 1995 was only achieved at the price of a regulation that is not readily discussed in public. According to this regulation, disabled children may be killed with a potassium injection in the heart while they are still in the birth canal. A cleft lip is cited as sufficient grounds for such measures. The scale of fees for physicians stipulates that the doctor performing this operation be paid 69.94 Euros.

During the sexual revolution in the 1960s, people rediscovered the idea of using children more for sexual pleasure. Of course, that is not how they put it; instead, they said it was about the "liberation of children's sexuality". One of the gurus of the sexual revolution was the controversial psychoanalyst Wilhelm Reich (1897–1957). He insisted that children, from the time of puberty, have "the right to completely free intercourse."[39] Even prepubescent children, he said, must not be prevented from developing their sexuality. The common conviction was that for centuries, a prudish society, hostile to sexuality, had been withholding sexual satisfaction from children. Now sexual science presented its latest insights. Eberhard Schorsch, one of the most respected sexual scientists in Germany, declared in 1970 at a public hearing in—of all places—the German Bundestag: "Non-violent sexuality between adults and children does not cause any harm to healthy children."[40] Was there a public outcry after this? No, not a peep. After all, it was "the state of science" at the time. In truth, of course, none of this was about children, but about adults who were sexually oriented toward children—a group that had been "discriminated against" and "criminalized" for their tendencies for centuries. After heterosexuals had been sexually liberated, followed by homosexuals, pedophiles were to be next on the agenda. The goal was within reach. There were pedophile magazines. Politicians—in the German Green party, for example—were roped into the campaign. There were resolutions and public confessions, and in 1989, the reputable official publishing arm of the German Society for Physicians released a book explicitly advocating the "decriminalization" of pedophilia. The Church was almost the only social institution that put up resistance and abstained from the sexual revolution's raid on this last stronghold. Yet no one put much stock in the Church's help; all the participants in the debate considered her outdated.

Of course, even within the Catholic Church, there were vastly different opinions at this time on the topic of sexuality. Progressive priests proved their progressive rebelliousness by having girlfriends— or boyfriends—more or less publicly. People were only open-minded when it came to sexuality. At this time, pedophiles—the kind who specifically sought out jobs that brought them into contact with children—found it relatively easy to act as a priest in a "sexually open-minded" way with children and adolescents. In contrast to the "progressive" Odenwaldschule [a private boarding school in southern Germany], where "emancipatory" sexual contact with children and adolescents was more or less supported by the leadership of the school, even becoming de facto the official house policy, pedophile priests everywhere had to hide, which was easier in times when regulations were less strict. But in no case did Catholic leaders approve of, much less actively support, pedophile activities. Therein lies a difference.

But then came the great awakening. Thanks to feminist counseling centers, it became clear at the beginning of the 1990s that there is no such thing as "nonviolent" sexuality between adults and children. There always remains an imbalance in power, as well as a fundamental misunderstanding. The child is looking for possible attention, acknowledgment, and maybe even tenderness in the pedophile "partner". The adult is looking for sex, and to this end he manipulatively utilizes attention, acknowledgment, and tenderness. At some point, the child notices that he has been cheated, and for many, this break of trust has a traumatic effect. Even more serious, however, is the case of abuse by a Catholic priest, because as such, he is—or should we say "was"—afforded a special credit of trust. When this trust is broken, it not only weighs on all the victims' future human relationships, but robs them of their trust in God, sometimes for their entire lives. The abuse of children and adolescents by Catholic priests is an especially perfidious crime.

In the early 1990s, the sexual abuse of children and adolescents finally became a public issue. And this was a good thing. But the climate soon got overheated. Self-proclaimed experts set out on a hunt for supposed abusers, using methods not unlike the "witch tests" of long ago. If a child sketched some sort of long image, it would be immediately taken by some zealous child-abuse hunter as a sure sign of abuse. Fathers were accused of abuse simply for having taken a bath with their children. One trial in Mainz marked the apex of this phenomenon, when a large family was accused of sexually abusing their sixteen children and adolescents. The case made headlines. All the children were put into orphanages. But after four years of court proceedings, it became perfectly clear that there had been no abuse. Through precise analysis, the respected psychologist Max Steller, a specialist in legal evidence, established beyond a shadow of a doubt that the case consisted merely of unintentionally suggested incidents that never actually took place. The court was shaken, and it apologized to those affected. The suffering of these children can hardly be imagined; not only were they kept away from their family members for years, but some of them were actually abused in the orphanage. Many families were shattered.

This case from Mainz became a guiding light. From then on, accusations were handled in a more responsible manner. At the time, the Church was still more or less unscathed. There had only been isolated—however disturbing—cases of abuse by clergy. Then in early 2002, the *Boston Globe* revealed a decades-long pattern of abuse and bureaucratic obfuscation within the Archdiocese of Boston. The story sparked a media wildfire, and dioceses across the United States came under intense investigation, sometimes with ghastly results. Nationwide, the Church responded with severity. Priests were defrocked and handed over to the authorities. The United States Conference of Catholic Bishops instituted the Charter for the Protection of Children and Young People. Parish rectories were reformed, lay investigative committees were established, and victims were paid generously— though of course money is hardly an adequate compensation for the trauma of sex abuse. Europe followed suit. In 2002, after the revelation of similar scandals on the Continent, the German Conference of Bishops established guidelines for addressing abuse. Similar measures were adopted in other countries. In 2003, there took place an international conference at the Vatican wherein leading international experts presented the most current research on the issue. These presentations and discussions were published. The German Bishops' Conference accepted the results and then brought in leading consultants to handle such cases as professionally as possible. Then there was the 2010 press conference at Canisius College in Berlin, a Jesuit prep school where some twenty students had been sexually manipulated in the 1980s.[41] Though the cases were old, the announcement triggered a global avalanche. Only then did many victims find the courage to go public and to face their suffering for the first time—a great blessing, to be sure. The dioceses became even more alert to these kinds of cases, taking precautions and drafting orders for prevention and intervention. In Germany and elsewhere, perpetrators confessed their guilt, and vows were made to improve. Pope Benedict XVI, who had already taken resolute action against abuse as a cardinal, supported all of these steps vigorously. In fact, over the course of just two years, he laicized almost four hundred priests for misconduct.[42] Pope Francis has shared in this resolve.

Yet 2018 proved an even more humiliating year for the Church, again with the United States in a starring role. In June, the Vatican suddenly removed from ministry Theodore Cardinal McCarrick, former archbishop of Washington, D.C., who was credibly accused of having molested an altar server in the 1960s. After this, the *New York Times* uncovered some fifty years of abuse at the hands of this influential cardinal, who preyed especially on eager young seminarians. With this story, there came to light, too, a whole underground "subculture" of homosexual activity in seminaries and rectories across the world—even in Rome. To make matters worse, in August, a grand jury in Pennsylvania released a nine-hundred-page report showing that at least a thousand children—probably many more—had been abused by Catholic clergymen across the state since the 1960s; at least three hundred priests were perpetrators, and all evidence pointed to a habit of denial and cover-up on the part of various ecclesiastical authorities anxious to avoid scandal. This public denunciation was unprecedented in scale, and dioceses across the nation came under fire, with many ultimately opting to release their own (ugly) records of abuse cases. The sheer volume of offenses caused many American Catholics to lose heart, and "crisis" became the word of the year. Pope Francis addressed the matter at a meeting of bishops in 2019: "In people's justified anger, the Church sees the reflection of the wrath of God, betrayed and insulted by these deceitful consecrated persons."[43]

Of course, the Church's response to all this did not much change the fact that her reputation had already suffered gravely from the abuse scandal. But to some on the outside, it was especially puzzling to see that pretty much only the Church stood in the spotlight. The chair of the German counseling center Zartbitter, an institution rather critical of the Church, stated in 2012 that there were just as many abuse cases in the Protestant churches as in the Catholic Church. Experts figure that far more cases have occurred within the German Olympic Sports Confederation. Yet these incidents attract only local attention; no one seriously asks why no special measures have been taken in response to them. Incidentally, it was the *Frankfurter Allgemeine Sonntagszeitung*'s excellent journalism, not the Catholic Church, that corrected the age's fatal impression that abuse was a specifically Catholic phenomenon. In this, the *Sonntagszeitung* picked up the trail left by other journalists in the 1990s regarding the progressive Odenwaldschule. Without question, most cases of sexual abuse occur not in institutions, but within families, with trusted relatives.

While some within the Church murmur that the celibate priestly lifestyle perhaps has something to do with the abuse, there is some scholarly evidence that, statistically speaking, celibacy actually reduces the risk. Speaking to the newspaper *Die Zeit*, Hans Ludwig Kröber— "the most prominent court-appointed expert in Germany" (as *Der Spiegel* puts it), a leading specialist who describes himself as an agnostic Protestant—used rather drastic words in this regard: "It's easier to get pregnant from kissing than to become a pedophile from celibacy."[44]

However, for the first time, the Catholic Church as an institution is now producing her own victims. This development is especially tragic because it stems from a desire, after the terrible shock of the abuse scandal, to do everything especially well, with a lot of good will, though sometimes unfortunately with little professionalism. The consequences are disastrous. Now a new group of victims has emerged: the falsely accused. Here, too, the media, with well-researched reports, have shed some light on this dark issue. The *Irish Times* gives the example of Father Tim Hazelwood of Killeagh, who fought an anonymous accusation for six years and in the interim lost not only his parish, but his credibility as a priest, even though the allegations eventually proved a total fabrication.[45] Similar stories abound. In Germany, practically the same thing that had led to a catastrophe in the fated Mainz case of 1994 was repeated again exactly twenty years later—in that same diocese of Mainz, of all places. This time, a kindergarten program was affected. The Church blamed herself "in an exemplary way" and had to admit in the end that the accusations against the kindergarten teachers had been hasty and that the diocese, in good faith, had overreacted. There are other cases along these same lines.

If we speak here about a second group of victims, this is no exaggeration. To be accused of sexual abuse *when one is innocent* is a traumatic experience, perhaps just as shattering as being sexually abused, especially if a person is wrongly robbed for the rest of his life of a good reputation, or even jailed. Because many of these people are abandoned after such an accusation, they are forbidden from returning to their job. Their colleagues no longer speak *with* them; instead people talk *about* them. Friends, neighbors, family members also become distant, and communicating with them is awkward. And for all these people, it is not easy psychologically to give up the estrangement once everything has eventually cleared up. The accused feels as if he were living in an almost unreal world, in a nightmare. To this day, there are few provisions made to prevent such catastrophes or at least to do as little harm as possible during the inevitable investigations. These latter victims have come to lament the same realities as the abused: no one speaks with them, they say. They are not taken seriously. Out of consideration toward the Church and the parish, they cannot not return to their old positions, even though that would be the only way to ensure full, doubt-free rehabilitation. Thus, whenever there is room for doubt in a case of abuse, it is urgently necessary to use the psychology of legal evidence, and to furnish those impacted—whether guilty or innocent—with an advocate who will stand by their side, as any good legal system would do. Then at the end of the process, in the event of innocence, their wish for complete rehabilitation should be met without reserve.

It's like a jinx. No matter what the Catholic Church does, she winds up the victim—in the worst case, the victim of her own efforts. But at the same time, there exist those spectacular Christians who see this victimhood as the Church's suffering on behalf of Jesus Christ as she follows him along his way. They do not let this suffering trouble them, but instead unite themselves to it spiritually. They are not worried about the praise of the world or about justice on this side of paradise, but concern themselves instead with justice before God's own judgment seat. Such a Christian attitude is not easy, but it is consistent, even though others will find it hard to understand.

XII

The Twenty-First Century

The Crisis of Christianity and the Refugees

1. Exonerations: Resistance and the Scalpel of Reason

At the end of this history of Christianity, the question arises: Why is common misinformation that has long been disproven by scholarship still so persistent? And why is the reaction to corrections of these errors, instead of friendly gratitude, often annoyance—"I don't believe you!" From a psychological perspective, why is the reaction often emotional rather than rational?

Religion deeply affects people; it is not something merely external, but above all something intimate, even for irreligious people. For they, too, often react with embarrassment if they are approached about religious topics unbidden. That can come across as inappropriate, in the same way it would if someone told a stranger about his love for his wife and his children. Every person has some concept of the meaning of the world and the meaning of life, no matter how vague it is. Everyone has worked on constructing this image of the world throughout his life little by little and has perhaps even fought for it against opposition. As soon as someone touches on a person's basic convictions, even if the conviction is the lack of any convictions, all the difficulties that person has suffered are suddenly brought back to him, and it is psychologically understandable if he does not want to stir them up again. In fact, a person who re-examined his basic convictions every day would be entirely unfit for life. This is the only way to explain how sometimes even highly rational people have highly irrational perspectives on the world, and refuse to subject their worldviews to any sort of operation with the scalpel of reason. After all, the more absurd such worldviews are, the greater the subconsciously felt danger that they will come tumbling down like a house of cards at the slightest breath of an argument. And what happens then? Is one supposed to start over completely with all these questions about meaning? It's these anxieties that people subconsciously resist, and these anxieties are likewise the source of the aggression that leads people to resent any questioning of their intellectual foundations. For this reason, rational, scientific arguments on these topics aren't an easy sell, even with those people who believe they have a "scientific worldview".

But there is another psychological reason for not wanting to accept the true history of Christianity that is outlined in this book. German history in particular, but also the entire history of the West in general, has known periods of very serious guilt. Think of the Holocaust, but also of the Crusades, the persecution of witches, the ruthless exploitation of other continents. It requires a strong sense of self-confidence to take up the burden of one's own past, even though that is the only way to maintain a healthy identity. But because this is so difficult, some find that it eases the burden to deny the oppressive parts of one's history and to assign them to others—a phenomenon that was apparent in the treatment of Pope Pius XII. For this socio-psychological service, society for some time now has been availing itself of Christianity and especially of the Catholic Church. The Old Testament knows this mechanism as the sacrifice of a scapegoat, who is ritually burdened with all the sins of the people and then with relief is sent out into the desert, where at some point it perishes along with its burden. French religious philosopher René Girard explained in an interview in the newspaper *Die Zeit* in March 2005, that we are in the process "of loading all the evil of the world onto the biblical religions, and we are pretty good at it, too. We unburden ourselves in doing so. If Christianity is blamed for everything, then we no longer have to admit our secret complicity with violence."[1] In this way, one can even feel progressive and morally superior, even though neither the blame nor the innocence really exists. However, it leads to bizarre results when one tries to convey the impression that an Italian pope was somehow to be blamed for the German Holocaust and a Polish pope would have to answer for the German genocide of the Jews. Such psychological attempts at explanations do not have to be overemphasized, but they can at least shed a little light on the strange irrational resistance that historical scholarship faces when it comes to insights on Christianity.

Only by facing one's own history does one develop healthy self-confidence, an adequate sense of one's own personal and national identity, and the ability to refrain from engaging in a bluster of bragging, both personal and national. This book is intended to make a contribution to the work of clearing up the facts. And it is therefore a book not only for Christians, but also for atheists who are free of prejudice, and who are not afraid of reality.

2. Burdens: Making Sacrifices for Victims

Ethnology is not aware of a single society without a religion. Religion has existed since the Early Paleolithic Age at least—in other words, for at least 40,000 years. It is remarkable that it is precisely the thinkers who are "tone-deaf when it comes to religion" who are bringing religion into play again these days, and real religion at that, not merely the dead ritualistic structure of it. Jürgen Habermas says that religion must not allow itself "to amount to nothing more than a cognitively undemanding accommodation of the religious ethos to the laws imposed on it by secular society."[2] Max Weber had already asked with concern what would happen when the embers of religion were completely extinguished, since so much in the modern world had been created through religion and in particular through Christianity. And philosopher Hans Jonas doubts "whether, without restoring the category of the sacred, the category most thoroughly destroyed by the scientific enlightenment, we can have an ethics able to cope with the extreme powers which we possess today and constantly increase and are almost compelled to wield." Hans Jonas' perspective is rather dramatic: "*We know the thing at stake only when we know that it is at stake.*"[3]

More than ever, this society is in need of a spiritual foundation that does not merely consist in promoting domestic demand in order to raise the GDP. The social and political problems that are coming to head can no longer be solved by technocratic means alone. And everyone knows that, too. Natural scientific perspectives alone are not going to help, either. Jürgen Habermas fears the "naturalization of the spirit": "The point of departure of this naturalization of the spirit is a scientific image of man that also thoroughly desocializes our self-conception."[4] No state can be built with cognitively adept, ruthlessly assertive individuals alone. The totality of the secularization of the twentieth century poses a new problem of legitimization to the state order. Since the state has to be neutral in terms of its worldview, the following famous statement by the former judge of the German Federal Constitutional Court, Ernst-Wolfgang Böckenförde, holds true: "The liberal, secularized state lives off premises that it cannot itself guarantee."[5]

But what if precisely these premises disappear? "You victim!" (*Du Opfer!*) is a nasty swear word today in Germany's schoolyards. Disparaging victims is an act of inhumanity, and not only that—it undermines the basis of our society. Sociologist Émile Durkheim called sacrifice indispensable, because "a sacrifice of one for the other", e.g., of the researcher for scholarship, is necessary for every society.[6] Without the readiness to make sacrifices, there would have been no resistance to the dictatorships of the twentieth century. Jürgen Habermas also considers it unavoidable to "accept sacrifices that promote common interests." But is his following observation enough, then? "All one can do is suggest to the citizens of a liberal society that they should be willing to get involved on behalf of fellow citizens whom they do not know and who remain anonymous to them, and that they should accept sacrifices that promote common interests."[7] What happens if the mere request is not enough? "That would not be my country", Chancellor Angela Merkel said with concern, in a decisive moment.[8] Is it enough that sacrifices for the sake of foreigners are merely agreed to instead of actively made out of conviction?

The immigrant crisis has highlighted the necessity for a reconsideration of the Christian roots of our societies. It was Christians and Christian parishes who out of a deep conviction took care of these people in need. If atheist Gregor Gysi was already worried years ago that a godless society might lose its solidarity, then in some areas in Germany these fears have already come true. Of course that does not mean that many atheists, out of a strong humanitarian impulse, were not ready to help and selflessly make sacrifices for the victims of cruel wars who were stranded in our midst. But that cannot be taken for granted.

It was a great cultural achievement to spiritualize the religious concept of sacrifice. The early Greek philosopher Heraclitus calls for spiritual sacrifices when he sarcastically speaks out against the temple sacrifices: "They vainly [try to] purify themselves with blood when they are defiled [with it]!"[9] And the prophet Isaiah proclaims a new divine spiritual message: "I do not delight in the blood of bulls, or of lambs, or of he-goats.... Seek justice, correct oppression; defend the fatherless, plead for the widow" (Is 1:11, 17). In the New Testament, Jesus cites the prophet Hosea twice: "For I desire mercy and not sacrifice, the knowledge of God, rather than burnt offerings" (Hos 6:6). The general tendency to make fun of religion can make one blind to such social impulses. René Girard only recently noted ironically that there hardly exists a work of religious history that does not compare the Christian Eucharist to a cannibalistic banquet whenever an opportunity presents itself. But this represents a complete misunderstanding of the social revolutionary potential of the Eucharist, where all the faithful without distinction receive the blood of Christ at the altar and are consequently truly of the same blood—related by blood.

Although Christians out of a religious impulse bind up the wounds of victims of religious violence, they must also answer the question of where Christianity stands on tolerance and violence. Recent anti-Christian polemics like to reference the Old Testament in this connection. But even there, even a fratricide is taken under protection when God gives Cain the "mark of Cain": "And the LORD put a mark on Cain, lest any who came upon him should kill him" (Gen 4:15). And not only contemporary Judaism, but also Christianity has known all along that they have to separate the archaic elements of the Old Testament, which arose from prevailing circumstances, from their spiritual meaning. Augustine explains it in the following way:

> And yet, in these precepts and commandments of the Law which it is not now lawful for Christians to use, such as the sabbath or circumcision or sacrifices or anything of this kind, such great mysteries are contained that every faithful soul realizes that nothing is more dangerous than to take whatever is there literally, that is, according to the word, while nothing is more healthful than a revelation according to the spirit.[10]

It is true that the New Testament is completely unsuitable for justifying physical violence. Again and again, when Christians have forgotten that, their Christian admonishers are at least able to put the words of their own Sacred Scriptures before their eyes, words that praise the peacemakers and even call on them to love their enemies, not by way of exception, but always. An agitator for war has never been able seriously to reference the New Testament. It is also no wonder that Christians have always been involved whenever it has been a matter of liberation, whether in Poland, in the DDR, or in the many missionary countries where missionary schools furnished the local liberators with arguments, so that the brittle European colonial systems came crashing down.

Tolerance, however, can never be understood as mere general indifference that "does not care". That would only cause social instability and call forth fundamentalist reactions. Ancient Christians' understanding of tolerance should nowadays be granted new and even world historical relevance. Thus, Frankfurt sociologist Karl O. Hondrich noted at the death of John Paul II: "The tolerance of this pope did not lie in theoretical concepts, but in being interiorly deeply turned even toward those who did not share his thoughts. Perhaps human sympathy is one word for it."[11]

Turning the history of Christianity and the Church into a scandal is itself a scandal. The state of international historical scholarship, which is presented in this book and which has painstakingly extricated Christianity from the sludge of hundreds of years of polemics—and has yielded surprising results—makes that abundantly clear. There is a reason that the discovery of the secret history of Christianity is mainly, though not exclusively, about the Catholic Church. In the past five hundred years, there has been no period in which Protestant publications were not considerably superior to Catholic public relations work. That is why this book has had to correct false reports about the Catholic Church so often. Protestantism, moreover, mostly denies any responsibility for mistakes made by Christians in the first fifteen hundred years of Christianity, and so the reader might have more easily gotten the impression that most of the scandals of Christian history have to do with "Catholic" topics. In any case, this book is only about the history of Christianity. Whoever is looking for arguments on the existence of God can consult my book, Gott— Eine kleine Geschichte des Größtens (God—A Short History of the Most High), and whoever is interested in getting to know the Catholic Church (or modern psychotherapy) better, might be interested in my

Der Blockierte Riese—Psycho-Analyse der katholischen Kirche (The Blocked Giant—A Psychoanalysis of the Catholic Church).

In the end, we have to remind ourselves that the Church was never predicted to take over the entire world. Christianity, in this sense, is not after success. If some people are disconsolate over the fact that few people go to church, they should be reminded that "church attendance" at the time of Jesus was in the end around 8 percent: only one out of twelve apostles persevered at the Cross, "the disciple whom he loved", John. And at the end of the world, the New Testament foresees the great apostasy, the antichrist; not paradise on earth, but the apocalypse, the dramatic end of the world.

3. The End: The Strengths of Weakness

The atheist ideologies of the twentieth century relied on the perfect society after world revolution and on irreversible progress without any errors leading up to it, or on a perfect race, which by necessity would have to rule the world. That is why it was such a catastrophe for Marxists when real existing socialism failed to meet the requirements of the ideology, and Hitler saw the downfall of the German people as a necessary consequence to their having lost the struggle for world domination. Christianity is different. It is the religion of the non-perfect, the sinners, who hope in the grace of God, which passionately moved Martin Luther. It is certainly no coincidence that Jesus made Peter, the traitor, the apostle to whom the Bible attributes the most weaknesses, into the leader of the Church. Thus, it is not surprising to Christians that the history of the Church has enough weaknesses to show for itself, even betrayal of its origins, which had been radical nonviolence. Again and again, the Bible talks about the weakness of men, who are given the mercy of God exactly because of this weakness, if they believe, hope, and love. Most false teachings did not want to accept that as true, despaired at the weaknesses of the Church and its clergy, and devoted themselves to "pure" teachings and allegedly "pure" gurus, mostly with inhumane consequences. There could be no society fit for men without mercy for and understanding of their weakness—nor could there be a Church fit for men.

On March 12, 2000, at Saint Peter's Basilica, Pope John Paul II made a confession of guilt for the Church at Mass on the first Sunday of Lent. He did so not as Karol Wojtyla, but as pope, as the 263rd successor of Saint Peter. At the time, it was called a "a historically unique act". The pope asked for forgiveness for the fact "that even men of the Church, in the name of the faith and morals, have sometimes used methods not in keeping with the Gospel in the solemn duty of defending the truth."

He prayed that Christians would confess "the sins committed by not a few of their number against the people of the Covenant" and that Christians have allowed themselves to be led "by pride, by hatred, by the desire to dominate others, by enmity towards members of other religions" and societal groups. He said that it is necessary to pray "for women, who are all too often humiliated and marginalized", and "for minors who are victims of abuse, for the poor, the alienated, the disadvantaged, and the unborn".[12]

The pope ended Mass with an act of self-commitment: "No more contradictions of love in the service of the truth, no more gestures against the communion of the Church, no more offenses against any people, no more recourse to the logic of violence, no more discriminations, exclusions, oppressions, degradations of the poor and the lowly [gli ultimi]."[13]

Pope Francis always takes the sins of the Church very seriously and repeatedly stresses that he, the pope, is a sinner, too. And he therefore never forgets to ask his audience at the end of his speeches to pray for him. For Pope Francis also says this: true Christians are not perfect.

The ideologies of the twentieth century have collapsed under the confession of their mistakes; Christianity has drawn new hope in the merciful God from the awareness of sin, whether alongside Luther 500 years ago, or alongside John Paul II at the turn of the millennium. Christians believe in the God who made this 2000-year history into salvation history, despite all the terrible human weaknesses, even on the part of Christians.

This book speaks about the so-called scandals of the Church. But the actual history of Christianity is not featured in it. That is the history of the saints, of spiritual beginnings, but also of those who suffer, both the great and, above all, the quiet sufferers. And it is the history of Christian beauty in the cathedrals of the Middle Ages charging toward heaven, in the frescoes of Michelangelo Buonarroti, and in Johann Sebastian Bach's Saint Matthew Passion.

NOTES

Preface

1. Joseph Ratzinger and Jürgen Habermas, *The Dialectics of Secularization* (San Francisco: Ignatius Press, 2005), 11.

Chapter I

1. Moses Finley, *The World of Odysseus* (New York: New York Review of Books, 2002), 20–22.

2. Jan Assmann, *The Price of Monotheism*, trans. Robert Savage (Stanford, CA: Stanford University Press, 2010), 41–42.

3. Jan Assmann, "Zur Geschichte des Herzens im Alten Ägypten", in *Die Erfindung des inneren Menschen. Studien zur religiösen Anthropologie*, Studien zum Verstehen fremder Religionen 6, ed. Jan Assman, (Gütersloh: Güthersloher Verlagshaus G. Mohn, 1993), 82.

4. Agobard of Lyon, "De unitate legis", in *Monumenta Germaniae Historica: Epistolae*, vol. 5 (Berolini: Weidmannos, 1899), 159.

5. *Apostolic Fathers*, vol. II, ed. and trans. Bart D. Ehrman (Cambridge, MA: Harvard University Press, 2003), 141.

6. Karl O. Hondrich, "Die Divisionen des Papstes", *Frankfurter Allgemeine Zeitung*, April 16, 2005, 8.

7. Karl O. Hondrich, "Konflikt der Kulturen—Auf der Suche nach dem, was die Menschen über die Verschiedenartigkeit der Kulturen hinweg zusammenhält", in *Christen und Muslime. Verantwortung zum Dialog*, ed. Evangelische Akademien in Deutschland (Darmstadt: WBG, 2006), 107.

8. Otto G. Oexle, "*Tria genera hominum.* Zur Geschichte eines Deutungsschemas der sozialen Wirklichkeit in Antike und Mittelalter", in *Institutionen, Kultur und Gesellschaft im Mittelalter*, ed. Lutz Fenske et al. (Sigmaringen: Thorbecke, 1984), 486.

9. Jochen Martin, *Spätantike und Völkerwanderung* (Oldenbourg-Grundriß der Geschichte 4) (Munich: Oldenbourg Wissenschaftsverlag, 1987), 78.

10. Heinz E. Tödt, "Demokratie (I. Ethisch)", in *Theologische Realenzyklopädie*, vol. 8 (Berlin: De Gruyter, 1981), 437.

11. Assmann, *The Price of Monotheism*, 11, 16.

12. Jan Assmann, "Gottesbilder—Menschenbilder: anthropologische Konsequenzen des Monotheismus", in *Götterbilder—Gottesbilder—Weltbilder. Polytheismus und Monotheismus in der Welt der Antike*, vol. 2, ed. Reinhard Gregor Kratz and Hermann Spiekermann (Tübingen: Mohr Siebeck, 2006), 328f.

13. Gary Remer, "Ha-Me'iri's Theory of Religious Toleration", in *Beyond the Persecuting Society. Religious Toleration before the Enlightenment*, ed. John Christian Laursen and Cary J. Nederman (Philadelphia: University of Pennsylvania Press, 1998), 87.

14. Günter Stemberger, "Juden", in *Reallexikon für Antike und Christentum*, vol. 19 (Stuttgart: Anton Hiersemann Verlag, 2001), 218.

15. Michael Toch, *Eznyklopädie Deutscher Geshichte*, vol. 44, *Die Juden im mittelalterlichen Reich* (Munich: Oldenbourg Wissenschaftsverlag, 1998), 2.

16. Bernard Lewis, *Islam and the West* (Oxford: Oxford University Press, 1994), 53.

Chapter II

1. St. Augustine, "Sermon 4", in *Sermons on the Old Testament*, trans. Edmund Hill (Brooklyn: New City Press, 1990), 196.

2. St. Thomas Aquinas, *Summa Theologiae*, 2nd ed., trans. Fathers of the English Dominican Province (New York: Benziger Bros., 1947), II-II, q. 25, a. 6.

3. Tertullian, *Apologeticum* 24.6.

4. Tertullian, *Ad Scapulam* 2.2.

5. Gratian, *Decretum Gratiani*, pt. II, causa XXIII, q. IV. c. I.

6. St. Augustine, *City of God*, trans. Henry Bettenson (New York: Penguin, 2004), XVI.2, 650.

7. St. Augustine, *Ep* XCIII.9.34; *Letters 1–99*, trans. Roland Teske (Hyde Park, NY: New City Press, 2001), 398.

8. St. Augustine, *City of God*, I.9, 16.

9. Gratian, *Decretum Gratiani*, pt. II, causa XXIII, q. 5, c. 33.

10. *Summa Theologiae* II-II, q. 10, a. 8.

11. Adolf von Harnack, *The Expansion of Christianity in the First Three Centuries*, vol. 2, trans. and ed. James Moffatt (New York: G. P. Putnam's Sons, 1905), 50.

12. Norbert Brox, *Das Frühchristentum. Schriften zur historischen Theologie*, ed. Franz Dünzl et al. (Freiburg: Herder Freiburg, 2000), 352.

13. St. Augustine, Ep CXCIX.48; *Letters 156–210*, trans. Roland Teske (Hyde Park, NY: New City Press, 2001), 351.

14. Monica Blöcker, "Volkszorn im frühen Mittelalter. Eine thematisch begrenzte Studie", *Francia*, no. 13 (1985): 124.

15. Rainer Forst, *Toleration in Conflict: Past and Present*, trans. Ciaran Cronin (Cambridge: Cambridge University Press, 2003), 39, 42

16. Tilman Nagel, *Islam. Die Heilsbotschaft des Korans und ihre Konsequenzen* (Westhofen: WVA-Verlag, 2001), 102.

17. Timo J. Weissenberg, *Die Friedenslehre des Augustinus. Theologische Grundlagen und ethische Entfaltung*, Theologie und Frieden 28 (Stuttgart: Kohlhammer, 2005), 512, 519, 521.

18. Johannes Hahn, *Gewalt und religiöser Konflikt. Studien zu den Auseinandersetzungen zwischen Christen, Heiden und Juden im Osten des Römischen Reiches (von Konstantin bis Theodosius II.)* (Berlin: De Gruyter, 2004), 293.

19. "The Bond of Anathema", in *From Irenaeus to Grotius: A Sourcebook in Christian Political Thought*, ed. Oliver O'Donovan and Joan Lockwood O'Donovan (Grand Rapids, MI: Eerdmans, 1999), 178–79.

20. Hans-Peter Hasenfratz, "Krieg und Frieden bei den alten Germanen", in *Krieg und Frieden im Altertum*, ed. Gerhard Binder and Bernd Effe (Trier: Wissenschaftlicher Verlag Trier, 1989), 204.

21. Hans Hattenhauer, *Das Recht der Heiligen* (Berlin: Duncker & Humblot, 1976), 121.

22. Hans-Dietrich Kahl, "Die ersten Jahrhunderte des missionsgeschichtlichen Mittelalters. Bausteine für eine Phänomenologie bis ca. 1050", in *Die Kirche des frühen Mittelalters*, vol. 2, bk. 1, *Kirchengeschichte als Missionsgeschichte*, ed. Knut Schäferdiek (Munich: C. Kaiser, 1978), 58.

23. Max Weber, *Economy and Society*, trans. Ephraim Fischoff et al. (Berkeley, CA: University of California Press, 1978), 562.

24. Hans Eggers, *Deutsche Sprachgeschichte*, 2nd ed., vol. 1, *Das Althochdeutsche und das Mittelhochdeutsche* (Reinbek: Rowohlt, 1986), 197.

25. Natural mummies found in the peat bogs of Denmark, Germany, England—TRANS.

26. Georges Tugene, *L'idée de nation chez Bède le Vénérable* (Paris: Brepols, 2001), 203–9.

27. Venerable Bede, *Vita Gregorii* 8.

28. Heinrich Heine, *Sämtliche Werke*, vol. 3, ed. Uwe Schweikert (Munich: Winkler Verlag, 1972), 518f.

29. Thomas Scharff, *Die Kämpfe der Herrscher und Heiligen. Krieg und historische Erinnerung in der Karolingerzeit* (Darmstadt: Wissenschaftliche Buchgesellschaft, 2002), 11.

30. Einhard, *Vita Karoli* 7.

31. *Capitulatio de partibus Saxoniae* 8.

32. Dieter Hägermann, *Karl der Große. Herrscher des Abendlandes* (Berlin: Propyläen, 2000), 241ff.

33. Andreas Platthaus, "Kaiser Rotohr lobesam. Sockel und Reich: Berliner Akademiestreit über Karl den Großen", *Frankfurter Allgemeine Zeitung*, August 25, 2003, 33.

34. Robert Bartlett, *The Making of Europe: Conquest, Colonization, and Cultural Change* (New York: Allen Lane, 1993), 269.

35. Stephen Allott, *Alcuin of York, c. A.D. 732 to 804: His Life and Letters* (York: William Session Limited, 1974), 74.

36. Johannes Fried, *Der Weg in die Geschichte. Die Ursprünge Deutschlands bis 1024* (Berlin: Ullstein, 1998), 108–10.

37. *Epistularum Fuldensium Fragmenta* 11.

38. Hans-Dietrich Kahl, "Was bedeutet: 'Mittelalter'", *Saeculum*, no. 40 (1989): 33, 37f.

39. Gerd Tellenbach, *Die westliche Kirche vom 10. bis zum frühen 12. Jahrhundert* (Göttingen: Vandenhoeck and Ruprecht, 1988), 72.

40. Karl Leyser, *Communications and Power in Medieval Europe*, vol. 1, *The Gregorian Revolution and Beyond*, ed. Timothy Reuter (London: Hambledon Press, 1994), 1–19.

41. Thomas A. Brady, "Reformation als Rechtsbruch—Territorialisierung der Kirchen im Heiligen Römischen Reich im europäischen Vergleich", in *Die Säkularisation im Prozess der Säkularisierung Europas*, ed. Peter Blickle and Rudolf Schlögl (Epfendorf: Bibliotheca Academica Verlag, 2005), 148.

42. Fried, *Der Weg in die Geschichte*, 34.

Chapter III

1. Michael Mitterauer, *Warum Europa? Mittelalterliche Grundlagen eines Sonderwegs* (Munich: C. H. Beck, 2003), 180, 198.

2. Harold J. Berman, *Law and Revolution: The Formation of the Western Legal Tradition* (Cambridge, MA: Harvard University Press, 1983), 2, 22, 531.

3. Michael Borgolte, *Christen, Juden, Muselmanen. Die Erben der Antike und der Aufstieg des Abendlandes 300 bis 1400 n. Chr.* (Munich: Siedler Verlag, 2006), 573, 583f.

4. Borgolte, *Christen, Juden, Muselmanen*, 9.

5. Hans-Georg Beck, *Ideen und Realitäten* (London: Variorum Reprints, 1972), ch. 12.

6. Steven Runciman, *History of the Crusades*, vol. 1 (Cambridge: Cambridge University Press, 1951), 84.

7. Runciman, 101.

8. Jonathan Riley-Smith, "Der Aufruf von Clermont und seine Folgen", in *Kein Krieg ist heilig. Die Kreuzzüge*, ed. Hans-Jürgen Kotzur (Mainz: Philipp von Zabern, 2004), 55–56, 59.

9. Christoph Auffarth, *Irdische Wege und himmlischer Lohn. Kreuzzug, Jerusalem und Fegefeuer in religionswissenschaftlicher Perspektive* (Göttingen: Vandenhoeck & Ruprecht, 2002), 125.

10. Benjamin Z. Kedar, *Crusade and Mission: European Approaches towards the Muslims* (Princeton, NJ: Princeton University Press, 1984), 60.

11. Radulfus Niger, *De re militari et triplici via peregrinationis Ierosolimitane (1187/88)*, ed. Ludwig Schmugge (Berlin: De Gruyter, 1977), III.91.

12. Rudolf Hiestand, "Juden und Christen in der Kreuzzugspropaganda und bei den Kreuzzugspredigern", in *Juden und Christen zur Zeit der Kreuzzüge*, ed. Alfred Haverkamp (Sigmaringen: Thorbecke, 1999), 153–208.

13. Robert Chazan, *European Jewry and the First Crusade* (Berkeley, CA: University of California Press, 1987), 193.

14. Steven Runciman, *The History of the Crusades*, vol. 1 (Cambridge, MA: Harvard University Press, 1951), 141.

15. Albrecht Noth, "Heiliger Kampf (Gihad) gegen die 'Franken'. Zur Position der Kreuzzüge im Rahmen der Islamgeschichte", *Saeculum*, no. 37 (1986): 240–41, 246.

16. John France, *Victory in the East: A Military History of the First Crusade* (Cambridge: Cambridge University Press, 1994), 355.

17. Kaspar Elm, "Die Eroberung Jerusalem im Jahre 1099", in *Jerusalem im Hoch- und Spätmittelalter*, ed. Dieter Bauer et al. (Frankfurt: Campus Verlag, 2001), 42–46, 50, 46–53; David Hay, "Gender Bias and Religious Intolerance in Accounts of the 'Massacres' of the First Crusade", in *Tolerance and Intolerance. Social Conflict in the Age*

of the Crusade, ed. Michael Gervers and James M. Powell (Syracuse, NY: Syracuse University Press, 2001), 3–10.

18. Jean Flori, *Pierre l'Eremite et la première croisade* (Paris: Fayard, 1999), 451.

19. William of Tyre, *Chronicon* 8.20.

20. Tilman Nagel, *Islam. Die Heilsbotschaft des Korans und ihre Konsequenzen* (Westhofen: WVA-Verlag, 2001), 113.

21. Quoted in Arnold Angenendt, *Toleranz und Gewalt. Das Christentum zwischen Bibel und Schwert* (Münster: Aschendorff Verlag, 2007).

22. Quoted in Angenendt, *Toleranz*.

23. Quoted in Angenendt, *Toleranz*.

24. Norman Tanner, ed., *Decrees of the Ecumenical Councils*, vol. 1 (London: Sheed and Ward, 1990), 203.

25. Erasmus of Rotterdam, *The Complaint of Peace*, trans. T. Paynell (Chicago: Open Court Publishing Co., 1917), 18, 22.

26. Martin Luther, *Tischreden*, no. 3552.

27. Radulfus Niger, *De re militari*, III.90, IV.12.

28. Rainer C. Schwinges, *Kreuzzugsideologie und Toleranz. Studien zu Wilhelm von Tyrus* (Stuttgart: Hiersemann, 1977), 242, 245.

29. Walter Sturminger, ed., *Die Türken vor Wien in Augenzeugenberichten* (Düsseldorf: Karl Rausch Verlag, 1968), 27.

30. Kedar, *Crusade and Mission*, 57–74.

31. St. Augustine, *Decretum Gratiani*, pt. II, causa 23, q. 5, c. 33

32. Jonathan Riley-Smith, *What Were the Crusades?* (San Francisco: Ignatius Press, 2009), 11.

33. Carsten Colpe, *Problem Islam*, 2nd ed. (Weinheim: Philo Verlagsges, 1994), 17f.

34. *The Summa Parisiensis of the Decretum Gratiani*, ed. Terence P. McLaughlin (Toronto: Pontifical Institute for Medieval Studies, 1952), d. 45, c. 1, 40.

35. Marie-Louise Favreau-Lilie, "'Multikulturelle Gesellschaft' oder 'Persecuting Society'? 'Franken' und 'Einheimische' im Königreich Jerusalem", in *Jerusalem im Hoch- und Spätmittelalter*, ed. Dieter Bauer et al. (Frankfurt: Campus Verlag, 2001), 92.

36. Ernst-Dieter Hehl, "Die Kreuzzüge. Feindbild–Erfahrung–Reflexion", in *Kein Krieg ist heilig*, 243f.

37. Riley-Smith, *What Were the Crusades?*, xiii.

38. Norman Housley, *The Crusaders* (Charleston, SC: Tempus, 2002), 180–81.

39. Egon Flaig, "Der Islam will die Welteroberung", *Frankfurter Allgemeine Zeitung*, September 16, 2006, 37.

40. Juan Luis Vives, *Opera Omnia*, vol. 5, *Politico-Moralia* (London: Gregg Press, 1964), IV.13.

Chapter IV

1. Quoted in Arnold Angenendt, *Toleranz und Gewalt. Das Christentum zwischen Bibel und Schwert* (Münster: Aschendorff Verlag, 2007).

2. Innocent III, Letter 228, *PL* 214.

3. *The Saxon Mirror: A* Sachsenspiegel *of the Fourteenth Century*, trans. Maria Dobozy (Philadelphia: University of Pennsylvania Press, 1999), I.1, 68.

4. Alexander Patschovsky, "Was sind Ketzer? Über den geschichtlichen Ort der Häresien im Mittelalter", in *'... Eine finstere und fast unglaubliche Geschichte'? Mediävistische Notizen zu Umberto Ecos Mönchsroman 'Der Name der Rose'*, ed. Max Kerner (Darmstadt: Wissenschaftliche Buchgesellschaft, 1987), 177.

5. Heinrich Fichtenau, *Ketzer und Professoren. Häresie und Vernunftglaube* (Munich: C. H. Beck, 1992), 11.

6. Helmut Feld, *Franziskus von Assisi und seine Bewegung* (Darmstadt: Wissenschaftliche Buchgesellschaft, 1994), 189–90, 195.

7. Walter Rüegg, ed., *Geschichte der Universität in Europa*, vol. 1, *Mittelalter* (Munich: C. H. Beck, 1993), 47.

8. Georges Minois, *Geschichte des Atheismus* (Weimar: Böhlaus Nachfolger, 2000), 86.

9. Kurt Flasch, *Das philosophische Denken im Mittelalter. Von Augustin zu Macchiavelli* (Stuttgart: Reclam, 1987), 406f.

10. Winfried Trusen, *Der Prozeß gegen Meister Eckhart. Vorgeschichte, Verlauf und Folgen* (Paderborn: Ferdinand Schöningh, 1988), 122–23, 177.

11. Martin Brecht, *Martin Luther*, vol. 1, *Sein Weg zur Reformation 1483–1521* (Stuttgart: Calwer Verlag, 1981), 371.

12. William J. Courtenay, "Inquiry and Inquisition: Academic Freedom in Medieval Universities", *Church History* 58, no. 2 (1989): 174.

13. Wolfgang Schild, *Alte Gerichtsbarkeit. Vom Gottesurteil bis zum Beginn der modernen Rechtsprechung* (Munich: Callway, 1980), 93.

14. Richard van Dülmen, *Theater des Schreckens. Gerichtspraxis und Strafrituale in der frühen Neuzeit* (Munich: C. H. Beck, 1985).

15. Winfried Trusen, "Der Inquisitionsprozeß. Seine historischen Grundlagen und frühen Formen", in *Zeitschrift der Savigny-Stiftung für Rechtsgeschichte: Kanonistische Abteilung*, no. 74 (1988): 168, 214.

16. Winfried Trusen, "Inquisitionsprozeß", in *Lexikon des Mittelalters*, vol. 5 (Stuttgart: Artemis Verlag, 1991), 441f.

17. Arno Borst, *Die Katharer* (Stuttgart: Hiersemann Verlag, 1953), 181.

18. Hans Hattenhauer, *Europäische Rechtsgeschichte* (Heidelberg: C. F. Müller, 1992), 227.

19. Kurt Victor Selge, ed., *Texte zur Inquisition* (Gütersloh: Mohn, 1967), 66.

20. Lothar Kolmer, *Ad capiendas vulpes. Die Ketzerbekämpfung in Südfrankreich in der ersten Hälfte des 13. Jahrhunderts und die Ausübung des Inquisitionsverfahrens* (Bonn: Röhrscheid, 1982), 158.

21. Yves Dossat, *Les crises de l'inquisition toulousaine au XIIIe siècle (1233–1273)* (Bordeaux: Imprimerie Bière, 1959).

22. Jean-Louis Biget, "L'inquisition en Languedoc, 1229–1329", in *L'Inquisizione. Atti del Simposio internazionale Città del Vaticano, 29–31 ottobre 1998*, ed. Agostino Borromeo (Vatican City: Biblioteca Apostolica Vaticana, 2003), 83–84.

23. Borst, *Die Katharer*, 132.

24. Dietrich Kurze, "Anfänge der Inquisition in Deutschland", in *Die Anfänge der Inquisition im Mittelalter. Mit einem Ausblick auf das 20. Jahrhundert und einem Beitrag*

über religiöse Intoleranz im nichtchristlichen Bereich, ed. Peter Segl (Cologne: Böhlau, 1993), 146.

25. Henry Charles Lea, *A History of the Inquisition*, vol. 2 (New York: Macmillan, 1922), 386.

26. Alexander Patschovsky, ed., *Monumenta Germaniae Historica*, vol. 11, *Quellen zur böhmischen Inquisition im 14. Jahrhundert* (Weimar: Hermann Böhlaus Nachfolger, 1979), 20.

27. Alexander Patschovsky, "Häresie", in *Lexicon des Mittelalters*, vol. 4 (Stuttgart: Artemis Verlag, 1989), 1936.

28. Gerd Schwerhoff, "Blasphemie vor den Schranken der städtischen Justiz: Basel, Köln und Nürnberg im Vergleich", *Ius Commune*, no. 25 (1998): 40.

29. Patschovsky, "Was sind Ketzer?", 181f.

30. Berthold Seewald, "Die unseligste Frau der modernen Geschichte", *Die Welt*, October 21, 2011, https://www.welt.de/kultur/history/article13672919/Die -unseligste-Frau-der-modernen-Geschichte.html.

31. Jacob Burckhardt, *Die Kultur der Renaissance in Italien* (Herrsching: Pawlak, 1981), 141.

32. Quoted in Arnold Angenendt, *Toleranz und Gewalt. Das Christentum zwischen Bibel und Schwert* (Münster: Aschendorff Verlag, 2007).

Chapter V

1. The Roman Catholic Church still acknowledges partial and plenary indulgences, rightly understood, although the purchase and sale of such indulgences is invalid.—TRANS.

2. Heiko A. Oberman, *Die Kirche im Zeitalter der Reformation* (Neukirchen-Vluyn: Neukirchener, 1981), 95.

3. Martin Brecht, *Martin Luther*, vol. 1, *Sein Weg zur Reformation 1483–1521* (Stuttgart: Calwer Verlag, 1981), 331.

4. Henry Kamen, *The Spanish Inquisition: An Historical Revision* (New Haven, CT: Yale University Press, 1997), 193.

5. Kamen, *The Spanish Inquisition*, 191.

6. Edward Peters, *Inquisition* (Berkeley, CA: University of California Press, 1989), 92.

7. Stephen Haliczer, *Inquisition and Society in the Kingdom of Valencia, 1478–1834* (Berkeley, CA: University of California Press, 1990), 79.

8. Henry Charles Lea, *A History of the Inquisition of Spain*, vol. III (New York: Macmillan, 1907), 2.

9. E. William Monter, *Ritual, Myth and Magic in Early Modern Europe* (Brighton: Harvester Press, 1983), 72.

10. Stephen Haliczer *Inquisition and Society in the Kingdom of Valencia*, 78.

11. Kamen, *Spanish Inquisition*, 187, 201.

12. Henry Charles Lea, *A History of the Inquisition of Spain*, vol. II (New York: Macmillan, 1906), 509.

13. Gustav Henningsen, "The Database of the Spanish Inquisition. The 'relaciones de causas'-project revisited", in *Vorträge zur Justizforschung. Theorie und Geschichte*, ed. Heinz Mohnhaupt and Dieter Simon (Frankfurt: Klostermann, 1993), 54.

14. Kamen, *Spanish Inquisition*, 203.

15. Quoted in Arnold Angenendt, *Toleranz und Gewalt. Das Christentum zwischen Bibel und Schwert* (Münster: Aschendorff Verlag, 2007).

16. John Tedeschi, *The Prosecution of Heresy: Collected Studies on the Inquisition in Early Modern Italy* (Tempe, AZ: Medieval and Renaissance Texts and Studies, 1991), 3, 8–9.

17. Peter Godman, *Die geheime Inquisition. Aus den verbotenen Archiven des Vatikans* (Munich: List Verlag, 2002), 357, 359.

18. Georges Minois, *Geschichte des Atheismus* (Weimar: Böhlaus Nachfolger, 2000), 174.

19. Minois, *Geschichte des Atheismus*, 174.

20. Hans Blumenberg, *Die Genesis der kopernikanischen Welt* (Frankfurt: Suhrkamp, 1981).

21. Arthur Koestler, *Die Nachtwandler. Die Entstehungsgeschichte unserer Welterkenntnis* (Frankfurt: Suhrkamp, 1980), 431.

22. Blumenberg, *Die Genesis der kopernikanischen Welt*, 470.

23. Carl Friedrich von Weizsäcker, *Der Garten des Menschlichen* (Munich: Hanser, 1977), 462.

24. Bertolt Brecht, *Werke*, vol. 24 (Frankfurt: Suhrkamp, 1945).

25. William Monter, "Heresy Executions in Reformation Europe, 1520–1565", in *Tolerance and Intolerance in the European Reformation*, ed. Ole Peter Grell and Bob Scribner (Cambridge: Cambridge University Press, 2002), 50.

26. Gerd Schwerhoff, "Blasphemie vor den Schranken der städtischen Justiz: Basel, Köln und Nürnberg im Vergleich", *Ius Commune*, no. 25 (1998): 76, 86.

27. Edward Peters, *Inquisition* (Berkeley, CA: University of California Press, 1989), 87.

28. Alain Cabantous, *Blasphemy: Impious Speech in the West from the Seventeenth to the Nineteenth Century*, trans. Eric Rauth (New York: Columbia University Press, 2002), 66–75.

29. Heiko A. Oberman, *Die Reformation. Von Wittenberg nach Genf* (Göttingen: Vandenhoeck & Ruprecht, 1986).

30. Quoted in Angenendt, *Toleranz*.

31. Dietmar Willoweit, "Katholische Reform und Disziplinierung als Element der Staats- und Gesellschaftsorganisation", in *Glaube und Eid. Treueformeln, Glaubensbekenntnisse und Sozialdisziplinierung zwischen Mittelalter und Neuzeit*, ed. Paolo Prodi (Munich: Oldenbourg, 1993), 130.

32. Francisca Loetz, *Mit Gott handeln* (Göttingen: Vandenhoeck & Rupert, 2002), 117.

33. Wolfgang Speyer, *Büchervernichtung und Zensur des Geistes bei Heiden, Juden und Christen* (Stuttgart: Hiersemann, 1981), 138.

34. Berndt Hamm, "Die Reformation als Medienereignis", *Jahrbuch für biblische Theologie*, no. 11 (1996).

35. Hubert Wolf, *Index. Der Vatikan und die verbotenen Bücher* (Munich: C.H. Beck, 2006), 13.

36. Thomas More, *Utopia*, trans. Clarence Miller (New Haven, CT: Yale University Press, 2001), 118.

37. Hubert Wolf, "Kontrolle des Wissens. Zensur und Index der verbotenen Bücher", *Theologische Revue* 99, no. 6 (2003): 452.

Chapter VI

1. Rita Voltmer and Franz Irsigler, "Die europäischen Hexenverfolgungen der Frühen Neuzeit—Vorurteile, Faktoren und Bilanzen", in *Hexenwahn. Ängste der Neuzeit. Begleitband zur gleichnamigen Ausstellung des Deutschen Historischen Museums*, ed. Rosmarie Beier-de Haan (Wolfratshausen: Edition Minerva Hermann Farnung, 2002), 33.

2. Wolfgang Behringer, *Hexen. Glaube, Verfolgung, Vermarktung* (Munich: C.H. Beck, 1998), 76.

3. Johannes Neumann, "Martyrium—Inquisition—Exorzismus", in *Angst und Gewalt. Ihre Präsenz und ihre Bewältigung in den Religionen*, ed. Heinrich von Stietencron (Düsseldorf: Patmos Verlag, 1979), 197.

4. Quoted in Arnold Angenendt, *Toleranz und Gewalt. Das Christentum zwischen Bibel und Schwert* (Münster: Aschendorff Verlag, 2007).

5. Rainer Decker, *Witchcraft and the Papacy: An Account Drawing on the Formerly Secret Records of the Roman Inquisition*, trans. H.C. Erik Midelfort (Charlottesville, VA: University of Virginia Press, 2008), 134–35.

6. Kim Siebenhüner, "Zwischen Justiz, Pädagogik und Bürokratie. Zur Gewalt der Römischen Inquisition (1600–1750)", in *Religion und Gewalt. Konflikte, Rituale, Deutungen (1500–1800)* (Göttingen: Vandenhoeck & Ruprecht, 2006), 385.

7. Arno Borst, "Anfänge des Hexenwahns in den Alpen", in *Ketzer, Zauberer, Hexen. Die Anfänge der europäischen Hexenverfolgung*, ed. Andreas Blauert (Frankfurt: Suhrkamp, 1990), 51.

8. Gerhard Schormann, *Hexenprozesse in Deutschland*, 2nd ed. (Göttingen: Vandenhoeck & Ruprecht, 1986), 42f.

9. Behringer, *Hexen*, 100.

10. Mathilde Ludendorff and Walter Löhde, *Christliche Grausamkeit an Deutschen Frauen*, 2nd ed. (Munich: Ludendorff, 1936), 7.

11. Mary Daly, *Gyn/Ecology. The Metaethics of Radical Feminism* (Boston: Beacon Press, 1981), 178–222.

12. Quoted in Angenendt, *Toleranz*.

13. Sibylla Flügge, "Rezension zu Gunnar Heinsohn, Otto Steiger, Die Vernichtung der weisen Frauen, Hemsbach/W. 1985", *Feministische Studien*, no. 1 (1986): 149–53.

14. Quoted in Angenendt, *Toleranz*.

15. Quoted in Angenendt, *Toleranz*.

16. Code of Hammurabi, § 2.

17. Wilhelm G. Soldan and Heinrich Heppe, *Geschichte der Hexenprozesse*, vol. 1, 3rd ed. (Hanau: Muller & Kiepenheuer, 1975), 116.

18. Richard Kieckhefer, *Magic in the Middle Ages* (Cambridge: Canto, 2000), 177–80.

19. Quoted in Angenendt, *Toleranz*.

20. Regino von Prüm, *Libri duo de synodalibus causis et disciplinis ecclesiasticis*, 371

21. Behringer, *Hexen*, 75, 32f.

22. Gerhard Schormann, *Hexenprozesse in Deutschland*, 26f.

23. Gregory VII, Letter 21.

24. *The Saxon Mirror: A* Sachsenspiegel *of the Fourteenth Century*, trans. Maria Dobozy (Philadelphia: University of Pennsylvania Press, 1999), 97.

25. Günter Jerouschek, "Vom Schadenszauber zum Teufelspakt: Friedrich von Spees Kampfschrift gegen ein Gesinnungsstrafrecht. Überlegungen zur Herausbildung von Hexereidelikt und Hexenprozeß aus rechtshistorischer Perspektive", in *Die politische Theologie Friedrich von Spees*, ed. Doris Brockmann and Peter Eicher (Munich: Wilhelm Fink Verlag, 1991), 142, 145.

26. Borst, "Anfänge des Hexenwahns in den Alpen", 61.

27. Quoted in Angenendt, *Toleranz*.

28. Winfried Trusen, "Benedict Carpzov und die Hexenverfolgungen", in *Recht und Kriminalität. Festschrift für Friedrich-Wilhelm Krause zum 70. Geburtstag* (Cologne: C. Heymann, 1990), 23.

29. *The Hammer of Witches: A Complete Translation of the* Malleus Maleficarum, trans. Christopher S. Mackay (Cambridge: Cambridge University Press, 2009), 75.

30. Günter Jerouschek and Wolfgang Behringer, "'Das unheilvollste Buch der Weltliteratur?' Zur Entstehungs und Wirkungsgeschichte des 'Malleus Maleficarum' und zu den Anfängen der Hexenverfolgung", in *Der Hexenhammer: Malleus Maleficarum*, ed. Wolfgang Behringer et al. (Munich: Deutscher Taschenbuch Verlag, 2000), 96.

31. Thomas Hobbes, *Leviathan* (New York: Penguin, 1985), 92.

32. Sönke Lorenz, "Zur Sprachpraxis der Juristenfakultät Mainz in Hexenprozessen", in *Hexenglaube und Hexenprozesse im Raum Rhein–Mosel–Saar*, ed. Gunther Franz and Franz Irsigler (Trier: Spee, 1995), 77.

33. Gerd Schwerhoff, "Die Erdichtung der weisen Männer. Gegen falsche Übersetzungen von Hexenglauben und Hexenverfolgung", in *Hexenverfolgung. Beiträge zur Forschung—unter besonderer Berücksichtigung des südwestdeutschen Raumes*, ed. Sönke Lorenz and Dieter R. Bauer (Würzburg: Königshausen und Neumann, 1995), 409.

34. Brian R. Levack, *The Witch-Hunt in Early Modern Europe*, 4th ed. (New York: Routledge, 2016), 82.

35. Gustav Henningsen, "La inquisición y las brujas", in *L'inquisizione. Atti del Simposio internazionale. Città del Vaticano, 29–31 ottobre 1998*, ed. Agostino Borromeo (Vatican City: Biblioteca Apostolica Vaticana, 2003), 584.

36. Günter Jerouschek, "Friedrich Spee als Justizkritiker. Die Cautio criminalis im Lichte des gemeinen Strafrechts der frühen Neuzeit", in *Friedrich Spee zum 400. Geburtstag. Kolloquium der Friedrich-Spee-Gesellschaft Trier*, ed. Gunter Franz (Paderborn: Bonifatius, 1995), 125.

37. Ingrid Ahrendt-Schulte, introduction to *Geschlecht, Magie und Hexenverfolgung*, ed. Ingrid Ahrendt-Schulte et al. (Bielefeld: Verlag für Regionalgeschichte, 2002), 10.

38. Levack, *The Witch-Hunt*, 84.

39. Rainer Decker, *Die Päpste und die Hexen* (Darmstadt: Primus Verlag 2003), 102.

40. Friedrich von Spee, *Cautio Criminalis oder Rechtliches Bedenken wegen der Hexenprozesse*, trans. Joachim-Friedrich Ritter (Munich: DTV, 1982), 3.

41. Quoted in Angenendt, *Toleranz*.

42. Spee, *Cautio Criminalis*, 134.

43. Quoted in Angenendt, *Toleranz*.

44. *Frankfurter Allgemeine Zeitung*, July 24, 2002.

Chapter VII

1. Jan Assmann, *Moses der Ägypter. Entzifferung einer Gedächtnisspur* (Munich: Carl Hanser, 1998), 73.

2. Immanuel Kant, *Perpetual Peace: A Philosophical Essay*, trans. M. Campbell Smith (New York: Macmillan, 1907), 164.

3. Tzvetan Todorov, *Die Eroberung Amerikas* (Frankfurt: Suhrkamp Verlag KG, 2005), 76.

4. Tzvetan Todorov, *Die Eroberung Amerikas*, 108f.

5. *History of the Expansion of Christianity*, vol. 3 (New York: Harper and Bros., 1939), 434.

6. Gratian, *Decretum*, dist. I, c. 7.

7. St. Thomas Aquinas, *Summa Theologiae*, 2nd ed., trans. Fathers of the English Dominican Province (New York: Benziger Bros, 1947), II-I, q. 94, a. 2.

8. Arthur F. Utz, ed., *Naturgesetz und Naturrecht. Theologische Summe, Fragen 90–97* (Bonn: Scientia Humana Institut, 1996), 221.

9. Aquinas, *Summa Theologiae* II-II, q. 60, a. 5.

10. Mariano Delgado, *Missionstheologische und anthropologische Gemeinsamkeiten und Unterschiede zwischen Katholiken und Protestanten im Entdeckungszeitalter*, ZMRW, no. 87 (2003): 109, 110.

11. Gudrun Hentges, *Schattenseiten der Aufklärung: Die Darstellung von Juden un 'Wilden' in philosophischen Schriften des 18. und 19. Jahrhunderts* (Schwalback: Wochenschau Verlag, 1999).

12. Quoted in Arnold Angenendt, *Toleranz und Gewalt. Das Christentum zwischen Bibel und Schwert* (Münster: Aschendorff Verlag, 2007).

13. Quoted in Angenendt, *Toleranz*.

14. Horst Gründer, "Genozid oder Zwangsmodernisierung?—Der moderne Kolonialismus in unversalgeschichtlicher Perspective", in *Genozid und Moderne*, vol. 1, *Strukturen kollektiver Gewalt im 20. Jahrhundert*, ed. Mihran Dabag and Kristin Platt (Opladen: Leske & Budrich, 1998), 139.

15. Gründer, "Genozid oder Zwangsmodernisierung?", 142.

16. Thomas More, *Utopia*, trans. Paul Turner (London: Penguin Books, 2003), 100.

17. Antonio de Montesinos, in *Witness: Writings of Bartolomé de Las Casas*, ed. and trans. George Sanderlin (Maryknoll, NY: Orbis Books, 1992), 66–67.

18. Francisco de Vitoria, *Relectiones. De Indis*.

19. Wolfgang Reinhard, *Geschichte der europäischen Expansion* (Stuttgart: Kohlhammer Verlag, 1988), 67–68.

20. Urs Bitterli, *Alte Welt—Neue Welt* (Munich: C. H. Beck, 1986), 96.

21. Roberto Fernandez Retamar, *Caliban and Other Essays*, trans. Edward Baker (Minneapolis: University of Minnesota Press, 1989), 58.

22. Alain Milhou, "Lateinamerika", in *Die Geschichte des Christentums. Religion, Politik, Kultur*, vol. 8, ed. Marc Venard and Heribert Smolinsky (Freiburg: Heribert Smolinsky, 1992), 795.

23. Pope Paul III, encyclical letter *Sublimis Deus* (June 2, 1537), translated in Francis Augustus MacNutt, *Bartholomew de las Casas: His Life, His Apostolate, and His Writings* (Cleveland, OH: Arthur H. Clark Co., 1909), 427–31.

24. Quoted in Gustavo Gutiérrez, *Las Casas: In Search of the Poor of Jesus Christ*, trans. Robert R. Barr (Eugene, OR: Wipf and Stock, 2003), 62.

Chapter VIII

1. Matthias Asche and Anton Schindling, ed., *Das Strafgericht Gottes* (Münster: Aschendorff, 2002), 34.

2. The division of Christianity into various confessional denominations— TRANS.

3. Heinz Schilling, "Die Konfessionalisierung von Kirche, Staat und Gesellschaft—Profil, Leistung, Defizite und Perspektiven eines geschichtswissenschaftlichen Paradigmas", in *Die katholische Konfessionalisierung*, ed. Wolfgang Reinhard and Heinz Schilling (Gütersloh: Gütersloher Verlagshaus, 1995), 41.

4. Johann Wolfgang von Goethe, *Goethes Werke*, ed. Erich Trunz, vol. 14 (Munich: C. H. Beck, 1999), 81; Wolfgang Neuber, Claus Zittel, and Thomas Rahn, introduction to *The Making of Copernicus: Early Modern Transformations of a Scientist and His Science*, ed. Wolfgang Neuber, Thomas Rahn, and Claus Zittel (Boston: Brill, 2014).

5. Friedrich W. Graf, *Moses Vermächtnis: Über göttliche und menschliche Gesetze* (Munich: C. H. Beck, 2006), 77.

6. Jean-Jacques Rousseau, *Émile, or On Education*, ed. and trans. Christopher Kelly and Allan Bloom (Hanover, NH: Dartmouth College Press, 2010), 454.

7. Max Weber, *General Economic History*, trans. Frank H. Knight (Mineola, NY: Dover, 2003), 365.

8. Quoted in Arnold Angenendt, *Toleranz und Gewalt. Das Christentum zwischen Bibel und Schwert* (Münster: Aschendorff Verlag, 2007).

9. Bernard Lewis, *The Crisis of Islam* (New York: Random House, 2004), 115ff.

10. Hartmut Hoffmann, "Kirche und Sklaverei im frühen Mittelalter", in *Deutsches Archiv für Erforschung des Mittelalters*, no. 42 (1986): 1–24, 21.

11. *The Saxon Mirror: A* Sachsenspiegel *of the Fourteenth Century*, trans. Maria Dobozy (Philadelphia: University of Pennsylvania Press, 1999), 126.

12. Gratian, *Decretum*, VI.33; *PL* 140: 772C.

13. Meister Eckhart, "The Nobleman", in *The Complete Mystical Works of Meister Eckhart*, trans. and ed. Maurice O'C. Walshe (New York: Herder and Herder, 2007), 559.

14. Francisco de Vitoria, "On the American Indians", in *Political Writings*, trans. and ed. Anthony Pagden and Jeremy Lawrance (Cambridge: Cambridge University Press, 1991), 242.

15. *The Complaint of Peace*, trans. T. Paynell (Chicago: Open Court Publishing Co., 1917), 29.

16. John Milton, "Areopagitica", in *Essential Prose of John Milton*, ed. William Kerrigan, John Rumrich, and Stephen M. Fallon (New York: Modern Library, 2007), 178.

17. Jürgen Habermas and Joseph Ratzinger, *The Dialectics of Secularization: On Reason and Religion* (San Francisco: Ignatius Press, 2005), 24.

18. Murray Gordon, *Slavery in the Arab World* (New York: New Amsterdam, 1989), 44.

19. Montesquieu, *The Complete Works of M. de Montesquieu*, vol. 1, *The Spirit of Laws* (London: T. Evans, 1777), 317.

20. Montesquieu, *Complete Works*, 1:315

21. Rodney Stark, *For the Glory of God: How Monotheism Led to Reformations, Science, Witch-Hunts, and the End of Slavery* (Princeton, NJ: Princeton University Press, 2003), 359f.

22. Peter Gay, *The Enlightenment*, vol. 2, *The Science of Freedom* (New York: W. W. Norton & Co., 1977), 410.

23. Christian Delacampagne, *Die Geschichte der Sklaverei* (Düsseldorf: Artemis & Winkler, 2004).

24. Robin Blackburn, *The Making of New World Slavery: From the Baroque to the Modern, 1492–1800* (London: Verso, 1997), 590.

25. Stark, *For the Glory of God*, 291, 293, 325.

26. Ephraim ben Isaak, "Biblical Literature: Hebrew Scriptures", in *A Historical Guide to World Slavery*, ed. Seymour Drescher and Stanley L. Engerman (Oxford: Oxford University Press, 1998), 93, 95.

27. Alexander Roberts and James Donaldson, ed., *The Ante-Nicene Fathers*, vol. 7 (New York: Charles Scribner's Sons, 1905), 151.

28. Egon Flaig, *Weltgeschichte der Sklaverei* (Munich: C.H. Beck, 2009), 978.

29. Cyprian, Letter 62.

30. Ambrose, "On the Duties of Clergy", in *A Select Library of Nicene and Post-Nicene Fathers*, vol. 10, trans. H. de Romestin (Oxford: James Parker and Co., 1896), II.28.136, 64.

31. Ambrose, "On the Duties of Clergy", II.28.136, 64.

32. Bishop Caesarius of Arles, *Caesarius of Arles: Life, Testament, Letters*, ed. and trans. William E. Klingshirn (Liverpool: Liverpool University Press, 1994), 25.

33. Adalbert Erler, "Loskauf Gefangener", in *HDRG*, vol. 3 (1984): 53.

34. Jean-Pierre Devroey, "Men and Women in Early Medieval Serfdom: The Ninth-Century North Frankish Evidence", *Past and Present*, no. 166 (February 2000), 30.

35. *The Saxon Mirror*, 125.

36. František Graus, *Pest—Geißler—Judenmorde. Das 14. Jahrhundert als Krisenzeit*, 2nd ed. (Göttingen: Vandenhoeck & Ruprecht, 1988), 105.

37. Eugene IV, papal bull *Sicut dudum* (January 13, 1435), quoted in Joel S. Panzer, *The Popes and Slavery* (New York: Alba House, 1996), 75.

38. Erasmus of Rotterdam, *The Education of Christian Prince*, trans. Neil M. Cheshire and Michael J. Heath (Cambridge: Cambridge University Press, 1997), 40.

39. Heiko A. Oberman, *Die Kirche im Zeitalter der Reformation* (Neukirchenen-Vluyn: Neukirchener, 1994), 128.

40. Stéphane Lebecq et al., "Sklave (Westen)", in *Lexicon des Mittelalters*, vol. 7 (Munich: Artemis and Winkler, 1995), 1979.

41. Rodney Stark, *The Victory of Reason* (New York: Random House, 2007), 28.

42. Norman P. Tanner, ed., *Decrees of the Ecumenical Councils* (London: Sheed & Ward, 1990), 1:223.

43. Seymour Drescher and Stanley L. Engerman, eds., "Moral Issues", in *A Historical Guide to World Slavery* (Oxford: Oxford University Press, 1998), 284.

44. Urban VIII, papal bull *Commissum nobis* (April 22, 1639), quoted in Arthur Utz and Brigitta von Galen, ed., *Die katholische Sozialdoktrin in ihrer geschichtlichen Entfaltung. Eine Sammlung päpstlicher Dokumente vom 15. Jahrhundert bis in die Gegenwart*, vol. 1 (Aachen: Scientia Humana Institut, 1976), 384.

45. Stark, *For the Glory of God*, 343.

46. Stark, *The Victory of Reason*, xiv.

47. Orlando Patterson, "Freiheit, Sklaverei und die moderne Konstruktion der Rechte", in *Die kulturellen Werte Europas*, ed. Hans Joas and Klaus Wiegandt (Frankfurt: Fischer Taschenbuch, 2005), 172–73.

48. Stark, *For the Glory of God*, 291.

49. Hans Joas, *Braucht der Mensch Religion? Über Erfahrungen der Selbsttranszendenz* (Freiburg: Herder, 2004), 127.

50. Rainer Forst, *Toleranz im Konflikt. Geschichte, Gehalt und Gegenwart eines umstrittenen Begriffs* (Frankfurt: Suhrkamp Verlag, 2003), 366, 567.

51. Jean-Edme Romilly, "Tolérance—Toleranz", in *Enzyklopädie. Eine Auswahl*, ed. Denis Diderot and Jean-Baptiste le Rond d'Alembert, trans. Günter Berger (Frankfurt: Fischer Taschenbuch, 1989), 279.

52. Jean-Jacques Rousseau, *The Social Contract*, trans. Maurice Cranston (New York: Penguin, 1968), 183.

53. Hartmut Lehmann, *Säkularisierung. Der europäische Sonderweg in Sachen Religion* (Göttingen: Wallstein Verlag, 2004), 91f.

54. Quoted in Arnold Angenendt, *Toleranz und Gewalt. Das Christentum zwischen Bibel und Schwert* (Münster: Aschendorff Verlag, 2007).

55. Quoted in Angenendt, *Toleranz*.

56. Quoted in Angenendt, *Toleranz*.

57. Quoted in Angenendt, *Toleranz*.

58. Michel Vovelle, *Französische Revolution—Soziale Bewegung und Umbruch der Mentalitäten*, trans. Peter Schöttler (Munich: Oldenbourg, 1982), 141.

Chapter IX

1. Otfried Höffe, "Christliche Sozialethik im Horizont der Ethik der Gegenwart", in *Christliche Sozialethik im weltweiten Horizont*, ed. Franz Furger and Joachim Wiemeyer (Münster: Aschendorff, 1992), 78–89, 87.

2. Pius VI, encyclical letter *Quod aliquantum* 11 (March 10, 1791), http://w2 .vatican.va/content/pius-vi/it/documents/breve-quod-aliquantum-10-marzo -1791.html.

3. *Quod aliquantum* 13.

4. Albert Soboul, *The French Revolution: 1787–1799, From the Storming of the Bastille to Napoleon* (New York: Routledge, 1989) 127.

5. Frank Maloy Anderson, *The Constitutions and Other Select Documents Illustrative of the History of France, 1789–1907*, 2nd ed. (Minneapolis: The H.W. Wilson Company, 1908), 59–60.

6. Pope Pius VI, quoted in Karl D. Erdmann, *Volkssouveränität und Kirche. Studien über das Verhältnis von Staat und Religion in Frankreich vom Zusammentritt der Generalstände bis zum Schisma, 5. Mai 1789–13. April 1791* (Cologne: Kölner Universitätsverlag, 1949), 297f.

7. Wilhelm Emmanuel von Ketteler, *Offenes Schreiben Kettelers als Deputierter der deutschen Nationalversammlung an seine Wähler (1848)*, in *Wilhelm Emmanuel von Kettelers Schriften*, ed. Johannes Mumbauer, vol. 1 (Kösel: Kempten and Munich 1911), 401.

8. Kurt Nowak, *Geschichte des Christentums in Deutschland* (Munich: Beck, 1995), 124.

9. Thomas Nipperdey, *Germany from Napoleon to Bismarck: 1800–1866*, trans. Daniel Nolan (Princeton, NJ: Princeton University Press, 1996), 339.

10. Kurt Nowak, *Geschichte des Christentums*, 548.

11. Leo XIII, encyclical letter *Immortale Dei* (November 1, 1885), no. 36.

12. Heinz E. Tödt, "Demokratie (I. Ethisch)", in *Theologische Realenzyklopädie* (Leipzig: Walter de Gruyter, 1981), 437.

13. Thomas Nipperdey, *Deutsche Geschichte 1866–1918*, vol. 1 (Munich: C.H. Beck, 1990), 465.

14. Karl Rohe et al., "Politische Gesellschaft und politische Kuktur", in *Das Ruhrgebiet*, vol. 2, ed. Wolfgang Köllmann et al. (Düsseldorf: Schwann im Patmos, 1990), 448.

15. Michaela Bachem-Rehm, *Die katholischen Arbeitervereine im Ruhrgebiet 1870–1914. Katholisches Arbeitermilieu zwischen Tradition und Emanzipation* (Stuttgart: Kohlhammer W., 2004), 239.

Chapter X

1. Joseph Mausbach, "Nationalismus und christlicher Universalismus", *Hochland* 9, no. 1 (1912).

2. Wolfgang J. Mommsen, "Die nationalgeschichtliche Umdeutung der christlichen Botschaft im Ersten Weltkrieg", in *"Gott mit uns": Nation, Religion un Gewalt*

im 19. und frühen 20. Jahrhundert, ed. Gerd Krumeich and Hartmut Lehmann (Göttingen: Vandenhoeck & Ruprecht, 2000), 258.

3. *Feldgesangbuch für die katholischen Mannschaften des Heeres* (Berlin: Verlag der Germania, 1914), 41.

4. Heinrich Missalla, *Für Gott, Führer und Vaterland* (Munich: Kösel, 1999), 52.

5. Thomas Nipperdey, *Deutsche Geschichte 1866–1918*, vol. 1 (Munich: C.H. Beck, 1990), 468.

6. Ralf Dahrendorf, *Versuchungen der Unfreiheit. Erasmus-Intellektuelle im Zeitalter des Totalitarismus* (Berlin: C.H. Beck, 2005), 5.

7. Martin Heidegger, "A Letter from Martin Heidegger to Elisabeth Blochman", trans. Alexander Moore, *The Review of Metaphysics*, 62, no. 3 (March 2019): 560.

8. Gerhard Besier, *Kirche, Politik und Gesellschaft im 19. Jahrhundert. Enzykolpädie Deutscher Geschichete* 48 (Munich: De Gruyter Oldenbourg, 1998), 9.

9. Quoted in Angenendt, *Toleranz*.

10. Manfred Kittel, "Konfessioneller Konflikt und politische Kultur in der Weimarer Republik", in *Konfessionen im Konflikt. Deutschland zwischen 1800 und 1970: ein zweites konfessionelles Zeitalter*, ed. Olaf Blaschke (Göttingen: Vandenhoeck & Ruprecht, 2002), 250.

11. Hans-Ulrich Wehler, *Deutsche Gesellschaftsgeschichte*, vol. 4 (Munich: C.H. Beck, 2003), 797.

12. Wehler, *Deutsche Gesellschaftsgeschichte*, 797.

13. Kurt Nowak, *Geschichte des Christentums in Deutschland* (Munich: Beck, 1995), 245, 256.

14. Rudolf Lill, "Konkordate", in *Theologische Realenzyklopädie*, vol. 19 (Berlin: De Gruyter, 2000), 469.

15. Gerhard Besier, *Kirche, Politik und Gesellschaft im 20. Jahrhundert* (Munich: De Gruyter Oldenbourg, 2000), 24f.

16. Werner K. Blessing, "'Deutschland in Not, wir im Glauben...' Kirche und Kirchenvolk in einer katholischen Region 1933–1949", in *Von Stalingrad zur Währungsreform. Zur Sozialgeschichte des Umbruchs in Deutschland*, ed. Martin Broszat et al. (Munich: Oldenbourg Wissenschaftsverlag, 1989), 45.

17. Jürgen W. Falter, *Hitlers Wähler* (Munich: C.S. Beck, 1991) 175, 177, 179.

18. Heinz Boberach, *Berichte des SD und der Gestapo über Kirchen und Kirchenvolk in Deutschland 1934–1944* (Mainz: Matthias-Grünewald, 1971), 356.

19. Günther van Norden, "Die evangelische Kirche und der Kriegsausbruch 1939", in *Evangelische Kirche im Zweiten Weltkrieg*, ed. Günther van Norden and Volkmar Wittmütz (Cologne: Habelt, 1991), 125.

20. Wehler, *Deutsche Gesellschaftsgeschichte*, 809, 817.

21. Helmut Moll, *Martyrium und Wahrheit. Zeugen Christi im 20. Jahrhundert* (Weilheim-Bierbronnen: Gustav-Siewerth-Akademie, 2005), 30.

22. Manfred Gailus, *Protestantismus und Nationalsozialismus: Studien zur nationalsozialistischen Durchdringung des protestantischen Sozialmilieus in Berlin* (Cologne: Böhlau, 2001), 13.

23. Gailus, *Protestantismus und Nationalsozialismus*, 11.

24. Nipperdey, *Deutsche Geschichte*, 444.

25. Herbert Schnädelbach, "Der Fluch des Christentums", *Die Zeit*, May 11, 2000, 15.

26. Immanuel Kant, *Religion within the Bounds of Bare Reason*, trans. Werner S. Pluhar (Indianapolis/Cambridge: Hackett, 2009), 110.

27. Kant, *Religion*, 41.

28. Kant, *Religion*, 51

29. Friedrich Nietzsche, *On the Genealogy of Morals*, trans. Douglas Smith (Oxford: Oxford University Press, 1996), 72.

30. Friedrich Nietzsche, *The Antichrist*, trans. H. L. Mencken (New York: Alfred A. Knopf, 1918), 43.

31. Nietzsche, *Antichrist*, 43.

32. Paul Veyne, *Bread and Circuses: Historical Sociology and Political Pluralism*, trans. Brian Pearce (London: Penguin, 1990), 33.

33. John Carey, *The Intellectuals and the Masses: Pride and Prejudice among the Literary Intelligentsia, 1880–1939* (New York: St. Martin's Press, 1993).

34. Pius XI, *Casti connubii*, no. 70.

35. Michael Schwartz, " 'Euthanasie'—Debatten in Deutschland", in Ingrid Richter, *Katholizismus und Eugenik in der Weimarer Republik und im Dritten Reich. Zwischen Sittlichkeitsreform und Rassenhygiene* (Paderborn: Schöningh, 2001), 266.

36. Kurt Nowak, *Geschichte des Christentums*, 268, 271.

37. Quoted in Angenendt, *Toleranz*.

38. David Flusser, "Paulus", in *Theologische Realenzyklopädie*, vol. 26 (Berlin: De Gruyter, 1996), 155.

39. Heinz Schreckenberg, *Die christlichen Adversus-Judaeos-Texte und ihr literarisches und historisches Umfeld* (Pieterlen and Bern: Peter Lang, 1982), 85.

40. Alexander Demandt, *Hände in Unschuld. Pontius Pilatus in der Geschichte* (Cologne: Böhlau,1999), 171.

41. Haim Cohn, *The Trial and Death of Jesus* (New York: Harper & Row, 1971), 188.

42. Philip Schaff, ed., *A Select Library of the Nicene and Post-Nicene Fathers of the Christian Church*, vol. VIII: *Saint Augustine: Exposition on the Book of Psalms* (New York: The Christian Literature Company, 1905), 106.

43. Origen, *Contra Celsum*, trans. Henry Chadwick (Cambridge: Cambridge University Press, 1953), 297.

44. Gregory of Nazianzus, *The Fathers of the Church: St. Gregory of Nazianzus: Select Orations*, trans. Martha Vinson (Washington, DC: Catholic University of America Press, 2003), 72.

45. Michael Toch, *Die Juden im mittelalterlichen Reich*, Eznyklopädie Deutscher Geschichte 44 (Munich: Oldenbourg Wissenschaftsverlag, 1998), 2.

46. "Birkat Ha Minim", Jewish Virtual Library, accessed December 18, 2019, https://www.jewishvirtuallibrary.org/birkat-ha-minim.

47. Michael Toch, *Juden im mittelalterlichen Reich*, 3.

48. Karl L. Noethlichs, *Die Juden im christlichen Imperium Romanum (4.-6. Jahrhundert)* (Berlin: Akademie Verlag, 2001), 95.

49. Alexander II, Letter from 1065, in Shlomo Simonsohn, *The Apostolic See and the Jews*, vol. 1 (Toronto: Pontifical Institute of Mediaeval Studies, 1988), 37.

50. Gregory IX, Letter of April 6, 1233, in Simonsohn, *The Apostolic See and the Jews*, 1:143f.

51. Nicholas IV, Letter of January 30, 1291, in Simonsohn, *The Apostolic See and the Jews*, 1:278f.

52. Solomon Grayzel, introduction to *The Church and the Jews in the XIIIth Century*, vol. 2 (New York: Jewish Theological Seminary Press, 1989), 21.

53. Shlomo Simonsohn, *The Apostolic See and the Jews*, vol. 7 (Toronto: Pontifical Institute of Mediaeval Studies, 1991), 467.

54. Kurt Schubert, "Das christlich-jüdische Religionsgespräch im 12. und 13. Jahrhundert", *Kairos. Zeitschrift für Religionswissenschaft und Theologie* 19, nos. 1–4 (1977): 185.

55. Avraham Grossman, *Pious and Rebellious: Jewish Women in Medieval Europe*, trans. Jonathan Chipman (Waltham, MA: Brandeis University Press, 2004), xiii.

56. Grossman, *Pious and Rebellious*, xiii.

57. Grossman, *Pious and Rebellious*, 154.

58. Michael Toch, *Juden im mittelalterlichen Reich*, 114.

59. Heinz Schreckenberg, *Christlichen Adversus-Judaeos-Texte*, 18, 21.

60. Innocent IV, Letter of July 5, 1247, in Simonsohn, *The Apostolic See and the Jews*, 1:194f.

61. Gregory IX, "Letter to the Bishops of Western France", in *Church, State, and Jew in the Middle Ages*, ed. Robert Chazan (West Orange, NJ: Behrman House, 1980), 109–110.

62. Quoted in Angenendt, *Toleranz*.

63. Stephen Haliczer, introduction to *The Jews of Spain and the Expulsion of 1492*, ed. Moshe Lazar and Stephen Haliczer (Lancaster, CA: Labyrinthos, 1997), ix.

64. Quoted in Angenendt, *Toleranz*.

65. Quoted in Angenendt, *Toleranz*.

66. Yosef H. Yerushalmi, *Assimilation and Racial Anti-Semitism: The Iberian and the German Models* (New York: Leo Baeck Insitute, 1982), 7.

67. Philippe Wolff, "The 1391 Pogrom in Spain. Social Crisis or Not?", *Past & Present*, no. 50 (1971): 18.

68. Yosef H. Yerushalmi, *Assimilation and Racial Anti-semitism*, 12.

69. Henry Kamen, "The Mediterranean and the Expulsion of Spanish Jews in 1492", *Past & Present*, no. 119 (1988): 44.

70. Horst Pietschmann, *Staat und Staatliche Entwicklung am Beginn der spanischen Kolonisation Amerikas* (Münster: Aschendorff, 1980), 12.

71. David Berger, "Christians, Gentiles and the Talmud: A fourteenth-century Jewish response to the attack on Rabbinic Judaism", in *Religionsgespräche im Mittelalter*, ed. Bernard Lewis and Friedrich Niewöhner (Wiesbaden: Harrassowitz, 1992), 120, 124.

72. Peter von der Osten-Sacken, *Martin Luther und die Juden. Neu untersucht anhand von Anton Margarithas 'Der gantz Jüdisch glaub' (1530/31)* (Stuttgart: Kohlhammer, 2002), 157.

73. Quoted in Angenendt, *Toleranz*.

74. Hubert Wolf, "Bekehrung galt als heikles Geschäft", *Frankfurter Allgemeine Zeitung*, July 5, 2003, 38.

75. John Raines, ed., *Marx on Religion* (Philadelphia: Temple University Press, 2002), 65.

76. Shulamit Volkov, *Die Juden in Deutschland 1780–1918* (Munich: R. Oldenbourg Verlag, 1994), 121.

77. František Graus, *Pest, Geißler, Judenmorde* (Göttingen: Vandenhoeck & Ruprecht, 1987), 277.

78. Quoted in Angenendt, *Toleranz*.

79. Olaf Blaschke, "Die Anatomie des katholischen Antisemitismus", in *Katholischer Antisemitismus im 19. Jahrhundert. Ursachen und Traditionen im internationalen Vergleich*, ed. Olaf Balschke and Aram Mattioli (Zürich: Orell Füssli, 2000), 8f., 11, 14.

80. Thomas Nipperdey, *Deutsche Geschichte*, 306.

81. Quoted in Angenendt, *Toleranz*.

82. Ronald Rychlak, *Hitler, the War, and the Pope* (Huntington, IN: Our Sunday Visitor Publishing, 2010), 568n231.

83. Hans-Ulrich Wehler, *Deutsche Gesellschaftsgeschichte*, vol. 4 (Munich: C. H. Beck, 2003), 505.

84. Gerhard Besier, *Kirche, Politik und Gesellschaft im 20. Jahrhundert* (Munich: De Gruyter Oldenbourg, 2000), 29f.

85. Helmut Gollwitzer, "Predigt über Lukas 3,3-14 am 16. November 1938", in *Dennoch bleibe ich stehts an dir ... Predigten aus dem Kirchenkampf 1937–1940* (Munich: Kaiser, 1988).

86. Quoted in Angenendt, *Toleranz*.

87. Burkhart Schneider, ed., *Die Briefe Pius XII. an die deutschen Bischöfe.* 1939-1944 (Mainz: Grünewald,1966), 239, note 1.

88. Quoted in Angenendt, *Toleranz*.

89. Dietrich Bonhoeffer, *No Rusty Swords: Letters, Lectures and Notes 1928–1936* (New York: Harper & Row, 1965), 224.

90. Quoted in Angenendt, *Toleranz*.

91. Margherita Marchione, *Pope Pius XII: Architect for Peace* (Herefordshire, UK: Gracewing Publishing, 200), 78.

92. Ian Kershaw, *The Nazi Dictatorship: Problems and Perspectives of Interpretation* (London: Bloomsbury Publishing, 2015), 295.

93. Quoted in Angenendt, *Toleranz*.

94. Karl-Joseph Hummel and Michael Kissener, ed., *Catholics and the Third Reich*, trans. Christof Morrisey (Leiden: Ferdinand Schöningh, 2018), 222.

95. Mary Gerhart and Fabian E. Udoh, ed., *The Christianity Reader* (Chicago and London: University of Chicago Press, 2007), 820.

96. Pope John Paul II, "Address to the Jewish Community—W. Germany", in John Paul II, *On Jews and Judaism* (Eugene J. Fisher and Leon Klenicki, eds.) (Washington: United States Catholic Conference, 1987), 35.

97. Quoted in Angenendt, *Toleranz.*

98. George Steiner, *Errata: An Examined Life* (New Haven: Yale University Press, 1998), 59.

99. Steven T. Katz, *Kontinuität und Diskontinuität zwischen christlichem und nationalsozialistischem Antisemitismus* (Tübingen: Mohr Siebeck, 2001), 43.

100. Yosef H. Yerushalmi, *Servants of Kings and Not Servant of Servants: Some Aspects of the Political History of the Jews.* Tenenbaum Family Lecture Series (Atlanta: Tam Institute for Jewish Studies, 2005), 17, 21, 23.

101. John Paul II, "The Roots of Anti-Judaism in the Christian Environment, from Pope John Paul II's Discourse during his Visit to the Rome Synagogue on 13 April, 1986", Vatican, last accessed December 18, 2019, http://www.vatican.va /jubilee_2000/magazine/documents/ju_mag_01111997_p-42x_en.html.

102. "Excerpts from the Apology by the Pope and Cardinals", *New York Times,* March 13, 2000, https://www.nytimes.com/2000/03/13/world/excerpts-from-the -apology-by-the-pope-and-cardinals.html.

103. "Excerpts from the Apology by the Pope and Cardinals".

104. Christoph M. Scheuren-Brandes, *Der Weg von nationalsozialistischen Rechtslehren zur Radbruchschen Formel. Untersuchungen zur Geschichte der Idee vom 'Unrichtigen Recht'* (Paderborn: Ferdinand Schöningh Verlag, 2006), 17.

105. John XXIII, encyclical letter *Pacem in terris* (April 11, 1963), nos. 10, 11, 14.

106. Vatican Council II, Declaration on Religious Freedom *Dignitatis humanae* (December 7, 1965), no. 2.

107. Vatican Council II, Pastoral Constitution on the Church in the Modern World *Gaudium et spes* (December 7, 1965), no. 74.

108. Georg P. Hefty, "Wie viele Wähler stellt der Papst?", *Frankfurter Allgemeine Zeitung,* April 5, 2005: 1.

109. Heinrich A. Winkler, *Germany: The Long Road West: Volume 2: 1933–1990,* trans. Alexander J. Sager (Oxford: Oxford University Press, 2007), 329.

110. Trutz Rendtorff, "Kirchenamt im Auftrage des Rates der Evangelischen Kirche in Deutschland", in *Evangelische Kirche und freiheitliche Demokratie. Der Staat des Grundgesetzes als Angebot und Aufgabe,* ed. Evangelische Kirche in Deutschland (Gütersloh: G. Mohn, 1985), 7.

Chapter XI

1. Thomas Nipperdey, *Deutsche Geschichte 1866–1918,* vol. 1 (Munich: C.H. Beck, 1990), 73.

2. Tertullian, *Ad uxorem* II.9 (*PL* 1:1302f.)

3. Paul Veyne, ed., "The Roman Empire", in *A History of Private Life,* vol. 1 (Cambridge, MA: Harvard University Press, 1987), 40.

4. Jean Gaudement, "Familie", in *Reallexicon für Antike und Christentum,* vol. 7 (Stuttgart: Anton Hiersemann, 1969), 340.

5. Christian Schulz, *Medizin und Christentum in Spätantike und frühem Mittelalter: Christliche Ärzte und ihr Wirken* (Tübingen, Germany: Mohr Siebeck, 2005), 139.

6. Peter Blickle, *Von der Leibeigenschaft zu den Menschenrechten* (Munich: C. H. Beck, 2003), 299.

7. *Decretum Gratiani*, pt. II, causa XXXI, q. II, c. IV.

8. Ivo of Chartres, *Decretum*, VIII.86 (*PL* 161:601C).

9. Jean-Jacques Rousseau, *Émile*, trans. Allan Bloom (New York: Basic Books, 1979), 324.

10. Regina Schulte, *Sperrbezirke: Tugendhaftigkeit und Prostitution in der bürgerlichen Welt* (Frankfurt: Syndikat, 1979), 168.

11. Ute Planert, *Antifeminismus im Kaiserreich* (Göttingen: Vandenhoeck und Ruprecht, 1998), 36.

12. Thomas Mann, "Die Ehe im Übergang", in *Das Ehe-Buch*, ed. Hermann Kayserling (Celle: Niels Kampmann Verlag, 1925), 214.

13. Nipperdey, *Deutsche Geschichte*, 69.

14. Michael Mitterauer, *Why Europe? The Medieval Origins of Its Special Path*, trans. Gerald Chapple (Chicago and London: University of Chicago Press, 2010), 95.

15. Gudrun Krämer, *Gottes Staat als Republik* (Baden-Baden: Nomos Verlagsgesellschaft, 2000), 158.

16. Musonius, *Diatribe* 12.

17. Seneca, *Ep* 122.7.

18. Paul Veyne, *Geschichte des privaten Lebens*, vol. 1 (Frankfurt: S. Fischer, 1989), 198.

19. St. Augustine, *De Bono Coniugali*, in *De Bono Coniugali, De Sancta Virginitate*, trans. P. G. Walsh (Oxford: Clarendon Press, 2001), 11.

20. St. Thomas Aquinas, *Summa Theologica*, trans. Fathers of the English Dominican Province (New York: Benziger Brothers, 1947), II-II, q. 26, a.11.

21. Heinrich Schipperges, "Grundzüge einer scholastischen Anthropologie bei Petrus Hispanus", in *Aufsätze zur portugiesischen Kulturgeschichte*, ed. Hans Flasche, vol. 7 (Münster: Aschendorff, 1967), 20–25.

22. Denis the Carthusian, "De doctrina et regulis vitae Christianorum", in *Doctoris ecstatici D. Dionysii Cartusiani: Opera omnia*, vol. 39 (Tournai: Typis Cartusiae S. M. de Pratis, 1910), 538, II.7.3.

23. Martin Luther, *Von Ehesachen* (Wittenberg, 1530).

24. Heinz Schilling, *Frühneuzeitliche Formierung und Disziplinierung von Ehe, Familie und Erziehung im Spiegel calvinistischer Kirchenratsprotokolle*, in *Glaube und Eid. Treueformeln, Glaubensbekenntnisse und Sozialdisziplinierung zwischen Mittelalter und Neuzeit*, ed. Paolo Prodi (Munich: De Gruyter Oldenbourg, 1993), 208.

25. Nipperdey, *Deutsche Geschichte*, 43.

26. Frank Schirrmacher, *Das Methusalem-Komplott* (Munich: Blessing Karl Verlag, 2004), 40.

27. Heinrich Schipperges, "Grundzüge einer scholastischen Anthropologie bei Petrus Hispanus", 20–25.

28. Adrienne Rich, *Of Woman Born: Motherhood as Experience and Institution* (New York: Bantam Books, 1977), 58.

29. Herrad Schenk, *Die Befreiung des weiblichen Begehrens* (Cologne: Kiepenheuer und Witsch, 1991), 130.

30. Alice Schwarzer, *Der kleine Unterschied und seine großen Folgen* (Frankfurt: S. Fischer, 1975), 181.

31. The US-specific material in this section has been added, with the author's approval, by the editors of Ignatius Press.

32. Bart Ehrman, ed. and trans., *Apostolic Fathers* (Cambridge, MA: Harvard University Press, 2003), 1:419.

33. Ehrman, *Apostolic Fathers*, 2:141.

34. Robert Jütte, "Vom Umgang mit der Geschichte in der Abtreibungsdiskussion", in *Geschichte der Abtreibung. Von der Antike bis zur Gegenwart*, ed. Robert Jütte (Munich: C.H. Beck, 1993), 16.

35. Wulf Schiefenhövel, "Fertilität zwischen Biologie und Kultur. Traditionelle Geburtenkontrolle in Neuguinea", *Neue Zürcher Zeitung*, March 13–14, 2004, 57.

36. Philippe Ariès, *Centuries of Childhood: A Social History of Family Life*, trans. Robert Baldick (New York: Vintage, 1965), 139.

37. Otto Hiltbrunner, "Patria potestas", in *Der Kleine Pauly. Lexicon der Antike*, vol. 4 (Munich: DTV, 1979), 552.

38. Bettina E. Stumpp, *Prostitution in der römischen Antike* (Berlin: Akademie Verlag, 1998), 29.

39. Wilhelm Reich, *Die Sexualität im Kulturkampf* (Copenhagen: Sexpol Verlag, 1936), 75.

40. Eberhard Schorsch, *Perversion, Liebe, Gewalt* (Stuttgart: Thieme, 1993), 166.

41. "Germany Shaken By 'Systematic' Sexual Abuse at Berlin Catholic School", *Der Spiegel*, February 1, 2010, https://www.spiegel.de/international/germany /jesuit-priest-admits-molesting-youth-germany-shaken-by-systematic-sexual-abuse -at-berlin-catholic-school-a-675331.html.

42. Silvano Tomasi, "Pope Benedict XVI Defrocked Nearly 400 Priests for Child Abuse", *The Guardian*, January 18, 2014, http://www.theguardian.com /world/2014/jan/17/pope-benedict-defrocked-400-priests-child-abuse.

43. Pope Francis, Address at the End of the Eucharistic Concelebration, Meeting on "The Protection of Minors in the Church" (February 24, 2019).

44. Quoted in Paul Badde, "Kommentar: Der Zölibat ist eine Liebesbeziehung", *Welt*, April 3, 2010, https://www.welt.de/debatte/article7038687/Der-Zoelibat -ist-eine-Liebesbeziehung.html.

45. Patsy McGarry, "Falsely Accused of Child Sex Abuse: Ordeal of Innocent Priests", *Irish Times*, February 12, 2017, https://www.irishtimes.com/news/social -affairs/religion-and-beliefs/falsely-accused-of-child-sex-abuse-ordeal-of -innocent-priests-1.2972906.

Chapter XII

1. Thomas Assheuer, "Jesus, unser Sündenbock. Was das Christentum über menschliche Gewalt lehrt: Ein Gespräch mit dem Religionsphilosophen René Girard", *Zeit Online*, March 23, 2005, https://www.zeit.de/2005/13/Interview _Girard.

2. Quoted in Arnold Angenendt, *Toleranz und Gewalt. Das Christentum zwischen Bibel und Schwert* (Münster: Aschendorff Verlag, 2007).

3. Hans Jonas, *The Imperative of Responsibility: In Search of an Ethics for the Technological Age* (Chicago: University of Chicago Press, 1985), 23, 27.

4. Jürgen Habermas, "2001 Acceptance Speech 'Faith and Knowledge' ", Friedenspreis des deutschen Buchhandels, last accessed March 13, 2020, https://www.friedenspreis-des-deutschen-buchhandels.de/sixcms/media.php/1290/2001%20Acceptance%20Speech%20Juergen%20Habermas.pdf.

5. Ernst-Wolfgang Böckenförde, *Recht, Staat, Freiheit. Studien zu Rechtsphilosophie, Staatstheorie und Verfassungsgeschichte* (Frankfurt: Suhrkamp, 2000), 112.

6. Émile Durkheim, *Soziologie und Philosophie* (Frankfurt am Main: Suhrkamp, 1996), 87.

7. Joseph Ratzinger and Jürgen Habermas, *The Dialectics of Secularization: On Reason and Religion* (San Francisco: Ignatius Press, 2007), 30.

8. Quoted in Hamed Abdel-Samad, "Frau Merkel, Multikulti ist gescheitert!", *The European*, June 25, 2018, https://www.theeuropean.de/hamed-abdel-samad/14233-brief-von-hamed-abdel-samad-an-kanzlerin.

9. Heraclitus, *Fragments: A Text and Translation with a Commentary by T. M. Robinson* (Toronto: University of Toronto Press, 1981), 13.

10. St. Augustine, "The Advantage of Believing", in *The Fathers of the Church*, vol. 4, *Saint Augustine: The Immortality of the Soul; The Magnitude of the Soul; On Music; The Advantage of Believing; On Faith in Things Unseen* (New York: Cima Publishing, 1947), 401.

11. Karl O. Hondrich, "Die Divisionen des Papstes", *Frankfurter Allgemeine Zeitung*, April 16, 2005, 8.

12. John Paul II, "Universal Prayer: Confession of Sins and Asking for Forgiveness", Vatican, last accessed December 3, 2019, http://www.vatican.va/news_services/liturgy/documents/ns_lit_doc_20000312_prayer-day-pardon_en.html.

13. Quoted in Aldino Cazzago, " 'Mai più'. La giornata del perdono", *Communio* (Italy), nos. 172–73 (2000): 25.